American Indian/First Nations Schooling

Books by Charles L. Glenn

The Myth of the Common School, 1988, 2002. Italian translation 2004; Spanish translation 2006.

Choice of Schools in Six Nations, 1989.

Educational Freedom in Eastern Europe, 1995.

Educating Immigrant Children: Schools and Language Minorities in 12 Nations (with Ester J. de Jong), 1996.

The Ambiguous Embrace: Government and Faith-based Schools and Social Agencies, 2000.

Finding the Right Balance: Freedom, Autonomy and Accountability in Education, I & II (with Jan De Groof), 2002.

Un difficile equilibrio: Europa continentale e mediterranea (with Jan De Groof), 2003.

Balancing Freedom, Autonomy, and Accountability in Education, I–III (with Jan De Groof), 2004.

Contrasting Models of State and School: A Comparative Historical Study of Parental Choice and State Control, 2011.

African American / Afro-Canadian Schooling: From the Colonial Period to the Present, 2011.

American Indian/First Nations Schooling

From the Colonial Period to the Present

Charles L. Glenn

AMERICAN INDIAN / FIRST NATIONS SCHOOLING
Copyright © Charles L. Glenn, 2011.

All rights reserved.

First published in 2011 by
PALGRAVE MACMILLAN®
in the United States – a division of St. Martin's Press LLC,
175 Fifth Avenue, New York, NY 10010.

Where this book is distributed in the UK, Europe and the rest of the world, this is by Palgrave Macmillan, a division of Macmillan Publishers Limited, registered in England, company number 785998, of Houndmills, Basingstoke, Hampshire RG21 6XS.

Palgrave Macmillan is the global academic imprint of the above companies and has companies and representatives throughout the world.

Palgrave® and Macmillan® are registered trademarks in the United States, the United Kingdom, Europe and other countries.

ISBN: 978–0–230–11420–3

Library of Congress Cataloging-in-Publication Data

Glenn, Charles Leslie, 1938–
  American Indian/First Nations schooling : from the colonial period to the present / Charles L. Glenn.
    p. cm.
    Includes bibliographical references.
    ISBN 978–0–230–11420–3 (hardback)
  1. Indians of North America—Education. 2. Indians of North America—Government relations. 3. Education and state—North America—History. 4. Church and education—North America—History. 5. Racism in education—North America—History. 6. Discrimination in education—North America—History. 7. North America—Race relations. 8. North America—Politics and government. I. Title.
  E97.G58 2011
  371.829'97073—dc22
                                                                    2011000363

A catalogue record of the book is available from the British Library.

Design by MPS Limited, A Macmillan Company

First edition: June 2011

With gratitude to Susan, Kate, and Megan

Contents

Preface	viii
Note on Terminology	x
Introduction	1
1 The Present Situation	5
2 Assumptions about Race	11
3 Making Christians	19
4 Wards of Government	29
5 The "Five Civilized Nations"	39
6 Churches as Allies and Agents of the State	49
7 Decline of the Partnership of Church and State	67
8 Separate Schooling Institutionalized	77
9 Problems of Residential Schools	93
10 Self-Help and Self-Governance	109
11 Indian Languages and Cultures	125
12 Navajo, Cree, and Mohawk	147
13 Continued Decline of Indian Languages	165
14 Indians in Local Public Schools	179
15 Have We Learned Anything?	193
Notes	201
References	221
Index	233

Preface

This account of the formal, "European-style" schooling of the children of the native peoples of North America over several centuries is written by a specialist in educational policy and administration, not by an academic historian, much less an expert on any of the dozens of peoples discussed. It is my engagement with the movements for social justice in the 1960s, followed by more than two decades as a government official responsible for educational equity and programs for those for whom English was a second language, that has informed my reading of the abundant material on the schooling of Indian children and youth in Canada and the United States, and the perspective from which I have, in turn, written.

For the past twenty years much of the focus of my work has been on how other countries have dealt and are dealing with cultural and linguistic differences, both those represented by "indigenous" language minority groups and also those caused by immigration. The occasion of a sabbatical after stepping down from administrative responsibilities at Boston University allowed me to reflect on my own country's efforts and failures in this respect.

I wrote this book in parallel with another, also to be published by Palgrave Macmillan, *African American / Afro-Canadian Schooling: From the Colonial Period to the Present*. While the experience of the two groups is different in many respects, it has been marked in both cases by the heavy influence of assumptions about race among the white majority, assumptions which have deeply influenced the manner in which schooling has been provided.

In the final chapter, I resume my more familiar role as a specialist on educational policy, and especially on equity issues, and make a number of recommendations that seek to relate the historical account to present developments and what can be learned from both history and our current successes and failures. The idea of "separate development" for Indians on rural and generally impoverished reservations is inconsistent with present realities.

The confrontation with the wider North American societies does not have to lead to cultural homogenization for those who choose to preserve elements of their ancestral culture and language. In our increasingly pluralistic societies, the stark either/or posed in nineteenth-century policy debates is no longer relevant. I suggest in this final chapter how a variety of choices with respect to ancestral heritage can be accommodated in the educational system without abandoning the goal that every child become capable of participating in the wider society and economy. Recent decades have seen structural innovations in American and Canadian education that make this possible.

Finally, it is remarkable how seldom Canada is mentioned in histories of education, or of the experience of Indian peoples, in the United States, and the same limited vision is true of histories of Canada. Remarkable because the parallels are striking, and the differences significant. This is not, strictly speaking, a study of comparative policies of the sort that I have written with my Belgian colleague Jan De Groof, but it seeks to show how much each nation has to learn from the other.

CHARLES L. GLENN
Boston University

Note on Terminology

The indigenous peoples of North America—"indigenous" in the sense of having been in what is now Canada and the United States for millennia before the arrival of European explorers and colonists—have over a thousand distinct identities and names for themselves; their cultures differ widely as do their languages. The most common term used to refer to them, and one which they have incorporated into their own intertribal identities, is "Indian," and that is the term that will generally be used in what follows, without the apologetic use of "scare quotes."

One reason for doing so is that it would have been awkward to keep writing "Native American / First Nations" in discussion of the many commonalities of the experience of native peoples on both sides of what is in terms of the historical existence of many of them an artificial and recently imposed international border.

In the United States, there has been for several decades an effort to replace "Indian" with "Native American," but the popularity of that phrase is fading and "Indian" continues to be used by the National Congress of American Indians, the American Indian Movement, and national and local American Indian Councils. In Canada, where the question of group identities has been exacerbated by the situation of Quebec, there is a government Department and Minister of Indian Affairs and Northern Development, though it is more politically correct to use the phrase "First Nations" (but see Flanagan's criticism), or the word "aboriginal."

Apart from their appearance in some quoted material, these labels will not be used in what follows, nor will the awkward phrase "American Indian / Alaska Native" be used, although Alaska Natives will be so identified when appropriate. If anyone is offended, my apologies.

Introduction

The account that follows is about the formal schooling, along the approximate lines of that provided to children of the white (or European-American) majority, of the children of the native peoples of North America. It is not about the education that has always been provided in countless ways by Indian communities outside of classrooms, in families and the shared rituals of religious and community life. It is thus to a considerable extent a history "from outside," focused on what public policies and private benevolence have sought to accomplish and on the changing assumptions of the white majority about the purposes and means of schooling Indian children.

Formal, European-style schooling was at times demanded by Indian peoples in their treaties with the national governments of Canada and the United States, and at other times resisted as an imposition and a threat to family and cultural integrity. The schooling actually provided was of very uneven quality and of very uneven relevance to the future lives of Indian children and youth, and the eagerness of Indian parents, in many cases, to ensure that their children received formal schooling that the parents themselves had not benefited from is a phenomenon that cannot fully be explained. After all, it was usually a matter of delivering their children over to an institution that had scant respect for the parents themselves or for their hard-acquired competence and their strongly held beliefs. It was often accompanied by a painful alienation between the generations as the children became more conversant in the ways of the majority society than were their parents, a phenomenon familiar also to immigrant parents. And, perhaps most cruelly, it did not in the great majority of cases actually lead to the hoped-for success of the children in Canadian or American society. All too often, the Indian youth who had reached the highest level of schooling offered and achieved everything expected of them by the available schools were then faced with accepting employment that required no such educational attainment.

Yet thousands of parents continued to believe that formal schooling could make all the difference for their children. We can only admire the triumph of hope over experience. And for some Indian youth, education did open doors to the wider society, as well as opportunities to mediate between their own communities and that society. My own Boston University is proud of its Medical School alumnus Charles Eastman (1889), a Santee Sioux who helped found the Boy Scouts and Camp Fire Girls and influenced American policies toward Indians at the national level. Many other examples of success could be cited . . . but not as many as one would like.

If the continued belief of Indian parents in the importance of formal schooling, over many discouraging decades, is somewhat of a mystery, a greater mystery is represented by the consistent policy choice, until late in the twentieth century, on the part of American governments at the federal, state, and local levels to maintain separate schools for Indian children, like that provided to Americans and Canadians of African ancestry. While the curriculum that they followed was commonly adapted in some way from that used at the same period for white pupils, Indian children and youth have seldom shared classrooms with white peers.

This came about for many different reasons. Geographical isolation, and the migratory habits of some native peoples, explains much of the separation. What requires an explanation, however, is why separate schooling was usually provided even under circumstances that would have allowed Indian and white children to be schooled together. Why did policy-makers in the United States and Canada assume, at almost all times, that separate schooling was only right and proper and in the interest of Indian pupils themselves?

This occurred, after all, in a society stubbornly committed to the "common school" and resolute—when faced with the flood of Catholic immigrants in the 1850s and beyond—in refusing to provide support for schools with an alternative religious character. We can understand separate Indian schooling more easily in the Canadian context of separate public schools for Catholics and Protestants, for English-speakers and French-speakers, but why, in the United States, with its quasi-religious commitment to the "common school," was an exception made so unhesitatingly for Indian children? Thousands were brought in the nineteenth century from the Dakotas to the Carlisle Indian School in Pennsylvania, more than a thousand miles away, surrounded by a white rural population; hundreds more to Hampton Institute in Virginia, where they were schooled with black pupils; and in the twentieth century, thousands to "Indian schools" in Los Angeles and other urban centers, while until recent decades few local public schools accepted the offer of government funding to serve Indian children living nearby.

To a very large extent, it must be said, the schooling of Indians is a shameful history, marked by persistent assumptions about the natural inferiority of these children and in consequence the need to provide them with unambitious forms of schooling, if indeed any formal schooling would not be wasted on them. The account has its brighter side, as well in the thousands of Indian and white teachers who committed themselves, often under great hardships, to educate Indian children, and their allies in religious and other benevolent organizations and, sometimes though not often enough, government officials and political leaders who supported such efforts.

Why was there so little willingness to see Indian pupils sitting on the "long school-bench" on which Horace Mann of Massachusetts, Egerton Ryerson of Ontario, and their many allies liked to imagine the child of the banker and of the working man learning side-by-side? The answer, surely, is that racial segregation is a deeply rooted tradition in American and Canadian education, and that this rested, in turn, on white assumptions about the significance of racial differences that "went all the way down," so fundamental that no education could overcome them.

With the massive movement of Indian families, after World War II, from reservations to cities in search of employment, this isolation has been overcome for many. More than half of Indian (and Alaska Native) fourth- and eighth-graders in the United States in 2009 attended public schools where they represented less than 25 percent of the enrollment, while almost 40 percent attended public schools where they were 25 percent or more of the enrollment. Only one in fourteen attended a federally supported Bureau of Indian Education school.[1]

Just as with African-American pupils, however, the end of segregation has not meant effective participation in the educational system. Indian pupils continue to lag behind in academic achievement, and also in engagement with their own schooling. No historical account can provide the solution to this problem, but perhaps it can suggest some of its causes.

CHAPTER 1

The Present Situation

Between 1980 and 1990, the number of Americans self-reporting as American Indian in the United States Census increased by an extraordinary 31 percent, with a further increase of 26.4 percent by 2000 and 26.7 percent beyond that by 2010. While the number of those who identified themselves only as Indian increased from 1,959,234 in 1990 to 2,475,956 in 2000 and 2,932,248 in 2010, an even more remarkable phenomenon appeared as a result of the adoption, for the 2000 Census, of the opportunity for individuals to list multiple racial or ethnic identities: 4,119,301 claimed to be at least partially Indian in 2000, rising to 5,220,579 in 2010. Thus, while those self-identified as only Indian were 0.9 percent of the US population in 2010, those claiming some Indian ancestry were 1.6 percent in 2010.[1]

Of these, in 2000 (2010 data not yet available), 2,416,410 (58.7 percent) listed a single tribe, 59,546 listed two or more tribes, and the balance listed a combination of Indian with other ancestries. There were almost 1.1 million Americans who listed mixed white and Indian ancestry, and 182,494 who listed mixed black and Indian ancestry.

Much of this growth in reported numbers was in urban areas and far from the traditional centers of Indian population in, for example, the Dakotas and New Mexico and Arizona. Between 1980 and 1990, the number of Americans identifying themselves as Indian jumped by 78 percent in New Jersey, 66.1 percent in Ohio, 64 percent in Texas, 62 percent in Virginia, and 58.3 percent in New York.[2]

Among the nearly 600 tribes—"each with different cultural values and attributes, political and social organizations, and histories"[3]—recognized by the American government, we will be giving particular attention to the two largest; the Cherokee and the Navajo represented, respectively, 11.6 percent and 11.1 percent of those individuals who claimed a single tribal identity in the 2000 US Census. A notable difference emerges—one that will be reflected in our account of their experiences with formal schooling—in comparing the "full-bloods" with those individuals who reported mixed ancestry. Only 38.5 percent of those with Cherokee ancestors reported only Cherokee ancestry, while 90.3 percent of those with Navajo ancestors reported only Navajo ancestry. As a result, individuals with any Cherokee ancestry represented 17.7 percent of all Americans who reported any Indian ancestry, while those with any Navajo ancestry represented only 7.2 percent. One would expect, from these data, that Cherokees would be much more assimilated into American society than Navajos, and one indication that this may be the case is that the achievement of Indian pupils on the National Assessment of Educational Progress (NAEP) is significantly higher in Oklahoma, where most Cherokees are concentrated, than in Arizona and New Mexico, home to the Navajo Reservation.

As of 2006, there were reported to be 1,678,235 Canadians with at least partial "aboriginal" ancestry, or 5.4 percent of the total population; of these, 512,150 or 1.6 percent of all Canadians, were of unmixed Indian ancestry.[4] There is a distinction between so-called Status Indians, registered members of bands (usually subdivisions of tribes), of whom there are about 700,000, and others of Indian ancestry, notably the mixed-blood Métis, descended generally from French-speaking trappers and traders and Indian women. About one quarter of the indigenous population of Canada live in Ontario, with about 16 percent each in British Columbia and Saskatchewan; 58 percent live on more than 2000 reserves. There are more than 600 recognized bands, though only eleven of these, mostly in Ontario and Alberta, have 2000 members or more.[5]

Over the last several decades Canada has been undergoing a crisis of conscience about its past treatment of its Indian population; indeed, as in the United States, there is much to be ashamed of. It may be because Canada experienced neither the agonies nor the triumphs of the Black Freedom Movement of the 1950s and 1960s that coming to terms with its past relationship with Indians has played a larger role in the national consciousness than has the parallel relationship in the United States. There is much talk of "reparations," and indeed the Canadian government committed $350 million for "community-based healing initiatives" over a four-year period.[6] In 2001, the Supreme Court of British Columbia awarded $500,000 to six aboriginal litigants because of their experiences in a residential school operated by the United Church of Canada under contract with the federal government.[7]

Neither Canada nor the United States has been able to find the right formula for ensuring the full participation of Indians in the benefits of post-industrial economies, with or without abandoning their distinctive cultural and communal traditions. The situation is further complicated by the fact that by no means do all Indians place a high value—at least as exemplified by their actions—on those traditions. The "acids of modernity" work powerfully against native languages and family patterns; the "expressive individualism" fostered by the electronic media in which most Indians, as much as anyone else, are submerged every day makes it less and less rewarding to devote the time and energy required to maintain traditional communal ceremonies and other interactions, much less languages that few can speak and vanishingly few as their only or dominant means of communication.

In an ideal world, perhaps, Indian youth would be so educated that, at adolescence, they could make a reasoned choice about whether to continue to speak their ancestral language and to follow their ancestral customs on the basis of the worldview of their ancestors or to turn their back on all of those and plunge wholeheartedly into the majority society and culture. The problem is that the sort of education that will make it possible to do the latter almost inevitably undermines the ancestral language, customs, and worldview. The Indian youth who has reached the point of reasoned choice may find that there is no going back. Formal schooling, in such circumstances, cannot be neutral in its effects.

Over the past century and a half, as predictions (discussed in the next chapter) that Indians would succumb to an unequal competition and disappear have faded away, they have been replaced by a series of promises on the part of policy-makers that, with just one more sustained effort along the lines proposed, the "Indian Problem" will be solved and government can stop concerning itself with Indians in a different manner than with other citizens. These predictions, like the others, have been falsified by experience. Governments in both Canada and the United States continue to be deeply involved in providing services to Indians in a way that they are not to other population groups, and it is not uncommon for Indian activists to claim a sort of dual citizenship, in their Indian "nation" as well as in the wider society, stressing one or the other as is more advantageous in a particular situation.

Whatever the reasons (and many have been advanced), Indians have on average—and, of course, there are thousands of exceptions—failed to flourish in North American societies. This is evident whether measured by the high rate of unemployment and welfare-dependency on reservations, the above-average prevalence of a variety of social pathologies, or the disappointing average achievement of Indian pupils. In the United States, this is the case in local public schools, in schools operated by the Office of Indian Education (of 184 schools, less than 30 percent made "Adequate Yearly Progress" in 2005–2006), or those operated by Indian tribes.

A national survey in 2003 found that 25.7 percent of Indians were living below the official poverty line, more than double the national average of

12.4 percent,[8] and data collected as part of the National Assessment of Educational Progress (NAEP) found that a lower proportion of Indian pupils than average had mothers who had graduated from high school.

One indicator of the low engagement of Indian pupils in their schooling is that they have the highest self-reported absentee rate from eighth grade of any of the racial/ethnic categories; almost two out of three reported that they had one or more unexcused absences in the preceding month: 33 percent reported no absences, compared with 44 percent for black, 43 percent for Hispanic, 45 percent for white, and 65 percent for Asian students. They also had the highest suspension rate, across the grades, of any group except blacks.[9] This seems to suggest that it continues to be true, as a national study of American Indian education found in the late 1960s, that in general "it appears that Indian pupils do not become enthusiastic about their schooling. They do not appear to exert themselves or to feel that school achievement is very important to them. However, they are not hostile to school."[10] Sociologist Alan Peshkin found the same indifference but not hostility toward school among the Pueblo students he interviewed and observed decades later.

Nor is their measured academic achievement satisfactory. On the various iterations of the NAEP, Indian pupils scored substantially lower than white and Asian pupils (though somewhat better on average than black and Latino pupils) on reading, math, science, and history/geography. They were less likely than any other group to take advanced coursework in high school. While other groups showed improvement between 2005 and 2007 (perhaps because of No Child Left Behind), Indian pupils did not.[11]

Similarly, in Canada, a parliamentary report in 1990 found that at least 45 percent of Indians living on reserves and more than half of the Inuit were functionally illiterate,[12] and school authorities in Arctic Quebec reported, in 1992, that most of the youth in their care dropped out of school without a diploma.[13] In Ontario, from 1983 to 1988, between 33 and 55 percent of the Indian ninth graders eventually completed high school.[14]

As might be expected, these indicators of academic difficulty are correlated with familial poverty among Indians. Of Indian fourth graders in the United States, 59 percent are eligible for free or reduced-price lunch based on their family incomes, compared with 36 percent of non-Indian 4th graders; the latter group, of course, includes black and Latino as well as white and Asian children.[15]

Are these indicators of the relative lack of success in contemporary educational and economic systems the result of unwise strategies employed by churches and governments over the course of many decades, or are they perhaps the result of the frequent changes in those strategies, and the halfhearted ways in which they have usually been pursued? Was it the wrong strategies or was it the inadequate implementation of the right strategies?

Or was it, perhaps, that the indigenous peoples of North America would require many generations to develop the capacities that Europeans and Asians had already developed before they arrived in North America and passed along culturally or even genetically (through previous natural selection) to their descendants here? This third hypothesis, as "politically incorrect" and unlikely as we may find it today, was frequently advanced during the nineteenth century, and the next section will consider some of the forms that it took, and how, to some extent, it was answered.

These questions, to which oceans of ink have been devoted in recent decades, will not be answered in the account that follows. It will be enough if we can trace the twists and turns of the policies and the measures taken by government and by benevolent organizations including churches, leaving it to the reader to reach conclusions. The fact that none of these twists and none of these turns has resulted in a marked degree of success in equipping Indian youth to participate on equal terms in the majority society and economy should, if nothing else, make us cautious of confident policy prescriptions. It should also, I would suggest, make us open to a great deal of responsible experimentation at the local level, and to respect what parents want for the education of their children.

CHAPTER 2

Assumptions about Race

One cannot make sense out of the historical record of the schooling—and often the nonschooling—of Indian children and youth apart from the changing ideas about the significance and influence of "race," a concept with little scientific meaning but enormous significance, in the United States and Canada, for how individuals and groups are perceived and also for how many individuals perceive themselves. "Race," in the sense in which the term has been used in North America, is entangled with ethnicity and thus with inherited culture and social networks, but it is also frequently taken to refer to an inherent and unchangeable disposition passed on, as we would now say, genetically.

Human populations and the differences among them have been classified in many ways, of which perhaps the classic is the five "varieties" identified by Blumenbach in 1795: Caucasian, Mongolian, Ethiopian, American, and Malay. The term "Caucasian" derives from his judgment that it was the Georgians of the Caucasus who represented the purest form of what also would be called the "Aryan" or "Indo-European" racial group. Soon, however, further differentiations were made; among Europeans "one began to hear of Nordic, Alpine, Mediterranean, Baltic, Dinaric, and God alone knows how many other races and subraces."[1]

Much has been written about the assumptions of the white majority about those considered racially different and usually inferior, and no attempt will be made here to repeat or even recapitulate what others have described in detail.[2] There are certain dimensions of this matter, however, which help to explain both the persistent practice of schooling Indian children separately and the nature of the debates over the character of that schooling.

In general it was the white majority, or its policy-makers, who determined until recent decades that Indian children would be schooled separately. It was thus the opinions and assumptions of the white majority about the significance of race that we will be exploring in this chapter. That should not be taken to suggest, however, that those whose children were being segregated had no views of their own, though often these are less available to us in the form of a written record. While there is a literature of "Indian oratory," it deals mostly with issues of war and peace and of white encroachment;[3] we have little record of the attitude of Indian parents toward formal schooling, though some indications of that will be supplied at appropriate points below.

Especially among the Navajo, recent decades have seen efforts to make separate schools instruments of cultural maintenance and renewal. Although, in some cases, Indian leaders and parents have themselves supported segregated schooling for reasons that had nothing to do with negative assumptions based on race, the significance of such decisions is of course entirely different from that of imposed segregation based on the racial attitudes of the white majority. It is these attitudes that this chapter is concerned with describing.

The prevailing assumption—at least at the level at which policies are debated and government programs determined and implemented—tended to be that Indians were not by nature inferior to whites but that they were many centuries behind Europeans in cultural development, and, unless somehow they could be helped to overcome that lag, they were fated to disappear through an unequal competition. Just as there were reasons to call into question the innate abilities of blacks as a justification for enslaving them, so there were reasons to emphasize the "noble savage" perception of Indians to encourage European settlement in North America.[4]

From the French colony of New France, Father Paul Le Jeune informed his fellow Jesuits that the Indians "are not so barbarous that they cannot be made children of God," and their minds are "of good quality. I believe that souls are all made from the same stock, and that they do not materially differ."[5]

Thomas Jefferson, for example, believed it important to vindicate the inherent qualities of Indians as he did of North American animals and birds, to answer European disparagement by the naturalist Buffon and others of the climate and conditions of the continent. Jefferson described the Indian as "a degraded yet basically noble brand of white man," capable of "strokes of the most sublime oratory; such as prove their reason and sentiment strong, their imagination glowing and elevated."[6] What was unclear, as we will see, is whether these noble creatures could survive the onslaught of rapacious white frontiersmen and land speculators from which Washington, Jefferson, and other early national leaders sought ineffectively to protect them.

There was and would be much romanticizing of Indians, in fact, including attributing to them such qualities as especially acute vision and hearing—since disproved[7]—suited to a people living by hunting or, more recently, a spirituality directed toward protection of the environment. These projections onto Indians of qualities that the white majority regard as desirable are almost as distorting as those other stereotypes of treacherous or drunken Indians unfit to play a role in contemporary society.

Not all "authorities" agreed. During the craze for Phrenology, when Horace Mann and others were convinced that the shape of the skull provided a scientific insight into personality and intelligence, one expert concluded from an analysis of Indian skulls that they were "savage and intractable." A visiting American speaker at a meeting, in 1841, of the British Association for the Advancement of Science insisted that "Red Men were an untameable species locked into a niche, and that 'civilization is destined to exterminate them' along with the buffalo. Since every effort to 'educate the Indians, has but deteriorated them' . . . the extinguishing of the tribes was a mercy killing of a tortured feral people unfitted to the creeping civilization. . . . 'their extinction will be a dispensation of kindness, not severity'."[8] Similarly, the author of *Types of Mankind* (1856) asserted that, despite "glowing accounts" from missionaries, there was no such thing as a "civilized *full-blooded* Indian." The shape of their skulls showed that they were missing the capacity for intellect and had a strong "animal propensity."[9]

Two courses of action toward Indians were considered at different times, and then combined uneasily. One was to educate Indians as rapidly as possible to fit into white society, as John Eliot sought to accomplish with the "praying Indians" in Massachusetts and as the Cherokee and other peoples, with white missionary help, sought to do for themselves in the early National period. Secretary of War John C. Calhoun (at that time, Indian affairs was one of the responsibilities of this office) wrote in 1820 that Indians "must be gradually brought under our authority and laws, or they will insensibly waste away in vice and misery. It is impossible with their customs that they should exist as independent communities in the midst of civilized society. . . . They should be taken under our guardianship; our opinions and not theirs ought to prevail in measures intended for their civilization and happiness."[10] This theme would be enunciated again and again by successive government officials responsible for Indians: they are doomed if we leave them to their own devices, and the only hope for their future is if we do what is best for them, whether they like it or not.

Others took an even gloomier view, that the North American indigenous peoples were fated to vanish, unable to compete in the struggle for survival in competition with white Americans and Canadians, and that benign neglect would be the kindest policy. President John Quincy Adams, seeking to resist pressure from Georgia and other Southern states to abrogate treaties with the Cherokee and other tribes and allow or cause them to be evicted from land coveted by white settlers and speculators, recorded in 1825 a conversation with his Secretary of State, Henry Clay of Kentucky.

> Mr. Clay said he thought. . . that it was impossible to civilize Indians; that there never was a full-blooded Indian who took to civilization. It was not in their nature. He believed they were destined to extinction, and, although he would never use or countenance inhumanity towards them, he did not think them, as a race, worth preserving. He considered them as essentially inferior to the Anglo-Saxon race, which were now taking their place on this continent. They were not an improvable breed, and their disappearance from the human family will be no great loss to the world. In point of fact they were rapidly disappearing, and he did not believe that in fifty years from this time there would be any of them left.[11]

Clay was not alone in this pessimistic assessment of the capacity of Indians to adapt to competition with White Americans and Canadians. An 1831 report by the head of the Federal Office of Indian Affairs in Washington said that Indians were "gradually diminishing in numbers and deteriorating in condition; incapable of coping with the superior intelligence of the white man; ready to fall into the vices, but unapt to appropriate the benefits of the social state; the increasing tide of the white population threatened soon to engulf them, and finally cause their extinction."[12] French visitor Alexis de Tocqueville, no doubt reflecting what he had heard from his white informants, wrote, "I believe that the Indian race of North America is condemned to perish . . . It is easy to foresee that the Indians will never want to become civilized, or that they will try it too late when they come to want it."[13]

A contemporary observer suggested that it would have been in the interest of the Indians to have been enslaved and thus learn the disciplines of life in an agricultural society, and that more of them would have survived "had we rigidly persevered in enslaving them."[14] Oliver Wendell Holmes (Sr.) suggested, in 1855, that it had been God's intention to place Indians in America only until "the true lord of creation," the white man, could claim it. Historian Francis Parkman's histories of the colonial period expressed a similar pessimism about the future of Indians in the face of white advance, which he saw as inevitable progress. "He will not learn the arts of civilization, and he and his forest must perish together."[15]

At the same period, in Canada, observers noted "the Indians' diminishing utility as Indians. As the nineteenth century progressed, Indians were becoming less valued for their original cultural attributes, whether as partners in the fur trade or as military allies. Settlement [of whites] assumed priority."

As a result of immigration, the Indian share of the total Canadian population fell to 1.5 percent by 1911, "and most were safely tucked away on reserves, no longer a threat to White settlement."[16]

The other proposed course of action, when education and "civilization" of Indians proved ineffective as a means of achieving a peaceful integration, was to isolate them in remote areas (often on land considered undesirable for white settlement) where they would be "protected" from the corruption and the aggressions of white society. The British government sought, in the eighteenth and early nineteenth centuries, to achieve this through restricting white settlement to east of the Allegheny mountains, and the system of reservations (in Canada called "reserves") was created to this end later in the nineteenth century.

When, through continued white encroachment and the agriculturally unproductive nature of most of the areas assigned to the Indians, it became clear that the reservations were not self-supporting economically, it began to seem to some policy-makers that it had been a mistake to shelter Indians from the pressures of living in areas of white settlement, where they "could have been compelled to acquire the civilized qualities of the whites."[17] New policies were adopted that sought to end the practice of communal ownership of reservation land and settle Indian families as farmers. There was a concomitant pressure to provide education that would permit Indian youth to function successfully in the wider economy and society. This process was often undermined by uncertainties about to what extent Indian youth could be expected to become culturally "white," and whether indeed this would be desirable.

Contrary to the gloomy predictions over many decades—and the popularity of depictions of the vanishing Indian, like the "End of the Trail" sculpture outside the Boston Museum of Fine Arts—the Indian population of the United States and Canada today is, as we have seen, by no means vanishing. It has in fact been growing remarkably rapidly, both through natural increase and also because more and more individuals are reclaiming (or perhaps in some cases inventing) Indian ancestry. "Since the 1970s, the United States census has steadily recorded huge increases in the number of Americans choosing to identify themselves as Indians, mostly in cities and suburbs far from reservations."[18] In Canada, since 1985, more than 105,000 Indians have reclaimed their status as members of recognized Indian bands. Indians are thus by no means dying out as predicted. On the other hand, they have remained disproportionately marginalized, in both the United States and Canada.

There has been at least as much—probably more—speculation about the unfitness of blacks as of Indians for full participation in American or

Canadian society, but in this case with an even more distinctly racist character. In some cases this involved comparisons between blacks and Indians, to the disadvantage of the former. In one of James Fenimore Cooper's popular novels, The Redskins (1846), an Indian character is contrasted with a black slave as "*vastly superior*" since he possessed "the loftiness of a grand nature" developed under "the impetus of an unrestrained, though savage, liberty." The slave, by contrast, "had suffered under the blight which seems to have so generally caused the African mind to wither." The Indian, though savage, is a "gentleman." A Canadian Anglican Church journal, later in the nineteenth century, noted that "[t]here is a certain innate dignity about the Indian that marks him off from the negro [*sic*], who in adaptability his superior, is his inferior in those qualities, which, when cultivated and developed place him on a level of acknowledged equality with civilized people."[19] Similarly, scientist and Harvard Professor Louis Agassiz, wrote contrasting the "indomitable, courageous, proud Indian" with the "submissive, obsequious, imitative negro [*sic*]" and—by the way—with the "tricky, cunning, and cowardly Mongolian".[20]

The contrasting stereotypes about the two groups owe something to the failure of the early attempts to turn captured Indians into slaves, in part because it was so easy for them to escape into the wilderness, while the Africans brought to replace them had far fewer options. Thus, the popular image of Indians came to be, at worst, that of a treacherous and dangerous enemy, while that of blacks came to be of a sort of semi-human domestic animal fit only to perform compelled labor.

Those who believed that observed racial differences rested on fundamentally different natures were implicitly—sometimes explicitly—rejecting the biblical account of a single creation. These "pluralists" argued that "the various human species were not blood-kin at all. Each species in its geographical home had a separate bloodline back to the beginning, which never connected to any other species." Samuel Morton, Professor of Anatomy at Pennsylvania Medical College, published *Crania Americana* in 1839, with descriptions of the skulls of more than 40 Indian peoples. Morton argued that they had been created in their homelands: "[H]is twenty-two great families of man consisted of nations that were initially unique and created on the spot." Others who studied the issue of race claimed to identify up to 63 distinct species of humans.

These "scientific" theories proved very convenient for those who wanted to deny any common humanity to which appeal could be made for abolishment of slavery or just treatment of Indians or blacks. The scientifically minded mocked those still clinging to the "religious dogma of mankind's Unity," to which a "trembling orthodoxy clutches like sinking mariners at their last plank."²¹ After all, Charles Darwin had concluded that the "mental characteristics [of the various races] are . . . very distinct." Late in the century, with the enormous influence of Herbert Spencer on thinking about public policy, in the United States as well as in Britain, it came to be widely accepted in circles that prided themselves on "advanced thinking" that "nothing could be done to improve the lot of the inferior races, and any attempt to lend assistance would simply run counter to the course of nature."²²

Some, as we have seen, took a more optimistic view of the potential of Indians to survive the competition of races. While Jefferson argued that Indians had the potential to become like whites, given enough time and the right education, he denied that possibility to blacks. In effect, Indians were different from whites because of the environment in which they had lived for many generations; blacks were different by their fundamental nature, and that could never change sufficiently.²³ In view of this long-standing tradition of denying to blacks the respect accorded to Indians, it became very common for educated Blacks to claim a measure of Indian ancestry, a fashion satirized by author Zora Neale Hurston when she wrote that "I am the only Negro in the United States whose grandfather on the mother's side was *not* an Indian chief."²⁴

CHAPTER 3

Making Christians

The intentions of European colonists and administrators toward the native peoples they encountered often included—along with less lofty motives—that of sharing with them sincerely held religious beliefs, in the conviction that acceptance of these beliefs and the accompanying behavioral norms was essential to their happiness in this life and beyond. There can be no question that the colonists also hoped that adoption of Christian beliefs and the associated (as Europeans understood them) behaviors would make the native peoples more tractable.

In an anticipation of what would continue to be a problem for the next three or four centuries, the good intentions articulated in official documents and instructions were frequently ignored or given a low priority by those grappling with practical problems in the presence of and in relationship with native peoples. What seem a straightforward goal from the perspective of Paris or London or Washington was not so simple to implement; all too often the good intentions did not take into account that the natives had their own goals, which seldom included welcoming a radically different worldview and manner of life, and that the complete *absence* of the native peoples often seemed more desirable to settlers than their converted *presence*.

In what would become Canada, the royal charter by Henri IV of France granted in 1603 to Pierre Dugua, the Sieur de Monts, to colonize and control the fur trade in "Acadia," required him "to seek to lead the nations thereof to the profession of the Christian faith, to civility of manners, an ordered life, practice and intercourse with the French for the gain of their commerce; and finally their recognition of and submission to the authority and domination of the Crown of France."[1] To this end, members of Catholic religious orders worked among Huron, Micmac, and other Indian peoples in the seventeenth century. While they were prepared to live among the Indians and follow them on their migrations, they hoped that "by the help of zealous persons in France, a boarding school might be established in order to bring up young

Indians to Christianity who might afterwards aid the missionaries in converting their countrymen." To their disappointment, a missionary priest explained in 1643, the "Seminary of the Hurons" had been shut down "because no notable fruit was seen among the Aboriginal constituency."[2]

Similarly, the relief expedition sent from England to the starving Jamestown colony in 1609 carried specific orders requiring the colonists to obtain from the Algonquians "some convenient number of their Children to be brought up in your language and your manners," as a means of ensuring the conversion of the natives, which remained "the most pious and noble end of this plantation."[3]

The royal charter awarded to the Massachusetts Bay Company, and the promotional materials developed to encourage investment and emigration, "considered Indian conversion integral to the Puritan goal of establishing a holy commonwealth in the New World. The colony's seal even depicted an Indian pleading, in the words of Saint Paul's vision reported in Acts 16:9, 'Come Over and Help Us'," holding an arrow pointed downward as a token of peaceful intentions—an image that is still found on the state shield. As a sign of its willingness to accept those Indians who became farmers like themselves as neighbors, in 1633 the Massachusetts legislative body declared "that all the lands any of the Indians in this jurisdiction have proved by subduing [that is, cultivating] the same, they have a just right unto."[4]

The goal of these efforts, it should be noted, was commonly based upon a recognition of the common humanity of the New World natives with Europeans, and an assumption that they could, relatively quickly, be "civilized" through basic education and acceptance of Christianity. The Indians were believed to be descendants of Adam and Eve and, like them, made in the image and likeness of God; this was, after all, before the rise of "scientific racism." Thus, in 1671 the government of Louis XIV ordered its administration in New France to "[a]lways strive by all manner of means to encourage all the clergy and nuns who are in the aforementioned country to raise among them the largest possible number of the said children in order that through instruction in the matters of our religion and in our ways they might compose with the inhabitants of Canada a single people and by that means also fortify the colony."[5]

Though several different strategies were employed to turn Indian children into French or English men and women, they were with very few exceptions unsuccessful. "Little by little, there was a realization on the part of the educators that Amerindian cultures were not easily eradicated, that traditional beliefs were well rooted, and that the colonial environment favoured many of the Amerindian customs and practices. . . . [T]hey were not impressed by European concepts of authority, morality, property, and work."[6]

Despite various good intentions, the results were meager; Indians "refused to fall into settled ways of life . . . Contact with the whites seemed only to deprive the Indians of their primitive virtues."[7] Margaret Connell Szasz, in her exhaustive account of efforts to convert and educate Indians in several Southern and Northern colonies, suggests that "[i]n many cases, the degree to which the Indian youth was affected by colonial schooling was in direct proportion to the extent of disruption experienced by that student's native culture."[8] Thus, the most extensive and relatively successful effort in the seventeenth century was in the Massachusetts Bay Colony, where "by the mid 1630s, European disease had reduced the population of the Massachusett tribe from over 24,000 to less than 750; meanwhile, the number of European settlers in Massachusetts rose to more than 20,000 by 1646."[9] Under these circumstances, the remaining Indians had much less capability of resisting white influence and retaining their tribal autonomy than did, for example, the Cherokees and Creeks in the Southeast, who to a considerable extent, adapted on their own terms.

During this period in which the English population was growing rapidly and that of the Indians declining equally rapidly, nearly one in four of the Indians in Southeastern New England became Christians, "the first large-scale conversion of Native Americans effected by English settlers in North America."[10] In Massachusetts, John Eliot, the pastor of the church in the town of Roxbury, took an active role in reaching out to the remaining Indians near Boston. In 1646, after Eliot experienced some success in preaching to Indians, the colonial legislature "passed a series of laws paving the way for a missionary program: the natives were forbidden to worship their own gods; two ministers were to preach to the Indians; and lands were to be purchased 'for the incuragment of the Indians to live in an orderly way amongst us'."[11] This land, interspersed among the communities of European settlement, was used to establish what, by 1674, were 14 "praying towns." Schools were established in each of these Indian communities; they, and the churches of Indian converts, were staffed primarily by Indians trained by Eliot at Natick, the first of the settlements. Early in his work among the Indians, in fact, Eliot wrote that he did not "expect any great good will bee wrought by the English . . . because God is wont ordinarily to convert Nations and peoples by some of their owne country men who are nearest to them, and can best speake, and most of all pity their brethren and countrimen." Thus Indian teachers and preachers were the "choyce instruments" of the missionary work, and they should be trained and sent "to invite theire countrymen to Pray unto God" as "the most effectuall and generall way of spreading the Gospel."[12]

Provision was also made, in the Massachusetts Bay Colony, for training Indians as teachers and preachers in institutions created for the children of the colonists; between 1656 and 1672, about 40 attended grammar schools, and four were admitted to Harvard, where a building was provided for Indian students. The results were disappointing: "[O]f these four, one died of consumption, one stayed only one year, one died of unknown causes, and one was killed by [other] Indians."[13] As the colony's official responsible for Indian affairs concluded, "In truth the design was prudent, noble, and good; but it proved ineffectual to the ends proposed."[14] How many times over the next three centuries and more could the same epitaph have been written for well-meaning efforts to solve the puzzle of how best to educate Indian youth!

Conversion and schooling of Indians occurred with more lasting success on the island of Martha's Vineyard, where the first European settler, Thomas Mayhew, his family, and a growing Puritan population lived on peaceful terms with about 3000 Wampanoags. Thomas Mayhew, Jr., pastor of the English church, learned the Wampanoag language and began to preach to the Indians, gradually gathering a congregation and starting a school. An English schoolmaster, Peter Folger, is reported to have taught reading and writing in both the Indian language and English in the school, which he opened in the 1650s.[15] Although young Mayhew and an Indian convert were lost at sea on a voyage to England in 1657, his father continued the work after his death.

The conversions in Martha's Vineyard are especially interesting because—unlike those elsewhere in New England but similar to those that would occur later to some extent among the Cherokee and other peoples in the Southeast—they did not occur in the context of population collapse and cultural and social disruption among the Indians. On the other hand, there was no effort to assimilate the Indians to their Puritan neighbors. "Neither the father nor the son, nor the converts themselves discussed the possibility of integrating converts within the English Christian community. All thought only of the creation of Christian Indian towns and churches which would be similar to those of the English, subordinate to them, and geographically separate."[16] The Vineyard Indians "adopted only those aspects of European culture that they chose. They acquired looms and ploughs or became deacons and magistrates as they continued to live in wigwams and preserve their Indian names."[17] Soon Indians had their own schools: there were two Indian schoolmasters on the Vineyard in 1658, and between 1661 and 1664 there were eight of them at work.[18]

There were also successful efforts to convert Indians in the Plymouth colony; by 1674 (before the outbreak of war) there were over a thousand Indians who professed to be Christians, and the number was approaching 1,500 by 1685. It is reported that 142 Indians had learned to read their own language by the earlier date, and nine had learned to read English. These "praying Indians" remained loyal to the colonists during King Philip's War. "It is true," we are told, "that the Pilgrims generally treated the natives as a race apart, but there is no evidence that, on the whole, they dealt more harshly with the Indians than with one another"![19]

The work of Eliot, the Mayhews, and the Plymouth missionaries, it should be noted, was supported largely by gifts from England, not by the colonists. The London-based Society or Corporation for the Propagation of the Gospel in New England, established by Parliament in 1649, provided funds to pay expenses incurred by Eliot and others, most notably for translation and publication of scripture and devotional works but also for missionary salaries, salaries for Indian teachers, and a variety of material goods that helped the Indians to adapt to the new economy created by the Puritan presence. Eliot thus was able to provide the "praying Indians" in Natick with "hoes, shovels, spades, mattocks, and crowbars, castoff clothing as well as new trade cloth; ox bells; cards and spinning wheels; apple trees and English herbs; and also medicines. In 1652 he also obtained 'winter supplies' for the new community. During the 1660s when the praying bands were under attack by the Mohawks, Eliot successfully urged the General Court to give them firearms."[20] He hired English craftsmen and farmers to teach the Indians carpentry, weaving, masonry, and English farming methods.[21]

It is currently fashionable to portray such measures as an unjustifiable imposition on an unspoiled Indian culture, indeed as a sort of "cultural genocide," but the fact is that—apart from Martha's Vineyard—the Indians of eastern Massachusetts were already in a situation of demographic and cultural meltdown as a result of the diseases introduced (unintentionally, it should not be necessary to add) by the English, and the clearing of land for farming all around them. It seems appropriate to credit Eliot and his allies, not only with good intentions, but also with effective efforts to improve the situation of the Indians, even if the positive results would in large measure be undone during the panic created by King Phillip's War.

> Eliot's program had some beneficial effects for the Indians. New goods and technologies helped the band adapt to a rapidly changing environment. Farming, woodworking, and spinning technologies, along with hunting game for sale to the English, berry gathering, and basket and broom making, all enabled the Indians to be producers in the colonial economy rather than an exploited underclass. His education initially allowed Indian scholars access to situations where they interacted with the English in a positive way. Literacy provided a basis for continued group identity and an important means of acquiring knowledge about the English. On a more concrete level, the fences Eliot encouraged the Indians to build reduced one of the major sources of

tension between natives and newcomers. Finally, the guns and ammunition, the meetinghouse, and the sawmill would also have functioned as symbolic reassurances that the Indians' own aspirations would be accorded fair scope by the increasingly powerful English.[22]

Perhaps, beyond these practical benefits, there were also aspects of the religious mission (which, of course, was central for Eliot, Mayhew, and other Puritans) that came to be important to the Indians who became Christian. Robert Naeher reminds us that the religion professed by the Puritans was not a matter of dry doctrinal instruction, but was profoundly concerned with changes in the heart. The believer—whether English or Indian—was expected to be able to describe to other Christians the sequence of religious experiences that had brought him to assurance of a converted state, and this had the effect of knitting communities together.

> Praying Church congregations were surrogates for fractured Indian kinship networks, and Praying Towns provided supportive communities for a disoriented population. Carved from territories formerly theirs and now free from European encroachment, Praying Towns thus offered Indians an opportunity to preserve their ethnic identity on "familiar pieces of land that carried their inner history." Indians chose "to pray" in order to enter into such sustaining arrangements, but once within them, the Indians were increasingly drawn to prayer as a means of giving meaning and order to their experiences. On taking this step, Indians entered into a deeper community with other truly Praying Indians. Eliot recounted how some Indians asked, "What is the reason, that when a strange Indian comes among us whom we never saw before, yet if he pray unto God, we do exceedingly love him: But if my own Brother, dwelling a great way off, come unto us, he not praying to God, though we love him, yet nothing so as we love that other stranger who doth pray unto God."[23]

The outbreak in 1675 of King Philip's War—during which the "praying Indians" suffered from both sides—brought an end to John Eliot's effort of encouraging the dwindling population of Indians in Massachusetts to create essentially Puritan villages, but Indian schools continued on Martha's Vineyard, protected by its isolation and the good relations between colonists and Indians.[24] On the mainland, the situation of Indians grew increasingly grim. Late in the eighteenth century the (white) pastor of the Natick church described an Indian community that was thoroughly demoralized. "He wrote of the Indians' drinking and 'eternal travelling around the country in a begging and destitute state.' He described the inroads made by war and disease between 1754 and 1760. In 1759 alone disease carried off whole families, with twenty Indians dying within three months."[25]

Efforts to provide schooling for the Indians were made in Virginia and the Carolinas as well. King James I had directed local parishes of the Church of England to take up special collections for "the erecting of some Churches and Schools, for the education of the children of those Barbarians," while under Oliver Cromwell's Commonwealth there was a successful fundraising effort in England for missions to the Indians. In a foreshadowing of the "outing" system developed at Carlisle Indian School in the 1880s, "sentiment in England" favored placing Algonquian children in the homes of English colonists as the most effective way of producing their "conversion and civility."[26]

The foundation of Virginia's William and Mary College in 1693 was "partially dedicated to the education of Indian students" and enrolled a number of them over the next decades, though "its Indian students shared only a tangential connection to the college course, with their instruction confined to a very elementary level."[27]

It was only belatedly, and as the colonists grew more secure and prosperous, that they began to devote some of their own resources to educate and convert the Indians. The Connecticut Assembly did so in 1717–1718, "finally determined to make up for lost time; for they and their forbears had been settled in the colony for over seven decades, and they had still failed to bring Christianity and schooling to the Indians." Under the influence of the evangelical religious revival that began in the 1730s, there was "a flurry of experiments in schooling for Indian youth," with Indian schools established in the colonies of Pennsylvania, New Jersey, Rhode Island, Connecticut, New York, and Massachusetts.[28]

While the primary instrument of the Great Awakening was preaching, the Protestant emphasis upon individual Bible study ensured a strong link between efforts to convert Indians to Christianity and efforts to teach them to read; this made the process more laborious than was the case, for example, in the Catholic missions to Indians in Canada, Florida, and Latin America. One of the New England missionaries to the Indians reported that, when he had asked them "what kind of being god was?" an Indian had replied, "Indians could not know that, because they could not read." The missionary then "further labored to show him how needful it was for them to learn to read . . . so they might come to the knowledge of those things that tend to their happiness."[29]

As this anecdote suggests, colonial missionary efforts among Indians, in a period before enforced dependence on reservations, often required seeking prior consent from Indian leaders. After Massachusetts authorities appointed a missionary to the Stockbridge Indians, in 1734, "no mission was started until the Indians themselves had been consulted and asked categorically whether they wished to be taught the Christian faith and to have a school for their children."[30]

It was Eleazar Wheelock who played the most important role in missionary and educational effort in Connecticut in the eighteenth century, as John Eliot had in Massachusetts a hundred years earlier. Wheelock founded, in 1754, a little boarding school in Lebanon, Connecticut, intended to remove Indian children from "the pernicious influence of Indian examples," a theme that we will see repeated again throughout the nineteenth and into the twentieth century in support of the residential school as the best form of education for Indians. As was often the case with later residential schools, the promoters were disappointed that, on return to their peoples, the graduates commonly reverted to the patterns of Indian life rather than serving as models for the transformation of their tribes. Thus, "Wheelock provided these girls with a practical skill, minimum reading and writing ability, and a Calvinist view of life, but he had failed to convince them that they should adopt the cultural traits of his own people. . . . Industry, diligence, frugality, and temperance were all aspects of Wheelock's character . . . It was ironic, then, that the cultural values that served Wheelock so well were the very qualities he was least able to transmit to his pupils."[31]

After 16 years, Wheelock relocated his school to Hanover, New Hampshire, where it metamorphosed into Dartmouth College, similarly dedicated to the education of Indians. He assured provincial authorities that if Indians were "brought up in a Christian manner . . . instructed in Agriculture, and taught to get their Living by their Labour" they would not "make such Depradations on our Frontiers." His school would prepare Indian teachers and preachers "for carrying the Gospel into the wilds of America." In response to his appeals, Wheelock was funded by provincial assemblies, New England churches, and mission-oriented organizations in England and Scotland. The actual impact upon the education of Indians, however, did not live up to the promises made during the fund-raising campaigns in England and Scotland. Wheelock told his sponsors that he intended to "cure the Natives of their Savage Temper" and to "purge all the Indian out" of his mostly Iroquois students, but he added the caution that "[f]ew conceive aright of the Difficulty of Educating an Indian and turning him into an Englishmen but those who undertake the trial of it."[32]

One is reminded of the gloomy conclusion of the Ursuline teaching sisters in New France who sought to educate Indian girls into suitable wives and mothers for an Indian population assimilated and loyal to the French colony, that "de cent de celles qui ont passé par nos mains à peine en avons nous civilisé une" [of a hundred of those who have passed through our hands we have civilized at most one].[33]

Some New England missionary efforts extended into the adjoining province of New York, where the five nations of the Iroquois were poised, in the eighteenth century, to provide crucial support to either the French or the British in the struggle for control of the Great Lakes region and the fur trade. The earliest missionary efforts had been by Catholic religious orders introduced by the French, but the Protestant Church of England also sent missionaries into upstate New York, and the English *Book of Common Prayer* was published in Mohawk in support of the efforts of the Society for the Propagation of the Gospel (SPG). The SPG founded a number of parishes across the region and provided the schooling necessary to participate in Anglican worship as well as in the developing economy. With the outbreak of the Revolution, the Indians under Anglican influence supported the Crown, while those under the New England Puritan influence took the other side. One of the effects of American independence was that many of the Iroquois relocated to what was then Upper Canada, now Ontario.[34] The SPG continued its educational efforts among them, providing a school in 1784, while the British colonial government was supporting a teacher among the Iroquois as early as 1785.[35]

CHAPTER 4

Wards of Government

Governments in the United States and in Canada have, since colonial times and continuing into the present, taken an active role in relation to the indigenous peoples on their frontiers and, eventually, within their borders. Frequently—though not consistently—these peoples have been treated as semi-sovereign nations, with which relations should be governed by negotiated treaties. Policy has wavered back and forth between seeking to assimilate Indians into the majority population, on an analogy with immigrants of various ethnic origins, and assuming that they would remain distinct and unassimilated. The conflict was faced clearly in 1873 when the then-Commissioner of Indian Affairs for the United States said that, while the Indians were claiming to be independent nations (as indeed the Constitution implied), they were actually only wards of white Americans. "The comparative weakness of the whites made it expedient in our early history to deal with the Indian tribes as with powers capable of self-protection and fulfilling treaty obligations, and so a kind of fiction and absurdity has come into all our Indian relations."[1]

Looked at from a long-term perspective, the native (pre-European) peoples of the United States were initially treated as a feature of the external environment of the nation; formal treaties were made with them, and an ever-retreating space was provided within which they could to some extent control their own destinies. In 1871, however, "Congress ended all treaty-making with tribes. This action marked a shift in government plans for the Indian, from relocation to the unsettled West to assimilation into the general population."[2]

In Canada, by contrast, the 1870s were a period of vigorous treaty-making between the federal government and Indian peoples. "The immediate stimulus to negotiating with various Indian groups was the resistance that certain Ojibwa bands manifested towards the passage of troops on their way to Red River, in the aftermath of Louis Riel's resistance to Canadian authority in the winter of 1869–1870." In these treaties, "it was the Natives who proposed the inclusion of guarantees of schooling . . . pursuant to Aboriginal rather than government prodding, that a provision was inserted in each of the seven treaties signed in the 1870s promising a school on their reserve 'whenever the Indians shall desire it.'"[3]

There is abundant evidence that nineteenth-century Americans and Canadians believed that the promotion of education among Indians was essential to the Indians' very survival, a belief that was strengthened when a popularized version of Darwinism created the conviction that the Indians could not survive in the "competition of the races" unless they somehow—not all were convinced that this was even possible—could be raised to something approximating "civilization." The American Commissioner of Indian Affairs asked, in 1856, what would become of "the rapidly wasting Indian tribes of the plains, the prairies, and of our new States and Territories?" It was certain that "these poor denizens of the forest [will] be blotted out of existence, and their dust be trampled under the foot of rapidly advancing civilization, unless our great nation shall generously determine that the necessary provision shall at once be made" for reservations and for "the blessings of education and Christianity."[4]

Similarly, a Joint Special Committee of Congress reported, in 1867, that "Indians everywhere, with the exception of the tribes within the Indian Territory [later Oklahoma], are rapidly decreasing in numbers" for a number of reasons, including "the irrepressible conflict between a superior and an inferior race when brought in presence of each other." The committee did not hesitate to place the primary blame upon "the aggressions of lawless white men"; nevertheless, it concluded, the evils of the situation "can never be remedied until the Indian race is civilized or shall entirely disappear."[5] Carl Schurz, the former Commissioner of Indian Affairs, stated as an established fact in 1881 that Indians were faced with "this stern alternative: extermination or civilization."[6]

In Canada, the Indian peoples had, under British rule in 1763, been "recognized as self-governing entities within the Empire." The Proclamation of 1763 by the British Crown had a specific and eventually superseded purpose, according to Sir George Murray, Secretary of State for the Colonies, in 1830. It had "reference to the advantage which might be derived from their [the tribes'] friendship in times of War rather than to any settled purpose of gradually reclaiming them from a state of barbarism and of introducing amongst them the industrious and peaceful habits of civilized life."[7] The intention in 1763 was to reserve all the land west of the Appalachian Mountains, in what became mid-western Canada and the United States, for "the several Nations or Tribes of Indians, with whom We [King George III] are connected, and who live under Our Protection." The attempt to limit encroachments by white colonists on the Indian hunting grounds, and alleged favoritism of the Crown toward the "merciless Indian Savages" mentioned in the *Declaration of Independence*, was one of the grievances that led to the American Revolution.[8]

In the peace negotiations in Ghent to end the War of 1812, the British sought to set aside the upper Ohio River valley as an independent Indian territory. John Quincy Adams, serving as one of the American negotiators, rejected this as based on "a profound and rankling jealousy at the rapid increase of population and of settlements in the United States, [and] an impotent longing to thwart their progress and to stunt their growth."[9] Ironically, as President a dozen years later, Adams would seek in vain to protect the Cherokee and other Indians of the Southeast from similar white population pressures.

Efforts to protect Indian territory in Canada experienced similar pressures by 1830, when white settlement was increasing rapidly and the Indians were becoming economically marginal and had lost their strategic importance. The Department of Indian Affairs was directed to improve the condition of Indian communities "by encouraging in every possible manner the progress of religious knowledge and education generally amongst the Indian Tribes." The Superintendent of Indian Affairs had already, in 1767, promised that "instruction in religion and learning would create such a change in their [the tribes'] manners and sentiments" as to "promote the safety, extend the settlements and increase the commerce of this country";[10] that would now become government policy.

In the new United States, the federal government, as in Canada, assumed responsibility for relations with Indian peoples wherever they lived, including making some gestures in the direction of education. It was by no means apparent that the states would allow the central government to assert its authority over Indian affairs, and in fact in the 1830s Georgia successfully repudiated treaties made by Congress with Indians who had been guaranteed rights to land within its borders.

The First Continental Congress adopted a resolution, in 1776, declaring that "a friendly commerce between the people of the United Colonies and the Indians, and the propagation of the gospel, and the cultivation of the civil arts among the latter, may produce many and inestimable advantages to both."[11] They set up a Committee on Indian Affairs and authorized it, among other duties, to employ "a minister of the gospel, to reside among the Delaware Indians, and instruct them in the Christian religion; a schoolmaster to teach their youth reading, writing, and arithmetic," and later appropriated funds to educate several Indian youth at Dartmouth College.[12] Article III of the Northwest Ordinance of 1787 provided that "the utmost good faith shall always be observed towards the Indians; their lands and property shall never be taken from them without their consent . . . laws founded in justice and humanity shall, from time to time, be made, for preventing wrongs being done to them and for preserving peace and friendship with them."[13]

From the beginning there was a recognition that the Indians had as much to fear from the settlers as the settlers had to fear from the Indians.

Henry Knox, secretary of war under the Confederation, reported to Congress in July 1788 the unprovoked and direct outrages against the Cherokee Indians by the inhabitants on the frontiers of North Carolina in open violation of the Treaty of Hopewell [1785]. The outrages were of such extent, Knox declared, "as to amount to an actual although informal war of the said white inhabitants against the said Cherokees." the action he blamed on the "avaricious desire of obtaining the fertile lands possessed by said Indians. . . . He recommended that Congress issue a proclamation warning the settlers to depart, and if they did not, to move in troops against them.[14]

President Washington offered a reward, in 1793, for the arrest of Georgians who had destroyed a Cherokee town.[15] Already—and despite the earlier efforts of British authorities to restrict settlement—whites outnumbered Indians west of the Appalachian Mountains. Others took an optimistic view of the relationship; characteristically, President Jefferson asserted, in 1803, that there was "a 'coincidence of interests' between the races. Indians, having land in abundance, needed civilization; whites possessed civilization but needed land."[16] In 1808, he assured the Western Indians that "the day will soon come when you will unite yourselves with us, join in our great councils, and form a people with us, and we shall all be Americans; you will mix with us by marriage; your blood will run in our veins and will spread with us over this great continent."[17]

Jefferson was not the only American then or subsequently who expected Indians eventually to be absorbed into the general population through intermarriage. An account of Hampton Institute, where both blacks and Indians were enrolled in the late nineteenth century, points out that the "essential difference . . . was that Indians could be candidates for amalgamation with the white race, while blacks could not . . . unlike their black counterparts, the Indian leaders had a specific goal to which they were to lead their race: amalgamation with the white race. The Indians, Helen Ludlow said straightforwardly, 'like our foreign elements . . . are being absorbed into our common population. The Indian problem is likely to disappear in the next century for want of a distinguishable Indian race.' No one at Hampton ever postulated such a future for the black race."[18]

In the meantime, the chosen instrument for regulating relationships with Indians was the formal treaty between the federal government and a tribe, in effect treating the tribe as a sovereign entity. Between 1803 and 1885, the American Senate approved almost 400 treaties with Indian peoples, of which 120 included promises that the government would provide education to the tribe, usually in exchange for land thus opened to settlers. Such treaties were by no means uncontroversial, since they could be interpreted as superseding the authority of state and territorial governments over Indian tribes and lands; refusal to recognize the authority of treaties or to enforce their conditions by restricting white encroachments was the basis of much injustice and many conflicts, leading to the expulsion of the Southeastern tribes in the 1830s.

A typical early treaty was that made in 1820 with the Choctaw, one of the Southeastern "civilized" tribes that would be pushed farther and farther westward until most of them ended up in Oklahoma. The treaty includes a provision that "fifty-four sections of one mile square shall be laid out in good land . . . and sold, for the purpose of raising a fund, to be applied to the support of the Choctaw schools, on both sides of the Mississippi River." As with other tribes, a missionary helped to advise the Choctaw and it was no doubt in part his influence that led to inclusion of the provision for schooling.[19]

It was not until 1819 that the American government made efforts to promote formal schooling among the Indians by establishing the "Civilization Fund," which was mostly used for grants to missionary organizations working among them. Initial reports of the results were optimistic; the Indians seemed responsive to the invitation to emulate white society. Choctaw leaders wrote to Calhoun in 1824, "We feel our ignorance, and we begin to see the benefits of education. We are, therefore, anxious that our rising generation should acquire a knowledge of literature and the arts, and learn to tread in those paths which conducted your people, by regular generations, to their present summit of wealth & greatness."[20] In that year there were, according to the federal government, 21 Indian boarding or day schools, operated by Christian missionaries, not federal employees, with altogether some 800 students.[21]

Benevolent intentions on the part of the federal government toward Indians could not long resist the political pressure of congressmen from the South and West (which at that point meant Alabama, Tennessee, Kentucky, and Ohio) to make Indian lands available for white settlement. The pressure became especially strong as the cultivation of cotton spread across the South. Soon the arguments for removal of the Indians to the undeveloped areas in the West that were still largely beyond white settlement were joined by others that claimed to be concerned with the best interests of the Indians themselves, protecting them from the encroachment of often-violent whites. "If the government and missionaries promised to carry their fostering aid west and continue there the original policy of enlightenment under quieter circumstances, would not this be best for the Indians and best for the rapidly expanding population of white Americans eager to settle and exploit the riches of the Mississippi Valley?"[22]

A strong supporter of civilizing efforts among the Indians modified his earlier positive views on what was being accomplished by missionary schools and the efforts of government agents after a tour of the frontier in 1827. He reported, for example, that Indians in the Northwest (that is, Ohio and neighboring areas) "pretend to nothing more than to maintain all the characteristic traits of their race. They catch fish, and plant patches of corn; dance, paint, hunt, get drunk, when they can get liquor, fight, and often starve." While some of the Southeastern tribes had benefitted from schooling, "these were, to my eye, like green spots in the desert." As a result of these observations, he had changed his view on the appropriate policy to support their removal to the West: "[A] sight of their condition, and the prospect of the collisions [with whites] which have since taken place, and which have grown out of the anomalous relations which they bear to the States, produced a sudden change in my opinion and my hopes."[23]

Perhaps the earlier commitment to promote the education of Indians could be better realized if they could be removed from the corrupting influence of white settlers, since "the contact of the Indians with white civilization had deleterious effects upon the Indians which far outweighed the benefits. The efforts at improvement were vitiated or overbalanced by the steady pressure of white vices."[24] A treaty with the Choctaw, in 1830, providing for their removal to west of the Mississippi to land guaranteed them in perpetuity (one of many broken promises), stated in Article XX that

> The U.S. agree and stipulate as follows, that for the benefit and advantage of the Choctaw people, and to improve their condition, there shall be educated under the direction of the President and at the expense of the U.S. forty Choctaw youths for twenty years. This number shall be kept at school, and as they finish their education others, to supply their places shall be received for the period stated. The U.S. agree also to erect . . . a Church for each of the three Districts, to be used also as school houses . . . [and] . . . twenty-five hundred dollars annually shall be given for the support of three teachers of schools for twenty years.[25]

In 1832, Congress established the position of Commissioner of Indian Affairs; the incumbent wrote in his *Annual Report* for 1838 that "the principal lever by which the Indians are to be lifted out of the mire of folly and vice in which they are sunk is education." An appropriate education for the Indian in his present state of civilization would involve improving his morals as well as his mind, including "by teaching him how to farm, how to work in the mechanic arts, and how to labor profitably." He welcomed a plan proposed by the Methodist Missionary Society, to establish "a large central school for the education of the Western Indians, with a farm and workshops." This, they argued, would be more effective than schools for the individual tribes, since by bringing together Indians from a variety of tribes, they would be forced to learn and use English. On the other hand, he pointed out, the funds available for Indian schools actually belonged, under the existing treaties, to the tribes themselves, and so it would not be feasible to cut off the small tribal schools, but the proposed central school could be a valuable supplement, by training teachers for the tribal schools.[26]

On the other hand, this civilizing work should be carried out at a safe distance from the corrupting influence of white settlements. As President Andrew Jackson put it, in his Message to Congress in December 1833, the Cherokee and Seminole could not continue to

> exist surrounded by our settlements and in continued contact with our citizens. . . . They have neither the intelligence, the industry, the moral habits, nor the desire of improvement which are essential to any favorable change in their condition. Established in the midst of another and superior race and without appreciating the causes of their inferiority or seeking to control them, they must necessarily yield to the force of circumstances and ere long disappear.[27]

There were parallel developments in Canada, though often somewhat later. Ashagashe, an Ojibwa leader, complained in 1827 that the Americans were providing schooling to Indians, but the British were not.[28] The population of Upper Canada (now Ontario) tripled between 1825 and 1842 to 450,000, and more than doubled again by 1851. Inevitably, this undermined the economic basis of the Indians' way of life. As Anglican leader John Strachan wrote in 1837, the Indians of Upper Canada "could no longer live by hunting as the settlements were extending through every part of the Province and unless something was done to induce them to alter their mode of life they must inevitably" perish. The preferred intervention, as would so often be the case in the future, was to seek to wean Indian children away from their families and tribes and thus prepare them to function in Canadian society. To this end, for example, a Methodist conference in 1837 called for establishment of a residential school that would remove Indian children "from their imperfectly civilized parents," placing them "under the exclusive direction of their religious and secular Instructors."[29]

The results over the next few years—as of so many such efforts—were discouraging; the report of a Canadian government commission concluded that the "benevolent experiment has been to a great extent a failure." Graduates of the boarding schools did not "seem to carry back with them to their homes any desire to spread among their people the instruction which they have received. They are content as before to live in the same slovenly manner . . . the same apathy and indolence stamp all their actions as is apparent in the rest of the Indians."[30] The problem, however, was not with the schools but with the conditions to which a graduate returned: reserves in which there was no individual land ownership and thus no opportunity to set up as an independent farmer and become "a full member of colonial society" like his white neighbors; the solution would be to distribute the commonly held land. This would in effect be to dissolve the tribes and treat Indians as individuals like any others.

In response to the growing distress of the tribes in Canada, the 1857 Act to Encourage the Gradual Civilization of the Indian Tribes promoted allotment of Indian lands held in common by the tribes to individual Indians, on the assumption that they would thus become independent farmers like the white settlers who were encroaching upon them. The Act provided that an Indian man who was literate in either English or French could apply to receive 50 acres of land from the common land of the reservation, and this would be inherited by his children.[31] This effort, which would be attempted several times over the following century in Canada and the United States alike, "redefined civilizing Indians from developing community self-sufficiency to assimilating them individually."[32]

Such proposals were resolutely opposed by tribal leadership, but advisors to the Canadian government insisted that "the longer the Indian is kept in a comparatively helpless condition, and treated as a child, the less inclined he will be to assume the responsibility for or taking care of himself." The transfer, in 1860, of authority for Indian matters from London to Ottawa opened the way for a succession of government actions designed to transform the situation of Indians.

With Canadian sovereignty attained in 1867, the new government's responsibility for Indian peoples was defined in Section 91.24 of the British North America Act, the Canadian Constitution. This had been preceded by the 1857 Act for the Gradual Civilization of the Indian and the 1858 Civilization and Enfranchisement Act, enacted by the British Parliament, and would be followed by Canada's 1876 Indian Act and 1884 Indian Advancement Act. A Canadian law adopted in 1868 authorized the government to use funds from the sale of Indian lands to help schools attended by Indian children, and over the following decade a number of treaties obligated the government to provide schools.[33]

In 1880, a government official in Canada wrote, "Let us have Christianity and civilization among the Indian tribes; let us have a wise and paternal Government . . . doing its utmost to help and elevate the Indian population, . . . and Canada will be enabled to feel, that in a truly patriotic spirit our country has done its duty by the red men."[34] In some quarters, at least, there was optimism that this could be achieved. "I believe that there is through Canada a kindly feeling towards the Indian race," wrote an Anglican clergyman active in the education of Indians in the 1870s, "that it is only their dirty habits, their undisciplined behaviour, and their speaking another language, that prevents their intermingling with the white people. I believe also that there is in the Indian a perfect capability of adapting himself to the customs of the white people . . . but he wants the advantages given him while young, and he requires to be drilled into the use of those advantages."[35]

The 1876 Indian Act "authorized the [Canadian] federal government to direct all of the activities of Indian people. . . . The act with its various amendments included, among other things, governance of the following: place of residence, access to travel, acquisition and sale of property or goods, education, and participation in traditional ceremonies."[36] The Act was also an attempt to place the situation of Indians within a legal context that provincial and local government and the courts could fit into their frame of reference; it "transformed loose groupings into rigidly defined communities, complete with membership lists, assigned reserves, and institutions of local government."[37]

Not all Indian peoples became wards of government in the full sense; the "Five Civilized Nations," in particular, were able with considerable success to maintain semi-independent status with an elaborated tribal government and a range of institutions similar to those of white society.

CHAPTER 5

The "Five Civilized Nations"

Perhaps the earliest instance of European-style schooling controlled by an Indian people was among the Cherokee. After several decades of government-funded missionary schools, the Treaty of 1835 provided an annual sum of $16,000 a year from the federal government to support Cherokee public schools. Although for some years the teachers were white, often recruited from New England, eventually almost all were Cherokees trained at the Cherokee-controlled secondary schools.[1]

The "Five Civilized Nations"—Cherokee, Creek, Choctaw, Chickasaw, and Seminole—were in their great majority driven from the traditional territories in the Southeastern United States in the 1830s and 1840s and settled in what for the rest of the nineteenth century was called "Indian Territory" before it became Oklahoma. Although there would be reservations of other Indian tribes in Oklahoma, the societies that these five peoples built were uniquely advanced as measured by the standards of White America.

A number of boarding schools had already operated among the Cherokee when they were living in the Southeast, as the result of initiatives by missionaries and in response to demand by the significant element of the tribe who were of mixed ancestry and wanted schooling for their children comparable to that received by white children. As early as 1714, "white traders were making annual trading trips to the Cherokee towns" in what later became western North Carolina. "Some settled in them and raised mixed-blood families. . . . By 1740, there were 150 traders buying up the Cherokees' pelts and furs by the thousands each spring."[2] Over time, men of mixed ancestry came to dominate many spheres of Cherokee life: in the early years of Brainerd Mission in Tennessee, founded by the American Board of Commissioners for Foreign Missions in 1816 to serve the Cherokee nation, the majority of the pupils were full-blooded Cherokee, but they were increasingly replaced by pupils of mixed blood.[3]

Members of the Cherokee Nation of mixed ancestry tended to marry those like themselves, "but it was due more to wealth, social behavior, and value differences than to purity of race." There was, however, a strong color bar against marriage with blacks, imitated from the surrounding white society, as "the Cherokees concluded that their survival as a nation depended upon their clearly distinguishing themselves from Africans. To treat blacks as equals would not raise the blacks in white eyes but would simply lower the red man. . . . The Cherokee renascence was consequently a grim imitation of the worst as well as the best in white culture."[4]

The contrast between full-blooded and mixed-blood would be decisive in subsequent Cherokee history, and the cause of repeated conflict; the remarkable level of prosperity and "civilization" noted by observers for the next hundred years would be largely confined to the minority of Cherokee with partial mixed ancestry, who characteristically had little interest in maintaining traditional customs.

> Numerous Tories had joined them in the war against the American colonists after 1776; some deserters from the ranks of the French and Spanish had become intermarried "countrymen." Their children did not speak Cherokee or know Cherokee customs. These white men and their foreign-speaking, European-dressed children, when grown, proved helpful in certain ways. They understood the language and customs of the whites and provided useful knowledge as well as serving as interpreters for the Cherokee leaders. . . . the children of mixed ancestry tended to marry their own kind, to raise their children as whites did, and to perpetuate a social group separate from the rest of the [Cherokee] nation.[5]

By the early nineteenth century, with the decline of their hunting grounds through overexploitation, Cherokees began to adopt the white farming practices spreading across the region, including—for the wealthier—the purchase of black slaves; some 200 out of 3,500 Cherokee families owned slaves. "White men who married Cherokees enjoyed the opportunity to become the owners of large plantations; land cost them nothing and they paid no taxes. Mixed-blood Cherokees who spoke English began to adopt the life style of surrounding white farmers. Gradually the Cherokees developed a landed elite and a small group of shopkeepers and entrepreneurs." By 1810, there was a substantial and growing difference between "the three hundred or so families who were prospering most through acculturation and the two thousand or more families who were still struggling to make ends meet each year." The former group—most of them mixed-bloods, who made up about 15 percent of the Cherokee nation—wanted formal schooling for their children, as a means of perpetuating their privileged position; only 94 out of more than 3000 school-aged children were attending school in 1809, and a year later the two Presbyterian schools closed, leaving 34 pupils in school[6] and a substantial unmet demand.

With the establishment of the federal Civilization Fund in 1819, and the growing activity by the American Board of Commissioners for Foreign Missions and by Methodists and Baptists among the Cherokee, the supply of schooling improved. Indeed, the Georgia legislature protested against the federal help to support these denominational schools because it tended to solidify the Cherokee presence on land that the state government was determined to claim for white farmers. In fact, however, "the largest proportion of missionary budgets had to be supplied by donations from the members of their churches or from local and state missionary societies organized for fund raising."[7]

Among the institutions that responded to the demand for white-style schooling was the Blue Springs, Kentucky, Choctaw Academy, an intertribal school opened in 1825.[8] In the 1820s, several Christian denominations opened schools in Cherokee territory, and these schools began to appear farther and farther west. The first across the Mississippi opened in 1819 as a result of Congregationalist efforts; they were followed by Moravians, Baptists, and others.[9] Despite the expanded availability of schooling, schoolmasters were often frustrated by the unwillingness of many Cherokee families to make it a priority.

> Because Cherokee parents were indulgent toward their children and did not comprehend the kind of discipline that required sitting behind a desk for long hours memorizing words in the white man's book, attendance at mission schools was irregular until the [Cherokee] Council passed a law in 1820 making attendance compulsory once a child had enrolled.[10]

As, increasingly, missionary schools met the need for primary instruction (at least of children from mixed-blood families), the Cherokee Council decided, in 1825, to establish an academy to prepare some of them to attend colleges;[11] while the prolonged disruptions that led eventually to expulsion from the Southeast frustrated such efforts, they were renewed when the Cherokees were at last settled in Indian Territory in the West.

A visitor from the North in 1830 found that "a spirit pervades the nation for amelioration, and in pursuit of economical and intellectual improvements and attainments." There were, he reported, well-attended schools where students learned English, the New Testament, grammar, and geography. "Some have received instruction in higher grades of learning, with whom you can discourse rationally on most subjects."[12] Article VI of the Cherokee Constitution adopted in 1839 echoed the language of John Adams in the Massachusetts Constitution of 1780: "Religion, morality, and knowledge being necessary to good government, the preservation of liberty and the happiness of mankind, schools and the means of education shall forever be encouraged in this nation."[13]

Determined to function as a self-governing "nation" after their forced exile to Indian Territory, the Cherokee National Council asserted its control over the education of its children by insisting that all schools must have their approval. "Although the Cherokee Nation permitted the missionaries to construct schools, these institutions remained private and were separate from the nation's school system. Like the Choctaw, the Cherokee secured funding through the education clause in their contested treaty of removal—the Treaty of New Echota—and through monies derived from direct land sales."[14] The Council established, in 1838, a committee responsible for creating a Cherokee-operated educational system. This was about the time, it should be noted, when the Massachusetts Legislature established a Board of Education, with Horace Mann as its first Secretary. In 1841, 11 Cherokee common schools were authorized, and the position of Superintendent of Education was created. By 1843, there were 500 pupils enrolled in the 11 schools, taught by two Cherokee and nine white teachers, and seven more common schools were authorized; by 1852, there were 1,100 pupils in 21 Cherokee schools, and by 1859 there were over 1,500 pupils in 30 Cherokee common schools.[15]

One of the most remarkable features of this achievement, compared with the situation of other tribes, was that more than half of the common school teachers, by 1854, were themselves Cherokees, and by 1858 "only two teachers in the entire [common] school system were not of Cherokee descent." On the other hand, there was a clear split within the tribe between the "progressive" elements, often of mixed ancestry, and the more traditional Cherokees, commonly full-bloods. "The progressive Cherokees certainly did not believe themselves 'primitive' and were determined to prove it by making their tribe a model of white society. These progressives wanted an educational system in order to 'uplift' the entire tribe, including poor full-bloods and some mixed-bloods."[16]

At the summit of this system would be separate academies—known as "seminaries"—for young men and young women, with instruction equivalent to that of secondary institutions elsewhere in the country. An academy education was at the time and for some decades after thought quite sufficient qualification for school teaching and a variety of other nonmanual occupations. In fact, "by 1859, fifteen of the twenty-six Female Seminary graduates had been hired to teach in the Cherokee public schools that did not give instruction in the Cherokee language."[17]

Establishment of the two seminaries was approved by the Cherokee National Council in 1846, with funding to be provided both by Cherokee funds and also by the trust funds promised by the federal government when it made a treaty with the Cherokee, in 1835, to surrender their lands in the Southeast and move west of the Mississippi. It should be noted that these schools were established by the Cherokees and not by the federal government.[18]

During the same period, the other "civilized nations" in Indian Territory were also creating boarding schools for pupils going on beyond the instruction in common schools, though in these other cases these schools were operated under agreements with missionary organizations, and the program of these schools was less exclusively academic and less relentlessly concerned to convey the High Culture of contemporary American society.[19]

The faculty for the new Cherokee academies were recruited in New England, the men graduates of Yale and Newton Theological seminary, the women of Mount Holyoke Female Seminary, which had a very strong orientation toward preparing young women to serve as missionary teachers on the frontier, in the overseas mission fields, and (after Emancipation) in the South; by 1856, 24 Mount Holyoke alumnae had taught among Indians.[20] The curriculum for the female and male academies was modeled on Mount Holyoke, on the one hand, and on Boston Latin School and Lawrenceville Academy, on the other.

What explains the consistent support, among the Cherokees, for the sort of education that middle-class white Americans and Canadians sought to provide for their own children? Cherokee leaders—who in almost all cases were of mixed ancestry—commonly explained it as a result of "the white blood that has made us what we are," as the superintendent of the Cherokee Female Seminary wrote in 1889, adding, "if missionaries wish to lift up [other] Indian tribes let them encourage intermarriage with whites . . . intermarriage will accomplish this purpose quickly." Another superintendent in 1909 "expressed his impatience with the full-blood girls by referring to the mixed-bloods as 'whiter' and therefore 'more intellectual'."[21]

There is an element of truth in this analysis; after all, the quickest way for children to acquire the English language and many of the cultural elements of European society was to have a white father (or, in fewer cases, mother), and intermarriage between colonial merchants, missionaries, and others had been occurring since the eighteenth century. By the end of the nineteenth, many leaders in the Cherokee community had three or four generations behind them of families who had lived according to white norms, and their sons and daughters arrived at the seminaries without any cultural gap to overcome. This was in sharp contrast with the situation in other Indian residential schools. "Whereas the federal boarding schools were controlled by white Americans, the Female Seminary was controlled by Cherokees who subscribed to the values of white Americans. . . . Also, at the seminary many students did not feel the loss of certain tribal customs—if they ever adhered to them in the first place. For many students, life at the seminary was not a great contrast to their home life."[22] A missionary noted, in 1853, that "in the Seminaries [as the academies were called] there are not more than four or five pupils of full-blood. The majority have so much white blood in their veins that a stranger would pronounce them entirely of white parentage."[23]

Obviously, the two Cherokee seminaries were elite institutions, equivalent to the English "Public Schools" like Eton and Harrow, and to the private boarding schools developing in New England and elsewhere in the late nineteenth century. Cherokee men were prepared by the Male Seminary for careers as physicians, lawyers, politicians, and bankers, usually after further study outside the Indian Territory. Indeed, the superintendent of Cherokee schools, in 1856, thought it necessary to point out that "each cannot be a professor, lawyer, doctor, preacher, school-master," and urged that the seminaries train in practical occupations, "engineers, agricultural experts, and skilled artisans—people who would build bridges, roads, and mills and do the work the [Cherokee] nation now had to pay whites to do."[24]

Women who attended the Female Seminary typically married alumni of its male counterpart, sometimes after a few years teaching school. The alumni of the Cherokee seminaries

> were unlike many members of other tribes who went to school and returned home only to find that they needed parts of both the white and Indian worlds but could not cope in either one. The women who moved from the Cherokee Nation to attend college found that upon their return they were accepted among their peers and faced little, if any, cultural confusion . . . Most of them married white men or men who had a smaller amount of Cherokee blood than they had. In some cases the husbands had a greater degree of Indian blood, but in every such instance they were physicians, politicians, or members of prominent Cherokee families (usually wealthy ones).[25]

There was no study of Cherokee culture, much less language, in Cherokee Female Seminary, and the social atmosphere clearly favored the girls from mixed-race families over full-blood (and hence darker) girls, who generally were from families less acculturated to white norms. At least 30 percent of the students who attended the Cherokee Female Seminary over the decades of its existence, Mihesuah found, were one-sixteenth Cherokee or less, "yet they still considered themselves Cherokees. Many of these girls had never heard the Cherokee language spoken." While these "nontraditionalists" were "intensely proud of their Cherokee lineage," they seldom bothered to learn the Cherokee language or to attend non-Christian tribal religious ceremonies. "The women of this highly acculturated subculture were not bicultural. Their feet were firmly planted in the portion of Cherokee society that adopted the ways of the white world."[26] Theodore Roosevelt, in one of his books about the frontier, wrote that "an upper class Cherokee is nowadays as good as a white";[27] in fact, of course, many had predominantly white ancestors.

Unfortunately, then, "in the long run, the Cherokee educational system, commendable as it was in principle, produced disunity; it increased rather than diminished class differences"[28] within Cherokee society. This was not, it should be emphasized, the result of either missionary intentions or government policy; it was something that the Cherokees did to themselves or, rather, which the acculturated elite did to emphasize the ways in which they and their families occupied and intended to retain a superior position.

Meanwhile, the number of black slaves owned by about 10 percent of the Cherokee families increased, in 1860, to between 3,500 and 4,000, giving the mixed-blood elite (about one-third of whom owned slaves) a strong incentive to side with the Confederacy in the Civil War . . . and many full-blood Cherokees to side with the Union.[29] This internal division reinforced that based upon acculturation to white society and use of English on the part of the mixed-bloods.

Other "civilized nations" relied more upon missionary management, though funding their schools by the same methods that the Cherokees used. The Choctaw schools were managed by missionaries, under an act of the Choctaw legislature in 1842 that established six boarding schools and "appropriated money for the support of these institutions and placed them under the direction of different missionary societies, which were to contribute additionally to their support."[30] Choctaw Academy, supported by federal funds owed to the Choctaw and by Baptist contributions, educated the Choctaw, Creek, and Pottawatamie until the Civil War.[31] The four schools founded by the Chickasaw were operated by Methodist or Presbyterian organizations. The Creek contracted with Methodists and Baptists to run several of their schools, though "the Baptists and Methodists who served at these schools were increasingly Creek themselves."[32]

Cherokee schooling was devastated by the Civil War, over which the tribe itself was divided, but the National Council had reopened 32 common schools by 1867, and doubled that number by 1870. Separate Cherokee schools were established for black pupils. A number of mission schools were also reopened. By 1880, 3,048 pupils attended Cherokee schools, and the number increased to 4,258 in 1899 and 5,505 in 1903, at the point when the Cherokee system was taken over and made part of the educational system of the new state of Oklahoma.[33]

The refuge from white settler encroachment that the Indian Territory was intended to provide to the Cherokee and other tribes was only temporary; "white people poured into the Territory like an animated flood. The existence of one republic inside of another had some most inviting concomitants for a class of men who had found life in the higher civilization uncomfortable." White outlaws found refuge from law enforcement in surrounding areas. Finally, in the Indian Appropriation Act of 1896, Congress declared it "to be the duty of the United States to establish a government in the Indian Territory which will rectify the inequalities and discriminations now existing in said Territory and afford needful protection to the lives and property of all citizens and residents thereof."[34] Former Commissioner Leupp wrote a few years later that "by degrees the condition of things there became so unbearably corrupt and dangerous that the government was forced to make a complete reorganization. This was done under the forms of agreements negotiated with the five tribes; but actually it was a plain taking-over of the territory, its reduction to the status of other territories, and finally its erection into a state, under the name Oklahoma."[35]

Thus, the period of largely independent self-government by the Five Civilized Tribes ended when Congress passed the Curtis Act in 1898, providing for distribution of the tribal lands held in common to individual members of the tribe, abolition of the tribal courts, and "assumption by the federal government of supervisory control over the tribal schools."[36] One of the results of this takeover was that the Cherokee people no longer possessed institutions perpetuating a tribal elite; while arguably this was a gain for intratribal equity, it was a loss for the development of leadership.[37] Oklahoma state institutions were controlled by the white majority, who far outnumbered Indians, and two-thirds of Indians lost their land allotments, "especially when Indian farms happened to have gold, oil, gas, or other valuable mineral deposits."[38]

Another result was a dramatic fall in the Cherokee literacy rate, attributed to the "almost complete alienation of the Cherokee community from the white-controlled public school systems."[39] In recent years, however, Indians in Oklahoma have performed significantly better than those in Arizona and New Mexico on the National Assessment of Educational Progress, presumably reflecting their much longer intergenerational experience of schooling and literacy.

On the other hand, the National Study of American Indian Education, completed in 1971, included a survey of different groups of Indians who were asked whether they rated "Indian Culture" or "White Culture" more highly. It was only the group in Oklahoma who rated White Culture more highly than their own.[40]

CHAPTER 6

Churches as Allies and Agents of the State

Government administrators and policy-makers in the nineteenth century in both countries frequently made use of churches and missionary organizations to promote government objectives with respect to Indian peoples, and had no hesitation about providing public funding for schools with explicitly religious goals. Indeed, government officials, a number of whom were themselves ordained Protestant ministers, did not hesitate to express the intention that Indians become Christian. This close alliance with missionary organizations was common practice in the United States until, in the 1880s, anti-Catholic prejudice on the part of the majority led to increasing restrictions on funding of religious schools among the Indians, and it remained the norm in Canada (where the role of the Catholic Church in education enjoys constitutional protection) until after the Second World War.

Despite this intermixing of government and church efforts, it is possible to distinguish them. The intention of missionary organizations was to "make Christians"; while this certainly included efforts to change behavior in many respects, missionaries also commonly accepted the distinctiveness of Indian peoples, often including their languages. In effect, missions to the Indians in North America were not fundamentally different from the contemporary missions to Africa and elsewhere around the world; they were not intended to "make Americans." By contrast, that was increasingly the goal of government policy, with schooling of Indians seen as in parallel with that provided to immigrants, with the goal of reshaping them into "Americans." There was, in consequence, a tendency on the part of denominational schools to be more accepting of various aspects of Indian culture, provided that they could be reconciled with Christian belief and practice. Catholic Archbishop John Ireland, quoted in the federal Bureau of Indian Affairs *Annual Report* of 1902, urged educators of Indians to focus on modification of behavior without emphasis on modification of identity:

> Teach the girls the ordinary industries for which they are fitted . . . and I believe it will do much more for the elevation of the race than teaching boys. Let the spirit of the home be what it should be, and the father and son will be all right. Teach the girls to take care of their homes and made them attractive, teach them cooking, teach them neatness, teach them responsibility. Teach the girls to milk and take care of poultry; and teach them how to serve a nice appetizing meal for the family; do this and I tell you you have solved the whole question of Indian civilization.[1]

In effect, the contrast, though never perfect, was between promotion of an essentially transnational goal of religious conversion (of course, mixed in practice with conscious and unconscious assumptions about the identity of Christianity and American or Canadian values) and promotion of a national goal of creating loyal subjects and eventually citizens. There was, arguably, more consistency in the approach of the churches to the education of Indians: for some four centuries, most missionary efforts have accepted the idea that the interests of Indians would be best served by maintaining a degree of separation from the majority society, while government in both countries has wavered between promoting the most rapid possible assimilation through residential schools, in the second half of the nineteenth century, to largely abandoning that goal in the early twentieth century, to a subsequent emphasis on integration of Indian children into ordinary public schools, and then beginning in the late 1960s to various measures to promote recovery of Indian identity and languages, with a de facto acceptance of segregated Indian schools under Indian control.

It is not surprising, therefore, that the leading nineteenth-century spokesman for and practitioner of the assimilation of Indians to American life, Richard Henry Pratt of the Carlisle Indian School, was hostile toward missionary efforts, writing in 1892 that "the missionary goes to the Indian. . . . He learns the language. He associates with him—makes him feel that he is friendly and has great desire to help him. He even teaches the Indian English. But the fruits of his labor, by all the examples I have seen, have been to strengthen and encourage him to remain separate and apart from the rest of us."[2]

Missionaries did, indeed, "come to regard previous approaches to assimilation as too hostile to Native cultures, so they advocated a more gradual approach that allowed Indians to maintain their racial pride as they adapted themselves to Euro-American society." As government policy in the United States shifted radically in the 1930s to promote the preservation of Indian traditions and religions, the missionaries found themselves outflanked and forced into the position of defending the changes that had occurred on many reservations as a result in large part of their efforts.[3] In particular, the Indian congregations that had gradually been gathered, often with Indian lay leaders and pastors, were in some circles no longer seen as positive expressions of adaptation, but as instances of "inauthenticity."

The situation was very different in the early Republic. Leaders of the newly independent United States were keenly aware of the presence of Indian peoples all along their Western border, and policy-makers starting with George Washington took various measures to seek to ensure peaceful relations with Indians as white population inexorably expanded westward. It was natural, given the sparse administrative machinery of the federal and state governments in the early national period, that policy-makers turned to churches and to benevolent agencies (almost all with a religious character) to establish a pacifying and "civilizing" presence among the Indians. These efforts were often in response to requests from the Indians themselves, as when the Seneca petitioned President George Washington in 1791 for "teachers to instruct their children in agriculture, cottage arts, reading, and writing." In addition, the terms of the treaties that the federal government entered into with Indian peoples, such as the Oneida, Tuscarora, and Stockbridge tribes in 1794, often obligated the government to provide funds for education.[4]

Although the American federal government—unlike those of several of the states—was barred from any "establishment of religion" by the First Amendment to the Constitution, it did not hesitate to support the work of various churches with the Indians; indeed, until the 1880s "the missionary was the prime civilizing element among the Indian tribes"[5] on behalf of the government as well as of the churches. Thomas Jefferson himself, despite his famous metaphor of the "wall of separation" between church and state, did not, when President, hesitate to sign a treaty in 1803 with the Kaskasia Indians of Illinois that included the provision that "whereas, the greater part of the said tribe have been baptised and received into the Catholic church to which they are much attached, the United States will give annually for seven years one hundred dollars towards the support of a priest of that religion, who will engage to perform for the said tribe the duties of his office and also to instruct as many of their children as possible in the rudiments of literature" and another $300 outright for the cost of building a Catholic church.

With or without government encouragement, Christian missionaries continued to go to the Indians as they had during the eighteenth century, and brought the latest styles of formal schooling with them. For example, a Presbyterian missionary, Gideon Blackburn, persuaded President Jefferson to provide some modest funding, and raised sufficient support from white churches to introduce Pestalozzi-inspired "manual labor" schools—one a boarding school, the other a day school—among the Cherokee in 1804. Results were encouraging, in part because many of his pupils had fathers who spoke English.

> The Cherokees soon discovered that the Presbyterian curriculum included considerable Christian training; the children were taught to read from the Bible and catechism, to say Christian prayers daily, and to sing Christian hymns. They were forbidden to speak Cherokee. The schoolmasters and their wives were ardent Christians; they also did their best to teach the children how to dress, eat, and behave according to the manners of whites. Mixed-blood parents had no objection to any of this, but full-blood parents were less pleased. Few full bloods attended; the schoolmasters spoke no Cherokee and had to rely on their students to translate. Blackburn was convinced that the sooner the Cherokees abandoned their language, the better.[6]

A dozen years later, in 1817, the American Board of Commissioners for Foreign Missions (ABCFM), supported largely by New England Congregationalists, established Brainerd Mission in Tennessee, named after an early missionary to the Delaware Indians, to serve the Cherokee nation. Buildings were erected, including the schoolhouse, a dining room, living quarters for teachers, a kitchen, a lumber house, a meat house, dormitories for the Cherokee students, a barn, a stable, a gristmill, and a carpenter's shop, and by May 1818 the school had 47 "promising" students. President James Monroe himself visited the school the following year, on his way to Nashville, and expressed his strong approval of how the Indian children were being "taught to work," which he believed was "the best, and perhaps the only way, to civilize and Christianize the Indians." Monroe promised additional federal funds to support the mission.[7]

One of the ABCFM missionaries, Samuel Austin Worcester, translated the New Testament and many hymns into the Cherokee language. He and another missionary later defied the state of Georgia through their support of the rights of the Cherokees and were sent to prison despite winning the Supreme Court case *Worcester v. Georgia*, when President Andrew Jackson chose to ignore the ruling of the Court; after his release, Worcester followed the Cherokee west and continued to live and work with them until his death in what later became Oklahoma in 1859.

In contrast with their justified suspicion of the white frontiersmen with whom they came in contact, Indians generally had a positive experience with missionaries, who "did not appear to share the hostility and contempt for Indians that most frontier whites did." One was pleased to be told by Moravian missionaries in 1799 that "we love all people, no matter what their color" and that so did the Great Spirit.[8]

> As the years progressed and humanitarian concern for the Indians deepened, still other aid came from missionary groups, who established missions among the tribes and who by and large subscribed to the principle that there was little hope of Christianizing the savages without first building a foundation of stable civilized existence. The missionaries were agricultural agents as well as messengers of Christ's Gospel and their centers were model establishments and practical schools which augmented the work of the government.[9]

In 1819, Congress appropriated $10,000 for a "civilization fund" to be administered by the Department of War. The enabling act stated that the intention of Congress was to make provision "against the further decline and final extinction of the Indian tribes, adjoining the frontier settlements of the United States, and for introducing among them the habits and arts of civilization." The President was thereby authorized "in every case where he shall judge improvement in the habits and condition of such Indians practicable, and that the means of instruction can be introduced with their own consent, to employ capable persons of good moral character, to instruct them. . . ."[10]

The notice issued by the Department of War to call for proposals for the use of the civilizing fund invited "such associations or individuals who are already actually engaged in educating the Indians, and who may desire the cooperation of the government" to apply, and specified that "Government cooperation will be extended to such institutions as may be approved, as well in erecting their necessary buildings as in their current expenses."[11] Secretary of War John C. Calhoun offered sponsors of mission schools two-thirds of construction costs,[12] though these efforts were complicated by the growing pressure to move the Southeastern Indians out of states and territories that were rapidly filling up with white settlers—and black slaves.

Funds raised by congressional appropriation or by land sales were used almost exclusively to support the work of denominational missions among the Indians, especially those in the Southeast. In 1819, Congress was informed that there were two missionary-run schools among the Cherokee, and two among the Seneca, as well as three other schools outside of the area designated as "Indian Country."[13] Progress was rapid; the director of the new Office of Indian Affairs in the War Department reported in 1824 that there were 32 Indian schools with 916 students, run by various religious groups.[14] Although the funds were administered by that office, which issued specific rules and regulations, the actual operation of schools serving Indians was left to the religious organizations, which obtained part of the necessary funding through submitting a formal request describing how the funds would be used to "civilize" Indian children. By 1842, the federal funds were supporting 37 schools established by missionary groups, with 85 teachers and 1,283 pupils.[15]

Much of the support for Indian schools was raised from the churches themselves along with the offerings that supported work in foreign mission fields, and government officials did not hesitate to see their work among the Indians in the context of worldwide Christian missions. "Great exertions," one informed Congress in 1818, "have, of late years, been made by individuals and missionary societies in Europe and America; schools have been established by those humane and benevolent societies in the Indies, amongst the Hindoos [sic], and the Hottentots; and, notwithstanding that superstition, bigotry, and ignorance have shrouded those people in darkness for ages, thousands of them have already yielded to instruction."[16] It was reasonable, therefore, to have confidence that similar efforts among Indians would produce similar results.

While Congress provided funding each year for missionary educational efforts, these could not have expanded as they did without the contributions of the churches, and the Indian tribes themselves provided substantial support for education through the funds owed to them by the federal government in exchange for the cession of land. In 1824, $12,708 of the funds for schools came from the government, $8,750 from the funds owed to the Indians in exchange for cession of land, and $170,148 from the contributions collected by the churches, or 89 percent from the churches, and the proportions were similar in 1825.[17]

Denominational missions were launched in Upper Canada (later Ontario) in the 1820s and after; Methodists, Anglicans, and Roman Catholics started day schools providing a manual labor curriculum for Indian youth. Anglican leader John Strachan appealed to the Church Missionary Society in England for help with his efforts to educate Indians, while Egerton Ryerson, commonly seen as the "Horace Mann" of Canada, began his career as a Methodist missionary among the Ojibway Indians, and learned their language. In 1830, the Methodists were operating 11 schools with 400 pupils among the Indians in Upper Canada.[18] By the 1850s, the government was providing yearly grants to some of the denominational schools, though the church sponsors "supplied the teachers, supervisors, and necessary equipment."[19] The Hudson's Bay Company, in the territory in the Far North, which it controlled, "was making annual grants to various religious denominations to encourage their educational endeavors."[20]

At the other end of the continent, in Southwestern Alaska, Western-style schooling was provided to Indians by the missions established by the

Orthodox Church during the period of Russian rule in the eighteenth and the first half of the nineteenth centuries.[21]

If missionaries and the churches that supported them played the dominant role in the education of North American Indians through much of the nineteenth century, it was in part because the administrative structures of the national governments were only weakly developed, in part because churches and other religious institutions were almost the only nongovernmental organizations concerned with education, but also because they were largely alone in their concern for the interests of native peoples. For example, in their efforts to avoid being expelled from their ancestral territory in the Southeast of the United States, the Cherokee

> had only one card left to play in their negotiations: to enlist the political aid of the distinguished and well-connected mission board of the newly arrived missionaries from New England. . . . They strongly preferred the original Indian policy of civilizing and incorporating the Indians and they firmly believed that the United States must live up to its treaty pledges.[22]

When, in 1830, congressmen from Tennessee introduced a bill to remove the Cherokee and other Indians to the West, Quaker groups from Pennsylvania and church and missionary societies in the Northeast expressed vehement disapproval, though eventually they proved unable to do more than delay the course of events; the Southern and Western senators were able to outvote those from New England and the mid-Atlantic states.[23]

The missionaries sent from New England "found intense hatred of the Indians among the whites everywhere on the frontier," and were unsuccessful in countering that attitude, as one of them wrote, "by showing that the Indians were capable of education and conversion to Christianity."[24] But the prevailing view in government until the "closing of the frontier" late in the century was that Indians must make way for whites, and that missionaries tended to stand in the way of the national interest because of their advocacy for the Indians through their connections in influential circles in the North, and through their encouragement of the Indians to adopt agriculture and other aspects of white society that made it more difficult to call for their expulsion.

General P. B. Porter, when serving as Secretary of War and thus as the official responsible for Indian policy, "argued against any kind of education for Native Americans because it tended to create a permanent missionary infrastructure that might actively oppose removal of Native Americans to the West. In Porter's view—one that was widely held outside of missionary circles—education did Indians more harm than good and, in the end, ruined them by undermining their culture, making them good-for-nothing."[25]

A congressman from Kentucky sought, in 1822, to abolish the Civilization Fund on the grounds that "all such attempts to civilize the Indians had ended in failure,"[26] but perhaps also motivated by concern over the de facto alliance between Southeastern Indians and Northern Evangelicals. In the same spirit, in his report on Indian Affairs to President Adams in 1828, Porter attacked the missionary schools as creating "half-educated" Indians who "finding no outlet for their intellectual skills and attainments among their degraded people," became either drunkards or troublemakers. The missionaries themselves, he charged, were acting "secretly to be sure, but not with less zeal and effect, to prevent . . . emigration" of Indians and thus to thwart the efforts of the government for their own selfish reasons. In 1830, this attitude led to a decision that henceforth grants from the Civilization Fund would be provided only for missionary schools west of the Mississippi.[27]

John Quincy Adams, as President from March 1825 to March 1829, sought to resist the pressure for removal of the Indians from their ancestral lands in Georgia and neighboring states; he later wrote that the country's Indian policy "is among the heinous sins of this nation, for which I believe God will one day bring them to judgement—but at His own time and by His own means." His Inaugural Address had praised the progress the previous administration had made in "alluring the aboriginal hunters of our land to the cultivation of the soil and of the mind," but he soon "came to realize, what was wanted was not the conversion of the native to the white man's ways; what was wanted was the native's land, nothing more, nothing less. Assimilation could result in such embarrassments as the Cherokee constitution, which, if it had been successful, would have deprived white land speculators of several hundred thousand acres of land."[28]

The leading evangelical politician of the period, Senator Theodore Frelinghuysen, gave a famous six-hour speech in Congress over the course of three days to oppose the removal of the Indians, but in vain. Frelinghuysen, who also opposed slavery and was allied with the Tappan brothers and others in that frustrating struggle, was a leader in a whole range of the benevolent associations that has been called the Evangelical United Front, including the American Bible Society and the American Sunday School Union, and serves as a reminder of how these causes and those promoting them were interrelated and often motivated by religious considerations.

The pressure to remove the Southeastern Indians beyond the Mississippi River—which would be completed by the army starting in 1838—increased the urgency for missionaries and the Indians themselves to demonstrate, by education, that they were fit to remain as neighbors of white settlers in Georgia and Alabama. As would occur some years later with "industrial schools" and then yet later with pedagogies associated with Progressive Education, the early efforts to provide schooling for Indian youth sought to employ the latest educational theories. In the first decades of the nineteenth century, this was the "monitorial" method of instruction associated with Joseph Lancaster and Andrew Bell and was initially employed to instruct orphans in India and urban working-class children in England.

The ABCFM, created by members of the Congregational Church in Massachusetts in 1810, decided in 1817 to extend their work to the Choctaw and other Indians, declaring their intention "to establish schools in the different parts of the tribe under the missionary direction and superintendence for the instruction of the rising generation in common school learning, in the useful arts of life and in Christianity, so as gradually to make the whole tribe English in their language, civilized in their habits and Christian in their religion."[29] Consistent with current pedagogical fashion, they announced that they would use the monitorial method in the schools they started. This involved training the more advanced among the pupils to teach their less-advanced peers, under the supervision of a single teacher. Instruction in basic literacy was combined with "inculcating 'habits of industry' through enforcement of strict discipline" and an emphasis upon practical skills. Pleased with the experiment, and support by government funding, the ABCFM opened a second school for Choctaw youth in 1818.[30]

The intimate connection between missionary enterprise and government policy was illustrated when the Osage Indians, like others, agreed to move out of territory they occupied—in this case, in Missouri—to make way for advancing white settlement. A Protestant mission had been established among them in 1821, and the government ordered, four years later, that "missionary establishments . . . for the benefit of the Osage Indians" be sold and reestablished "at the principal villages occupied by these Indians," noting that "those missionaries may have objections to this removal, but their establishments were built upon individual and public contributions for the special benefit of the Indians & to answer the purpose of their institutions they must be located amongst Indians."[31] The government cut off its funding of the Indian schools operated by the ABCFM in 1830 because "the Government by its funds should not extend encouragement and assistance to those, who thinking differently upon this subject, employ their efforts to prevent removals,"[32] and after 1832 the federal government "offered generous subsidies to move missions west."[33]

Already in this early period there were indications of the specialization of mission focus that would characterize the denominational work with Indians throughout the nineteenth and well into the twentieth century. For example, "the Moravians (United Brethren) and the Presbyterian Board of

Missions taught the slave-owning, mixed-blood Cherokee elite, whereas the Methodists and the Baptists learned Cherokee and lived with the common people, usually full-bloods, as itinerant ministers. . . . [T]he Baptists and Methodists used Cherokee exhorters (lay preachers) and were able to convert the poor."[34] Since Methodists (and Baptists) did not insist upon extensive education for their preachers, they were younger, and "some of them were married to Cherokees. They had no large mission establishments but rode from village to village on horseback, sleeping in the cabins of the Cherokees, sharing their food, treating them as equals." In the 1830s, when most Northern missionaries with withdrawn as a result of the hostility of Southern state governments, the Baptist and Methodist congregations were sustained by Cherokee converts

> who, in their own language and style, spoke of what Christianity could mean in their lives on their terms. From these native preachers and from other converts, the Cherokees learned how Christianity could be a source of help and power that did not make them feel inferior to whites and that did not compel them to become just like whites. . . . Through it they found a new order, meaning, and direction in their lives.[35]

When the Cherokee and other Southeastern Indians were forced to relocate to the Indian Territory, the missionaries went with them, starting their own schools and also staffing the public schools established by the Cherokee Nation. In 1847, out of 21 teachers in the public schools, five were Congregationalist, three Baptist, and two were Methodist missionaries, in addition to ten schools operated by missionary organizations on the Cherokee reservation.[36]

Despite the low status in general of the Catholic Church in the United States in the nineteenth century, and the suspicions directed toward it by the Protestant majority, Catholics were strongly involved in the government-subsidized educational efforts among Indians; by 1832, they were operating three of the 51 schools receiving government support, and this effort continued to expand.

The alliance with religious organizations to provide schooling for Indians was a matter of conviction and not simply of convenience, as when government makes use of nonprofit organizations, which are already, for their own charitable and other reasons, engaged in the work. The 1832 *Annual Report of the Commissioner of Indian Affairs* mentions the "very salutary effect" that could be expected from the development of a code of laws for Indians, "especially as co-operating with the influences derivable from the education of their youth, and the introduction of the doctrines of the christian religion, all centering in one grand object—the substitution of the social for the savage state." Without such measures, he warned in terms that would be repeated with increasing frequency throughout the nineteenth century, "it may be a matter of serious doubt whether, even with the fostering care and assured protection of the United States, the preservation and perpetuity of the Indian race are at all attainable."[37]

Despite occasional unseemly rivalries among denominations, their partnership with the government in providing schooling to Indians was almost unchallenged for the first hundred years of American independence. "In every system which has been adopted for promoting the cause of education among the Indians," Commissioner of Indian Affairs William Medill wrote in 1847, "the Department has found its most efficient and faithful auxiliaries and laborers in the societies of the several Christian denominations, which have sent out missionaries, established schools, and maintained local teachers among the different tribes. . . . the Department has not hesitated to make them the instruments, to a considerable extent, of applying the funds appropriated by the government for like purposes."[38]

After the Civil War, when the resources and activities of American government expanded enormously, and during a period of extensive (though largely ineffective) federal intervention to provide schooling for the children of free slaves in the South, government also made gestures toward a systematic approach toward schooling for Indian youth. Despite pledges to the tribes, however, a government-operated system of Indian schooling was slow to become a reality, and officials continued to express their support (financial as well as moral) for the efforts of the churches.

"Peace" was a popular slogan in the United States after four years of a bloody Civil War, and Congress appointed a blue-ribbon Peace Commission to seek agreements with the Indian tribes that were resisting the advance of white settlement into the Great Plains. "The peace policy was a praiseworthy effort. A product of the idealism of the reconstruction era, it won enthusiastic backing from both politicians and reformers. Unfortunately, like so many ambitious schemes of the postwar period, it did not work."[39] Again and again the advance of white settlement and its encroachment on Indian lands, as well as its frequent influence on Indian mores, undermined the ability of Indian peoples to make a successful transition to the new circumstances that they faced. In a striking image, the new Commissioner of Indian Affairs in 1868, a former Methodist minister, wrote that "[b]eyond the tide of emigration and hanging like the froth of the billows upon its very edge is generally a host of law-defying white men, who introduce among the Indians every form of demoralization and disease with which depraved humanity and in its most degrading forms is ever afflicted."[40]

This would be the theme of Hamlin Garland's popular novel *The Captain of the Gray-Horse Troop* (1902). Garland portrays a Western politician, in the 1890s, whose policy, since he was restrained "by men with hearts and a sense of justice," from simply killing off the Indians as he would have preferred, was "a process of remorseless removal from point to point, from tillable land to grazing land, from grazing land to barren waste, and from barren waste to arid desert." Garland also describes a well-meaning Commissioner of Indian Affairs complaining that

> "The Injun has it—let's take it away from him," seems to be the universal cry. I am pestered to death with schemes for cutting down reservations and removing tribes. It would seem as if these poor, hunted devils might have a thumb's-breadth of the continent they once entirely owned; but no, so long as an acre exists they are liable to attack. I'm worn out with the attempt to defend them.[41]

Already three decades earlier, the Peace Commission appointed by Congress in 1867 asked, "Have we been uniformly unjust? We answer, unhesitatingly, yes!"[42] In response, President Grant announced the government's Peace Policy in 1869. This had three major elements. The first, an attempt to eliminate corruption and to improve the quality of the supervision of the reservations, was that church and mission boards were asked to assume supervision over particular tribes and to nominate individuals to serve as agency and reservation personnel and thus as government employees. The Kiowa-Comanche Agency in Oklahoma, for example, was entrusted to the Society of Friends, which appointed a farmer from Iowa as the agent in charge.

> A thorough-going Quaker whose temperament meshed perfectly with the humanitarian goals of the Peace Policy, Tatum faced an enormous task. Before him were more than six thousand Indians from ten tribes speaking nine languages and occupying an area the size of Connecticut. An earnest and eager agent, Tatum soon discovered that enlightened conduct . . . was sadly out of step with the realities of the reservation. . . . "[T]here was no more incongruous spectacle than that of a Quaker agent preaching the virtues of peace and agriculture to a plains warrior, treating this man . . . as a simple, misguided soul who could be brought to see the error of his ways by compassion and sweet reason".[43]

By 1875, on this reservation, only eight Indians had abandoned their traditional dress for what was called "citizen clothing," and only 60 out of some 600 Indian children were in school.[44]

The second element of the Peace Policy was an expansion of federal support for Indian education. The Commissioner of Indian Affairs had written, in 1866, that education was "the means of saving any considerable portion of the race from the life and death of heathen."[45] To this end, Article 7 of the 1868 Treaty of Fort Laramie with the Sioux and their allies specified that "[i]n order to insure the civilization of the Indians entering into this treaty, the necessity of education is admitted . . . they therefore pledge themselves to compel their children, male and female, between the age of six and sixteen years, to attend school." It should be noted that this was at a time when few of the states had adopted compulsory school attendance laws for white children. Article 7 went on to the government's pledge "that for every thirty children between said ages who can be induced or compelled to attend school, a house shall be provided and a teacher competent to teach the elementary branches of an English education shall be furnished."[46] The treaty with the Navajo, the same year, contained almost identical language;[47] unfortunately, in both cases, the government was as slow to provide schools as Indian parents were to accept the importance of formal schooling.

On the Kiowa-Comanche reservation, for example, "the government failed from the beginning to meet its obligations. At no point in the agency's history were there sufficient facilities, and the Indian Office never came close to providing anything resembling enough schools for the children entitled to them." In fact, the first school opened on the reservation was provided, not by the government, but by the Society of Friends.[48]

The third element of the Peace Policy was that the president would appoint a Board of Indian Commissioners made up of philanthropists and reformers with a special concern for the welfare of Indians. This was simply an advisory group with no authority over Indian affairs, but it paved the way for the influential role that would be played by the Lake Mohonk Conference of the Friends of the Indian for several decades after its founding in 1883. In its first report, in 1869, the Board urged that "[s]chools should be established, and teachers employed by the government to introduce the English language in every tribe. It is believed that many of the difficulties with Indians occur from misunderstanding of either party, the teachers employed should be nominated by some religious body having a mission nearest to the location of the school. The establishment of Christian missions should be encouraged, and their schools fostered. . . . The religion of our blessed Saviour is believed to be the most effective agent for the civilization of any people."[49]

Indeed, at this point the federal government had little alternative to the religious organizations in seeking to stabilize its relationship with the various Indian peoples. The first report of the new Board, in 1869, could identify only the mission schools, on the one hand, and those of the Cherokee and other "civilized nations," on the other. It was not until 1870 that Congress appropriate $100,000 for schools on the "industrial" model for which Hampton Institute was an example.

Resistance to the Peace Policy began at once. "Politicians, who coveted the Indian Service with its growing number of field appointments as an endless source of patronage, and the Indian Office, which frowned on any attempt to reduce its control over the administration of Indian affairs, . . . began a campaign to frustrate and emasculate the power of the church boards to appoint agency officials."[50] Sporadic outbreaks of violence on the ever-expanding frontier—for which both Indians and settlers were responsible in varying degrees—led to demands to leave the implementation of policy toward the Indians up to the Army, which could confine them on their reservations, safely out of the way of the farmers, ranchers, and miners who were filling the West.

The exception that seemed to show that Indians could in fact be civilized was the "Five Civilized Nations" that, as we have seen, had been displaced from the Southeast and were now settled in the "Indian Territory" (later to become Oklahoma). The *Annual Report of the Commissioner of Indian Affairs* for 1868 provided an optimistic account of what had been accomplished:

> The blanket and the bow are discarded; the spear is broken, and the hatchet and war-club lie buried. . . . Schoolhouses abound, and the feet of many thousand little Indian children—children intelligent and thirsting after knowledge—are seen every day entering these vestibules of science; while churches dedicated to the Christian's God, and vocal with His praise from the lips of redeemed thousands, reflect from their domes and spires the earliest rays and latest beams of that sun whose daily light now blesses them as five Christian and enlightened nations so recently heathen savages. . . . [T]heir average intelligence is very nearly up to the standard of like communities of whites.[51]

What was needed now, he argued, was to apply the same strategy with the Cheyenne, Arapahoe, Apache, Kiowa, Comanche, Sioux, "and all our other tribes," including confining them on reservations, introducing the idea of individual property, and finally, "the great coadjutor in the whole work in all its progress, the Christian teacher and missionary."[52]

For most tribes, the treaties' provisions, including those for funding, were administered through religious and mission organizations until the 1870s, when the federal government began to take a direct role in educating Indian children. However, several tribes controlled their own schools and thus their own treaty funds. Most notable among these tribes were the Choctaw and Cherokee, who combined had nearly 200 schools when the Indian Territory was dissolved in the early 1900s;[53] many of these were managed under contract between the tribes and missionary organizations.

There was a long way to go. In 1876, the Indian Office estimated (with suspicious exactness) that there were 266,151 Indians living in the United States, excluding Alaska; of these 104,818 wore "citizens' dress" and 25,622 could read English. There were, according to the report, 437 teachers educating 6,028 boys and 5,300 girls in 63 boarding schools and 281 day schools,[54] but, as we will see, the conditions and the effectiveness of this instruction was highly questionable.

In 1882 the Commissioner of Indian Affairs wrote

> Civilization is a plant of exceeding slow growth, unless supplemented by Christian teaching and influences. I am decidedly of the opinion that a liberal encouragement by the government to all religious denominations to extend their educational and missionary operations among the Indians would be of immense benefit. I find that during the year there has been expended in cash by the different religious societies for regular educational and missionary purposes among the Indians the sum of $216,680, and doubtless much more which was not reported through the regular channels . . . but insignificant in comparison with the healthy influences created by the men and women who have gone among the Indians . . . for the higher and nobler purpose of helping these untutored and uncivilized people to a higher plane of existence. In no other manner and by no other means, in my judgment, can our Indian population be so speedily and permanently reclaimed from the barbarism, idolatry, and savage life, as by the Christian people of our country. . . . [I]t is not only the interest but the duty of the government to aid and encourage these efforts in the most liberal manner. No money spent for the civilization of the Indian will return a better dividend than that spent this way.[55]

Three years later came the assurance from the Commissioner that "the Government can, and does, fairly and without invidious discrimination, encourage any religious sects whose philanthropy and liberality prompts them to assist in the great work of redeeming these benighted children of nature from the darkness of their superstition and ignorance."[56]

The regular congressional appropriations in support of the "civilizing" work of religious organizations, which had begun with $10,000 in 1817, reached $100,000 by 1870, and in 1876 there were 54,473 Indians in agencies supervised by Methodists, 40,800 supervised by Baptists, 38,069 by Presbyterians, 26,929 by Episcopalians, 24,322 by Quakers, 17,856 by Catholics, 14,476 by Congregationalists, and 21,974 by other denominations.[57]

To take just one example, the Presbyterian missions agency, between 1837 and 1893, sent over 450 male and female missionaries to at least 19 tribes, where they operated day and boarding schools, offering "at their best" a wide menu of academic work: "English, arithmetic, algebra, history, geography, chemistry, botany, physiology, natural philosophy (the sciences), natural history (geology and biology), Latin and Greek, and sometimes—for pragmatic reasons—literacy in tribal languages. During class, Sunday School, and throughout the mission the teachers attempted to provide 'a thorough knowledge of the great truths of religion, in its most simple and practical form.'"[58]

During the period of expansion of the federal government's role after the Civil War, the churches continued to provide generously for Indian schools operated under government contracts. "The increase in enrollment between 1887 and 1888, for example, was substantially greater in the contract schools than in the government schools because the contract schools had increased their [physical] accommodations more than the government schools".[59]

Starting in 1883 and continuing for decades, the Lake Mohonk Conference of Friends of the Indian brought together representatives of churches, philanthropists, and reformers; for the rest of the nineteenth century they had a strong influence on federal policy toward Indians, including support for residential schooling that would more effectively insulate Indian youth from the influences of family and tribe. One of the elements of a comprehensive program adopted at Lake Mohonk in 1884 was a resolution that "[t]he Indian must have a knowledge of the English language, that he may associate with his white neighbors and transact business as they do. . . . He must have a Christian education to enable him to perform duties of the family, the State, and the Church. Such an education can best be acquired apart from his reservation among the influences of Christian and civilized society. . . . The Christian people of the country should exert through the Indian schools a strong moral and religious influence. This the Government cannot do, but without this the true civilization of the Indian is impossible." This led to the conclusion that residential schools like Carlisle, located in areas where Indian pupils could be "placed in the families of farmers and artisans," should be supported and multiplied.[60]

Carlisle and subsequent off-reservation residential schools in the United States were in general, although not exclusively, operated by the government itself and not by denominational agencies, unlike in Canada. Prime Minister Macdonald told the Canadian House of Commons in 1883 that "secular education is a good thing among white men but among Indians the first object is to make them better men, and, if possible, good Christian men by applying proper moral restrains, and appealing to the instinct for worship that is found in all nations, whether civilized or uncivilized."[61] Already for decades the development of schools for Indians had been largely promoted by missionary organizations that commonly would start schools without prior authorization and then seek government subsidies on a per pupil basis. These subsidies were almost never adequate; in British Columbia, "the greater part of the money was found by the respective church, with, in some cases, a small grant from the federal government."[62] As discussed below, the miseries associated with residential schools that would be the cause of public repentance on the part of church and state alike, together with reparations, were to a large degree caused by funding inadequate to feed and house the Indian pupils adequately, or to attract really capable and stable staff to teach and to manage the schools.

The treaties with Indian tribes negotiated by the Canadian government between 1870 and 1877 frequently included provision for schooling, with the characteristic language being that "Her Majesty agrees to maintain a school on each reserve hereby made, whenever the Indians should desire it." Often missionaries, already on the spot, were advisors to the Indians as they negotiated these treaties, and the "government's treaty promises in the area of education gave the churches a lever to provide funding for schools and teachers. They did not hesitate to use it," to such an extent that a member of Parliament complained in 1907 that "the clergy seem to be going wild on the subject of Indian education and it is time some limit should be placed on their demands." It was reported in 1927 that "Churches have been pioneers in the remote parts of the country, and with missionary funds have put up the buildings and induced the [government] to provide funds for maintenance." As a result, "the churches expanded the system according to the light of their mission strategies and budgets. The Department then followed as best it could in the face of constant petitions."[63]

An example of this process was the founding of a Catholic school for Indians in British Columbia. The government had postponed action on a request for a school for four years when the bishop, in 1898, appealed to the government minister, "telling him that in anticipation of a grant the missionary responsible for the project had gone ahead and built a school large enough for fifty pupils and would proceed to open it. 'Surely,' the bishop concluded, 'the government will not leave him exposed to the impossibility of opening the school for want of means to care for the intended pupils.'" The grant was approved.[64]

In the Yukon, which remained almost entirely untouched by white Canadians until the Klondike Gold Rush beginning in 1896, it was the Anglican bishop who urged the government to provide schools for the natives. "Because White settlement was not increasing," however, "and because the

Natives could continue their harvesting activities, the federal government saw no benefit in educating or relocating [into consolidated settlements] the Native population." Although the bishop was convinced that "schooling is the most hopeful branch of mission work," he had great difficulty obtaining contributions from either Church or State. The Minister of the Interior was emphatic in 1908: "I will not undertake . . . to educate the Indians in the Yukon. In my judgement they can, if left as Indians, earn a better living." It was only gradually, with extreme difficulty and uncertain results, that schooling was provided here and there in that vast territory. Government "tightfistedness, evident from 1910 to the end of the Second World War, forced the clergy to operate their schools on an extremely small budget." With the collapse of the fur market, and the growing dependence of Inuit and Indian families on government welfare support that required children to attend school, the quality and quantity of schooling improved in the Far North.[65]

CHAPTER 7

Decline of the Partnership of Church and State

During the second half of the nineteenth century, the frontier was rapidly closing across North America and native peoples—who included, in Canada, the mixed-race Métis—were no longer beyond the borders of advancing "civilization" but increasingly surrounded by it. The population of the United States west of the Mississippi rose from seven to more than 11 million during the 1870s. In the Dakota Territory, for example, there had been twice as many Indians as whites in 1870, but a decade later the Indians were outnumbered by more than six to one. "More area came under the plow in the half-century following the Civil War than had been broken in all of the years since the landing at Jamestown."[1] This changed the context within which schooling was provided, but not, for some decades, either the purpose or the dominant role, in pursuing public as well as charitable goals, of Christian religious organizations.

This collaboration and division of labor began to come under pressure in the United States in the 1880s, although as we have seen, the Commissioner of Indian Affairs expressed support for public funding of religious schools for Indians as late as 1882, writing in his annual report: "I am decidedly of the opinion that a liberal encouragement by the government to all religious denominations to extend their educational and missionary operations among the Indians would be of immense benefit. . . . No money spent for the civilization of the Indian will return a better dividend than that spent this way."[2]

Belying this assurance to the denominational associations, federal policymakers planned a comprehensive system of schooling for Indians, to be owned and operated by the federal government. In 1887, there were 41 boarding schools (mostly on-reservation) with 2,553 students, and 20 day schools with 1,044 students operated under contract with the Indian Bureau, mostly by religious organizations.[3] The Commissioner of Indian

Affairs provided assurances, in 1889, that "Indians, like any other class of citizens [though actually Indians did not become citizens by right until 1924], will be free to patronize those schools which they believe to be best adapted to their purposes,"[4] but in fact there was declining support for public funding of nongovernment schools.

Some opponents of government encouragement of missionary efforts were concerned that these encouraged Indians to retain their distinctiveness. As we have seen, Richard Henry Pratt, the best-known educator of Indians in North America, was an ardent critic of church efforts among the Indians, charging that missionaries, "in their efforts to build Christian congregations, frequently ignored the larger business at hand—preparing Indians for citizenship in the white man's civilization."[5] He went so far as to charge that "using religion as a racial separating wall became perpetual purposes in missionary enterprises and a leading influence in establishing the segregating, reservating government system."[6] Certainly it was the case that, as we will see, on many reservations the only use of Indian languages in a written form was in connection with Bible-reading and hymn-singing, and that some of those languages would not have remained in use as long as they have without the functions they served in churches and Bible studies.

A more important cause of the change of policy that would occur in the 1890s, however, was the growing opposition to Catholic schooling in general, which turned policy-makers against Catholic schools for Indians. The change of political climate was closely related to contemporary controversies over the growth of Catholic schooling of immigrants in a number of cities across the country. Rather than joining with Catholics in calling for public funding of all church-sponsored schools serving the Indians, most Protestant groups came to oppose such funding even for their own schools in order to be consistent with their opposition to public funds for urban parochial schools. Protestant denominations began to withdraw from the contract school system for reasons they ascribed to the principle of separation of church and state—which had not apparently troubled them previously—and urged all religious denominations to do the same. In 1890, Catholics received $356,957 from the federal government, compared with $47,650 to Presbyterians and about half that to Congregationalist, Episcopalian, and Quaker educational efforts among the Indians.[7]

In 1892, the General Assembly of the Presbyterian Church reported, "It is the policy of the Government to give a thorough English education, and to instruct in the duties and responsibilities of American citizenship, thus doing for the children of the Indians precisely what the common schools are doing for the children of foreigners who are crowding to our shores—assimilating and Americanizing them. . . . Finding the mission schools at hand, often in the very locality they wished to occupy, instead of founding new schools, they resolved to subsidize the mission school . . . the Government was to appropriate a certain amount of the public money, and was to be admitted to a certain measure of control, on condition that the sectarian schools should cease to be sectarian so far as to avoid the appearance of sectarianism. The plan was essentially a vicious one . . ."[8] This despite the fact, it should be noted, that Presbyterian educational efforts among Indians had enjoyed such support for more than 70 years.

The same (election) year, the Methodist General Conference adopted a resolution requesting "missionary societies working under its sanction or control to decline either to petition for or to receive from the national Government any moneys for education work among the Indians," and similar resolutions were adopted by Episcopalians, Congregationalists, the American Missionary Association, and the Quakers; Baptists had never taken any federal funding for Indian education. A spokesman for the National League for the Protection of American Institutions warned the Board of Indian Commissioners, "All over this country at the present time the power of ecclesiasticism [meaning Roman Catholicism] is asserting itself in local, state, and national political issues. It is a present and pressing peril."[9]

In 1889, a Methodist minister, Daniel Dorchester, had been appointed Superintendent of Indian Education. Although the Commissioner of Indian Affairs, Thomas Morgan, was also a Protestant minister, Dorchester was a more prominent anti-Catholic; he had been active in the public school controversy in Boston in 1888[10] and in that year published a book called *Romanism versus the Public School System*, attacking Catholic schooling. "Its crying defect," he wrote, "is that its teaching is not only un-American but anti-American, and will remove every one of its pupils, in their ideals, far from a proper mental condition for American citizenship, and enhance the already too difficult task of making them good citizens of a republic." As Prucha comments, "With such a man in charge of Indian schools, it is no wonder that the Catholics feared for the future of their Indian schools."[11]

The Friends of the Indian, a group dominated by reformers active in Protestant circles, began to have second thoughts about church involvement in the education of Indians, while continuing to insist that this education should be marked by a Christian (that is, Protestant) character. The president of the Lake Mohonk Conference in 1891 declared that "the time for fighting the Indian tribes is passed." What was needed now was an "army of Christian school-teachers. . . . We are going to conquer the Indians by a standing army of school-teachers, armed with ideas, winning victories by industrial training, and by the gospel of love and the gospel of hard work."[12] On the other hand, the influential reformers gathering each year at Lake

Mohonk were more than dubious about the growing Catholic presence in Indian work. A speaker at the Lake Mohonk Conference in 1892 charged that "much Roman Catholic teaching among the Indians does not prepare them for intelligent and loyal citizenship."[13]

In fact, it was increasingly Catholic missionary efforts that were taking the lead in educational work with Indians. Between 1889 and 1897, of the $4,437,339 appropriated by Congress for the support of private Indian schools, Catholic institutions received $3,094,247, or three quarters.[14] This preponderance was in large part the result of decisions by Protestant denominations to decline further government subsidies, largely as a way of building a case against support for Catholic Indian schools, a parallel process that had begun a generation before with respect to nongovernment schools serving the majority population.

In 1893, the Bureau of Catholic Indian Missions (BCIM) reported that it ". . . conducts the following schools under contract with the United States Government: thirty-nine boarding schools, with 3,265 pupils, and thirteen day schools, with 292 pupils. The total compensation for the above service amounts to $369,535. In addition to the foregoing the Bureau of Catholic Indian Missions supports five other Indian schools at its own expense. About $50,000 for support of teachers and scholars is expended by the Catholics themselves."[15]

In response to this evolving climate of opinion, a new Commissioner of Indian Affairs spelled out a new policy in his *Annual Report* of 1891, writing that "the rapid development of the public-school system has brought the Government schools into a position where it is entirely feasible for them at an early day to assume the whole charge of Indian education, so far as it is carried on by the Government. . . . I believe that the Government ought to assume, absolutely and completely, the control of Indian education, and these wards should be trained in the Government institutions with the specific end of fitting them for American citizenship, and that no moneys from the public Treasure should be devoted to sectarian or church institutions."[16]

That principle could not be implemented immediately, without abandoning dozens of Indian schools for which the government had no replacement in the short term, and attempts to force Indian parents to send their children to government-operated schools rather than church-operated schools sometimes encountered strong resistance. In one case, "a 'renegade' Indian band—which menaced Indians as well as whites for transferring students—prompted the government to reexamine its compulsory attendance policy; the decision to abandon it was made in 1892 when it was scarcely a year old. . . . [T]he Indian Affairs Office still asserted that Indian parents 'have no right to designate which school their children shall attend'."[17]

In the Appropriations Act of 1895, Congress declared that "it is hereby declared to be the settled policy of the Government to hereafter make no appropriation whatever for education in any sectarian school";[18] note that this was not justified on First Amendment grounds. A plan for gradual termination of federal financial support for church-sponsored Indian schools was put into place, and by 1897 only Catholic institutions continued to receive federal Indian funds, and those in diminishing amounts.[19] Between 1896 and 1900, federal appropriations for Indian education provided by faith-based schools were reduced by an average of 20 percent per year.[20]

The BCIM insisted, quite reasonably, that the new policy direction was based upon religious prejudice and was in any case disingenuous:

> If we are to give the Indians, and the Indian children especially, any Christian teaching whatever, that teaching will be, and in the very nature of things must be, sectarian. . . . [M]uch might be taught that would be nonsectarian as between the views of the leading Protestant denominations, but which would be sectarian as to Catholics. . . . God forbid that I should find fault with any honest effort to Christianize the Indians. What I do object to is that the effort now being made to secularize, to "non-sectarize" the Indian schools, is a dishonest, hypocritical one, whose sole aim and purpose it is to drive the Catholic Church out of the Indian educational and missionary field . . . and to substitute for its influence and teachings the influence and teachings of other religious bodies. . . . The Catholic Church only objects and regrets that it is not love for the Indian that underlies the "nonsectarian" clamor, but pharisaical hatred of itself."[21]

The Office of Indian Affairs had paid St. Boniface Indian School in California $125 per student each year; after 1900, the BCIM tried to make up the loss of federal funding by giving the schools $100 a year from Catholic sources for each student.[22]

Catholics argued that much of the funding they received for educating Indians were not federal funds but rather treaty and trust funds belonging to the Indians, and in 1906 this argument was supported by an opinion of the U.S. Attorney-General. President Roosevelt, according to his Commissioner of Indian Affairs, "ordered that an Indian who was entitled to participate in a tribal fund should be permitted to contribute his share, or any part of it, toward the support of any mission school he preferred. Two denominations, the Catholics and the Lutherans, took advantage of the order, and presented petitions numerously signed by Indians interested in some particular school, praying for the diversion of so much of the respective shares as might be necessary to support and educate a certain number of children at that school."[23]

However, the Indian Rights Association, a white organization founded with an explicitly anti-Catholic agenda, instituted a suit in the federal courts seeking an injunction against funding of Indian schools with a religious character. The Court of Appeals for the District of Columbia observed that "it seems inconceivable that Congress should have intended to prohibit them from receiving religious education at their own cost if they so desired it; such an intent would be one 'to prohibit the free exercise of religion' amongst the Indians." In May of 1908, the U.S. Supreme Court heard the case of *Reuben Quick Bear v. Leupp*, 210 U.S. 50 (1908) on appeal, and insisted that "we cannot concede the proposition that Indians cannot be allowed to use their own money to educate their children in the schools of their own choice because the Government is necessarily undenominational."[24] In an anticipation of its decision almost a hundred years later in *Zelman v. Simmons-Harris*, 536 U.S. 639 (2002), upholding the voucher program in Cleveland, the Supreme Court thus upheld the use of public funds for faith-based schools, provided it was not government itself that was making the decision on how the funds would be allocated.

In fact, "[a]fter a sharp decline, attendance in mission day and boarding schools slowly increased between 1900 and 1926, from 4,081 to 7,571 students."[25] The 1928 Meriam Report, which did so much to set a new direction for policy toward the education of Indians, noted that

> From the earliest time the national government has accepted the cooperation of private citizens and private agencies in many of its activities, and there is no reason why it should not continue to do so in the Indian educational enterprise. . . . [A]t the present time mission schools might be justified on at least four different grounds: first, as needed supplementary aid to existing facilities; second, to do pioneer work not so likely to be done by public or government schools; third, to furnish school facilities under denominational auspices for those who prefer this; and fourth, to furnish leadership, especially religious leadership, for the Indian people. . . . In general the principle has been accepted in the United States that parents may if they prefer have their children schooled under private or denominational auspices. There is no reason why Indian parents should not have the same privilege. . . . In the case of Indian mission schools the national government should exercise its right, as most of the states now do, to supervise denominational and other private schools. It is important, however, that this supervision be of the tolerant and cooperative sort rather than inspectional in character."[26]

During the 1930s in the United States, dozens of government schools for Indians were established, frequently in direct competition with mission schools, but there is some evidence that many Indians continued to prefer the latter, according to a former Bureau of Indian Affairs Supervisor of Indian schools.[27]

To a growing extent, however, missionary work among Indians became symbiotic upon government institutions through, for example, running YMCA and other programs in BIA boarding schools that were "an important point of contact between missionaries and Indians. With thousands of Indian youth concentrated in a dozen or so large boarding schools, missionaries had a form of access to the Indians unparalleled on sparsely populated reservations." Beginning in the mid-1930s, however, John Collier and the "Indian New Deal" sought to end this special—though informal—relationship. For Collier, with his strong sympathy for traditional Indian religions (discussed below), the privileged access of Christian missionaries to Indians was highly inappropriate. "This was a striking contrast to the usual encouragement reiterated in previous regulations," wrote one missionary leader.[28] On the other hand, government staff actually running schools had often considered "[n]ative religions as an obstacle to the Indians' moral, intellectual, and physical well-being," and relied on the help of the missionaries in their understaffed schools.[29]

The partnership between church and state persisted much longer in Canada, with its constitutional protections for the role of the churches, though Baptists in Toronto objected, in 1892, to public funding of Indian schools.[30] Despite scattered concerns, in contrast with "the United States where federal policy began to encourage children into public schools during the interwar years, in Canada the symbiosis between state and church was too comfortable to be altered until it became absolutely impossible to ignore changing times."[31] In 1931, government funds were helping to support 44 Catholic, 21 Anglican, 13 United Church, and two Presbyterian residential schools for Indians. Nevertheless, by 1959 Anglican leaders were complaining that "[t]he old spirit of co-operation of Church and Government working together for the good of the Indians [sic] children has been lost; . . . more and more . . . our Principals are tending to become simply servants of the Government." Ten years later, the Canadian government ended its long-standing partnership with churches in managing of residential schools, "effectively secularizing this element of Aboriginal education."[32]

It is fashionable, in academic circles, to be highly critical of the efforts of Protestant and Catholic missionaries and teachers to minister to the Indian peoples. Certainly there was much insensitivity to religious aspects of Indian identity, and thus to the distinctive Indian worldviews that have been much emphasized in recent years.[33] The efforts to preserve or revive aspects of Indian culture, discussed below, have sometimes—though not always—entailed a rejection of much of what the missionaries taught. On the other hand, those efforts would have been far more difficult if the churches and at least some of the schools established by the missionaries had not in many cases preserved the local Indian language and aspects of tribal culture. In an example that could be multiplied, some of the Navajo-speaking teachers who made it possible to reintroduce the language for instruction in the celebrated school at Rough Rock were literate in Navajo because they had attended mission rather than government schools.[34] Interviews with Navajo teachers in another community revealed the contrast between their government schooling exclusively through English and their encounters with the Navajo language in church.

> Linda Henley wrote, "One time my mother took us to church. . . . I was very impressed when I saw the community people . . . and they had never had English education go up on the stage and they sang Christmas songs all in Navajo. Some of them actually held song books and looked at the words while singing." Charlene Begay remembered, "When I was about seven years old, my grandmother took me to the Presbyterian Church. There I sat with her and she would be holding a Bible and the preacher would be reading the verses in Navajo. I looked at the Bible while sitting by my grandmother." Marie Kiyannie recalled, "The church services were usually conducted mostly in Navajo. . . . I remember sitting there reading the Bible and singing the hymns with the grownups."[35]

Once government-funding for church-operated schools was terminated in Canada, in 1969, and the Department of Indian Affairs took over the management of Indian schools, the churches became more free to form alliances with Indian leaders to demand more just policies toward native peoples.[36] In a sense, government support had made the churches clients of Ottawa; when it was ended, they became more effective advocates, and this opened the way to a new relationship. The same process had occurred early in the century in the United States, where "[n]ot only did the Catholic missions survive the Protestant attacks, they succeeded in identifying themselves with the concepts of Indian freedom of choice and, at least on the limited question of sectarian or nonsectarian education, self-determination."[37]

Over time, in fact, missionary efforts on some reservations led to creation of churches with Indian leadership, and to a mutual adaptation between Christian and native forms of expression; by 1923, "out of 438 ordained Protestant ministers on Indian reservations, more than 260 were Native Americans." "Indigenous leadership" and adaptation to native cultures were part of the discussion of mission strategy worldwide, which was occurring around 1900. "Years of experience with cultural change taught most missionaries to see assimilation as a gradual process involving slow progress toward the ultimate goal. They found greater success when they taught their subjects to read their own tribal language first and when they sought to build upon existing cultural values."[38]

Chief Dan George, in British Columbia, wrote about the breakdown of Indian cultural and social life as a result of white settlement and the hostility of many of the settlers. "It is no wonder we turned to the only people who did not steal and who did not sneer, who came with love. They were the missionaries and they came with love and I for one will ever return that love."[39] In the same spirit, the Seneca Arthur C. Parker, editor of the *Quarterly Journal* of the Society of American Indians wrote that "between the church and the state, if a comparison were drawn, the church understands better and responds more intelligently to the vital necessities of the race because its concern is with the man and not his property."[40] A similar judgment was rendered by the long-time chairman of the Board of Indian Commissioners in the United States:

> Too much of the record of the white man's relation to the primitive Americans for the last three centuries has been humiliating, not to say revolting; but the resolute persistence of missionary endeavor has been a bright page on a dark history. It is often, to be sure, a tale of pathetic failure. Often the missions have been obliterated as the tide of migration swept westward, or the best efforts of the missionaries have been defeated by the cruelty and rapacity of the conquering race; but still it is a splendid story . . .[41]

Particularly interesting is the comment by Francis Leupp, who had been Theodore Roosevelt's Commissioner of Indian Affairs, writing several decades after the end of the partnership between the American government and the missionary organizations to provide schooling. According to Leupp, "[I]n dimensions, in scholastic scope, and in material equipment the Government school system as it stands to-day is an enormous advance on the old mission school system; but in real accomplishment as proportioned to outlay it does not begin to equal the latter, and in vital energy it must always be lacking." The reason, Leupp argued, was that "except in magnificence, no governmental enterprise can compare with the same thing in private hands." Some of the government schools serving Indians were "as nearly ideal as they could be made under the adverse conditions inseparable from public undertakings which have a strictly human side; but in a general way it must be confessed that they lack a certain all-pervading spirit which distinguishes so many schools supported by private benevolence." The teacher in a government school "may be sincerely interested in the Indians. But there is something in such a position as his, with the deadly letter of the law ever staring him in the face, with the formalism and routine, and the statistical comparisons, and the rule of level and plummet, which is bound to have its effect, in course of time, on the noblest man alive."[42]

CHAPTER 8

Separate Schooling Institutionalized

In a 1957 article criticizing the efforts of the federal government to follow through on Reconstruction in the former Confederacy, Edgar Wesley concluded that "the crime of federal neglect is made more glaring when one contrasts the cruel abandonment of the freedmen with the relatively generous outpouring of supplies, equipment, schools, and teachers that have been showered upon the Indians for more than a century and a half."[1] Whether the government resources have indeed been generous, there is no question that the involvement of the federal governments with Indian affairs, including education, has continued over many decades, in contrast with the intermittent attention paid to the situation of black Americans and Canadians.

Probably the most controversial aspect of Indian education in North America has been the role of boarding (or "residential") schools that took Indian youth, sometimes as young as seven or eight, away from their families for most or all of the year, often for a number of years, in order to provide them with education in a "total institution"[2] designed, in the words of its most influential proponent, to "kill the Indian in him and save the man." As a result,

> in Indian country, the subject of boarding schools always evokes an emotional response, of all the issues that whirl around Native American education history, none is more driven by raw emotion and painful memory than this institution. Within this context, most critics target the boarding schools run by the Bureau of Indian Affairs (BIA), which still looms as the symbol of assimilation.[3]

Similarly, in Canada, "the residential school has become a metaphor for the history of Aboriginal education in British Columbia, as in Canada more generally. . . . Instead of becoming agents of assimilation, they served, so students' recollections attest, as vehicles for marginalizing generations of young men and women both from the Canadian mainstream and from home environments."[4] Typical is a report that appeared in Canada's most widely distributed newspaper:

> A representative of four British Columbia native bands said yesterday that they intend to call churches and governments to account—morally and financially—for the damage done to their communities through the religious residential school system . . . the council of four Shuswap Indian bands decided to mount the conference after the community started to conquer widespread alcoholism and social problems in recent years and realized that the self-destructive behaviour had been masking the pain of the residential school experience.[5]

We will use the term "residential school" to refer to the off-reservations schools that served youth from several tribes, in contrast with the "boarding schools" on reservations that often were simply a convenience for families who lived too far from schools for daily attendance from home. Thus, the celebrated Navajo schools at Rough Rock and Rock Point were boarding schools, but they were not residential schools in the sense in which we are using the term. While our sources sometimes use "boarding school" to refer to off-reservation institutions, like the famous Indian school at Carlisle, Pennsylvania, we will use "residential school" in those instances. This has the added advantage of making the terminology consistent for Canada and the United States.

On the other hand, there is a significant difference between the schools in the two countries. Residential schools in Canada were operated by various Christian denominations, with inadequate per-pupil funding from the federal government in Ottawa, until well after the Second World War. In the United States, while church-operated boarding schools have always played a role, by the 1890s public funds were being used almost exclusively to support government-operated schools; the big residential schools like Carlisle were created and operated by the Bureau of Indian Affairs, and seem in general to have been more adequately funded than their counterparts in Canada.

Recent critics have tended to paint a very negative picture of the role of residential schools for Indians—Milloy, for example, entitled his book about the Canadian experience *"A National Crime": The Canadian Government and the Residential School System,* charging that "it is clear that the schools have been, arguably, the most damaging of the many elements of Canada's colonization of this land's original peoples and, as their consequences still affect the lives of Aboriginal people today, they remain so," and that the residential "schools produced thousands of individuals incapable of leading healthy lives or contributing positively to their communities."[6] Although "half or fewer British Columbia Aboriginal children of past generations actually attended residential school," another author asserts, "numbers were sufficient for family life to deteriorate" among Indians.[7] A Canadian psychologist reported Indians "who had attended residential schools said they felt the experience had affected their sexual relations, their ability as parents, their feelings about religion and non-Indians, and their use of alcohol. In addition, those whose fathers had attended residential school said their fathers were stricter and less affectionate with their children, and more frequently beat their wives."[8]

Similarly, a book about the American experience with residential schools is entitled *Education for Extinction: American Indians and the Boarding School Experience*,[9] and there have been frequent claims that "the process of taking Indian children out of their communities to place them in institutions has broken up the family life of many Indians and has also weakened parental responsibility. These patterns have been passed down to the next generation of Indian children, who, whether or not they attend a boarding school, are affected by their familial environment."[10]

These are strong charges, focused above all on the presumed damage to the relationship between Indian children and their parents, their ancestral culture, and their ability to function as members of their tribal societies. Arguably, the residential school for Indians was another example of the common theme of government-mandated schooling as a deliberate alternative to the socializing effects of family and community, a strategy anticipated by Plato, attempted by the Jacobins during the French Revolution, and implemented with increasing determination by many Western governments during the course of the nineteenth century.[11] As the power of resistance of Indians waned, so the ability of Indian parents to refuse to allow their children to be taken to faraway schools waned as well. In 1896, the Commissioner of Indian Affairs, when asked whether Indian parents had a right to decide where their children would go to school, gave a decided "No".[12]

Recent scholarship, on the other hand, has tended to focus on previously overlooked benefits of the residential school experience on the formation of Indian leadership in the United States and Canada. "Ironically," write the editors of one recent collection, "the American boarding school and Canadian residential school experience for many native American children provided new skills . . . that strengthened their identities as Native Americans."[13] In Alberta, "the brass bands, sports teams, and school spirit of Qu'Appelle and St. Mary's laid the foundation for such present-day Indian cultural institutions as the Qu'Appelle Pow Wow and the Mission War Dance Festival."[14] For some Indian youth in both countries, "boarding schools were places of refuge and safety where they were able to make lasting friendships, despite the oppressive atmosphere."[15] And interviews with alumni of a former residential school in Oklahoma found that they "value the school as the place they 'learned to work.' They believe the attitudes and skills associated with working hard, and working well, in whatever field, did carry over strongly into adult life."[16]

Residential schooling broke down tribal exclusiveness and created leaders with a pan-Indian identity, equipped to advocate effectively for the interests of their own tribes in alliance with leaders from other tribes with whom they had attended school. "Boarding schools, which were established to destroy tribal identity, ended up helping to create an Indian identity."[17] Arguably, if the tribes had remained in their geographical and linguistic isolation without the residential schools to bring together their future leaders, there would never have been an Indian Rights Movement or the subsequent changes in government policies toward native peoples. "The Cherokee anthropologist R. K. Thomas discusses the growth of the modern pan-Indian movement in the United States in terms of the links to the "boarding school experience of nineteenth and twentieth-century Indians." That educational experience, in Canada as well as in the United States, increased the Indians' mobility and contacts with other groups, and resulted in "greater knowledge and concern about each other's character and interests, and a consequent common sense of identity. . . . The residential schools which succeeded the industrial schools similarly produced trained and politicized personnel for modern Indian-rights movements."[18] The first organization that brought together representatives of Indian peoples from across the United States, the Society of American Indians, was founded by graduates of residential schools who had developed skills and relationships across tribal boundaries.[19] Similarly, in Canada, "an astonishingly high proportion of the male leadership of Native political organizations, especially from the 1940s until the 1980s, were the products of residential schools."[20]

Origins of Residential Schools for Indians

The early forms of residential school were intended to respond to the nomadic character of many Indian tribes as they followed the animals they hunted or, in the case of some tribes in British Columbia, made long fishing voyages; they were a way to gather a sufficient number of children in one place where there was a resident missionary, and keep them there long enough for him (or, in some cases, her) to provide a course of instruction. The population of Indian communities was often so small that, as Canadian officials pointed out, "the number of children of an age to attend school on each Reserve, would not justify the expense necessary to establish a school."[21] A missionary at Moose Factory in the Canadian frontier of Rupert's

Land wrote in his journal in 1841 that the Indians' "restless and wandering dispositions and habits" prevented maintenance of a well-regulated school and a "civilized" community.[22] Already in 1820 the Hudson's Bay Company had appointed a missionary teacher for what was then known as the Red River Settlement, the present Winnipeg.[23]

At the Chilocco Indian School in Oklahoma, many children who attended, even in the 1920s and 1930s, came from isolated communities where there were no public schools or reservation day schools available.[24] Even after the Second World War there continued to be practical circumstances that made residential schools desirable in some cases. The leadership of the Sechelt Indian Band in British Columbia, concerned that their children had been getting into trouble, pointed out that "the fathers of the Sechelt Band children are fishermen and loggers and must leave home for long periods of time so that there is no systematic paternal control over their children during these periods. It is the day school children who break the laws of Canada, while residential school children do not get in trouble with law enforcement." George Manuel, a Canadian Indian leader who wrote eloquently about his own bad experiences at a residential school, nevertheless called for an increase in residential school places to meet the needs of "Indian people in isolated areas who move from place to place at different seasons of the year seeking employment."[25] Indeed, the two Navajo schools that were most often cited as exemplars of local control and the preservation of Indian culture, Rock Point and Rough Rock, were both boarding schools, since many Navajo families were too widely spread to send their children to a day school.

Over time, however, a second purpose emerged, to shield the pupils from what was seen as the regressive influences of their families and the Indian community in general. Methodists in Upper Canada in 1837 decided to build a "Central Manual Labour School" for Indian youth, in part to remove them "from their imperfectly civilized parents" and place them instead "under the exclusive direction of their religious and secular Instructors."[26] "The worst of it was," those concerned with the "civilization" of Indians often observed, "that the natives seemed 'content and happy; happy in their degradation and filthiness; seemingly content to remain as they are with little ambition to change for the better.' In such an environment, a day school was next to useless. . . . An agent to the Sioux came directly to the point: 'I regard all expenditures on . . . day schools in this tribe as a waste'."[27]

In Canada, the report of the Bagot Commission (1844–1845) urged that "education was, of all the elements of the civilizing system, the most important. They proposed, therefore, as well as the continuation of on-reserve common schools, the beginning of "as many manual labor or Industrial schools" as possible. . . . In such schools, under the supervision of non-Aboriginal teachers and isolated from 'the influence of their parents,' pupils would 'imperceptibly acquire the manners, habits and customs of civilized life'." The report suggested that efforts directed at Indian adults would be fruitless and that, instead, graduates of residential schools "would be the civilized Aboriginal people of the future; they 'would recommend themselves to the confidence of . . . their White friends, and at the same time be rendered to occupy places of trust and profit'" in relation to their tribes, thus serving as the "leaven of civilization."[28]

The importance of preparing Indian children for a better future than seemed possible for their parents—marked as they were considered to be by "the well-known inferiority of the great mass of Indians in religion, intelligence, morals, and home life"—justified using the authority of government to make residential schooling compulsory so that at least the children could be guided "to the proper channel."[29] A Canadian government official expressed his doubts, in 1886, about whether anything useful could be made out of Indian adults, who were "physically, mentally and morally . . . unfitted to bear such a complete metamorphosis." Nor could they function adequately as parents; as late as 1912, five Canadian Catholic bishops urged the government to take Indian children as young as six away from their parents, so that they could be "caught young to be saved from what is on the whole the degenerating influence of their home environment."[30] If Indian youth could be put into a boarding school early enough, wrote the superintendent of a school serving the Kiowa-Comanche-Apache Reservation in 1899, it would be possible "to change them forever."[31]

Not that, the promoters of residential schools conceded, it was necessarily the fault of the Indians' backwardness alone. Along the coast of British Columbia, where there were many culturally and linguistically distinct Indian peoples, "the conditions of those tribes which had had contact with white people was, in many respects, deplorable." Over the course of the nineteenth century their territories (which, in contrast with those of the Plains Indians, were relatively stable and distinct) had been penetrated "by the traders who brought goods to barter for furs, but who also brought measles, smallpox, tuberculosis, syphilis, and alcohol. The old way of life was destroyed not only by disease and alcohol but also by the changing pattern of life brought on by the new economic system based first on the fur trade but expanding into lumbering, farming and mining industries which required land—Indian land."[32]

Efforts by Christian missionaries to "civilize" the coastal Indians through on-reservation day schools had limited success, compounded by the "baneful influence of White men . . . who live among and freely mingle with them chiefly for the gratification of evil desires." The Indian Commissioner for the new province reported, in 1878, that "Indians have not been isolated from the corrupting influences of bad associations, not is it possible under such circumstances to interfere materially with irregular habits and customs incident to life in the wigwam, the destruction of which is so necessary ere the much desired higher life can be obtained. . . . [T]he impressions made upon the child or youth are quickly lost in the greater attraction of his later associations." As a means of responding to these problems, "missionary day schools as at present conducted" were inadequate. "The migratory habits of the Indians and the questionable utility of endeavoring to educate in this way children who attend most irregularly, and who spend much greater intervals amid the opposing but more attractive scenes of camp life tend to frustrate the object in view." The only solution was the establishment of residential schools, in almost all cases founded and supported by the churches, with the assistance of inadequate government grants.[33]

An official report of the Canadian government in 1880 urged that

> the Indian youth, to enable him to cope successfully with his brother of white origin, must be dissociated from the prejudicial influences by which he is surrounded on the reserve of his band. And the necessity for the establishment more generally of institutions, whereat Indian children, besides being instructed in the usual branches of education, will be lodged, fed, kept separate from home influences, taught trades and instructed in agriculture, is becoming every year more apparent.[34]

Similarly in the United States, the 1878 *Annual Report of the Commissioner of Indian Affairs* argued that "education of their children" was the quickest way to civilize Indians, but that it needed to be provided "to children removed from the examples of their parents and the influence of the camps and kept in boarding schools." In the same report, Richard Henry Pratt described Indian youth in residential schools as "hostages for good behavior of [their] parents,"[35] a theme that was employed in Canada as well.

A Canadian government official wrote in 1895 that "it is disheartening to find the wide-spread indifference manifested by Indian parents with regard to regularity of, or indeed any, attendance by their children at the day schools." Eight years later he wrote that "pagans outside the sphere of civilization are disposed to regard education as an attempt to erect a barrier between themselves and their children,"[36] and indeed their perception was accurate; this tended often to be the effect of formal schooling. As a study, decades later, in Alaska concluded, "The material quality of the schools and the general excellence of the staff—as evaluated within white educational standards—leave us with no villains. . . . Yet . . . it appears that the better the school is by white standards, the more erosive becomes the educational experience" for Alaska natives.[37] Contrary to many of the criticisms of residential schools, it may have been precisely their strengths rather than their weaknesses that made them disruptive to Indian lives.

A third, related, purpose of residential schools was to promote proficiency in English through a "language bath," bringing Indian children from different tribes together in a situation in which their only common language was English. The American Commissioner of Indian Affairs wrote, in 1873, that it was almost impossible "to teach Indian children the English language when they spend twenty hours out of the twenty-four in the wigwam, using only their native tongue."[38]

Among the presumed virtues of residential schools was that they brought together youth from different language groups who were thereby forced to use English to communicate with one another, which was not the case at day schools or even at reservation boarding schools where, it was reported, "As they but rarely hear any English outside of school, . . . they cannot be brought to see the need of it, and its use can be insured only by disciplinary measures." At Carlisle, Pratt assigned Indian youth speaking nine different languages to a single dormitory, and "some students began to lose touch with their native tongue." At the Haskell Institute in Kansas, Indian youth were organized into five companies, each of mixed origin; they were assigned to dormitories and to mess hall seating by company, thus requiring them to talk English among themselves.[39] The same natural process occurred at residential schools in Canada, where English or French served as a common language among youth from different linguistic groups.[40]

The "residential industrial school" was, in the 1840s, a recent concept, developed in the United Kingdom as a way to deal with the growing number of poor and neglected urban children. The "Industrial Feeding Schools" of Aberdeen in Scotland were created in connection with adoption, in 1845, of a law forbidding begging; boys and girls were rounded up by the police, washed and fed, and invited to return for schooling and regular meals. In England, Parliament adopted the Industrial Schools Act in 1857, allowing magistrates to commit disorderly youth to residential schools. The schools were called "industrial" because they were intended to develop in neglected youth habits of working—that is, of industry in its original sense—and to teach them trades. A similar law would be enacted for Ireland in 1868. In fact, industrial schools were established during this period in Australia, Britain, France, and Ireland, as well as the United States and Canada.[41]

We should not assume that the residential school was in all cases a model of schooling imposed on Indians; it was adopted also by the Cherokee

Nation after the Civil War as more appropriate for Cherokee-speaking children than the English-medium schools that served the children of the mixed-blood elite: "[T]he teachers would speak and teach in English, but the full-blood children would [unfortunately] keep their own language by working, learning, and learning with children who spoke Cherokee."[42]

The Hampton Institute in Virginia was founded in 1868 with funding from the Congregationalist American Missionary Association to provide freed slaves with an "education that combined cultural uplift with moral and manual training, or as [its superintendent General Samuel Chapman] Armstrong was fond of saying, an education that encompassed 'the head, the heart, and the hand'."[43] A decade later, a first group of Indians—prisoners from frontier warfare—were brought to Hampton by their custodian Richard Henry Pratt, an army officer who would become the most celebrated proponent of residential schooling for Indians. Pratt had been sent east with these prisoners in 1874 and attracted attention by his success in beginning their education while at Fort Marion in Florida. When Pratt was authorized to seek a boarding school for some of them, the only one that responded was Hampton, whose superintendent saw this as a chance to expand the school's mission while also attracting new financial support from the government and from northern philanthropists, who were beginning to find Indians more intriguing than freed slaves as a target for their benevolence.

Armstrong used his connections in Washington to gain approval for government funding for 120 Indian students each year, and Pratt was sent to the Dakota Territory to recruit the first group of students. The program designed for the Indians had to be quite different from that already in place for black students, since the former came to the school with far less exposure to whites and to the English language. It was necessary to set up a separate Indian school within Hampton to teach basic skills, and tensions between the races led to separate dormitories, different food, and separate dining facilities.[44]

Booker T. Washington, by then a graduate of Hampton and not yet the founder of the Tuskegee Institution and the best-known black American of his time, was asked by Armstrong to serve as "house father" for some 75 newly arrived Indians at Hampton from 1880 to 1881. In his autobiography, Washington described them as "for the most part perfectly ignorant." "The things that they disliked most," he wrote, "were to have their long hair cut, to give up wearing their blankets, and to cease smoking, but no white American ever thinks that any other is wholly civilized until he wears the white man's clothes, eats the white man's food, speaks the white man's language, and professes the white man's religion."[45]

In the early years of the schooling of Indians at Hampton Institute, they were allowed "to use their own languages before breakfast and after supper during the week and all day on Sunday, but by the late 1880s federal authorities were (as we will see) seeking to suppress the use of Indian languages, and "Armstrong felt under pressure to comply, declaring that English speaking 'is the law of the school'."[46]

Although Pratt transferred his efforts to the Carlisle army barracks in Pennsylvania in 1879, Hampton continued as a government-subsidized residential school for Indians until 1912, when "pressure in Congress, particularly from representatives of Native American ancestry, forced the removal of the government subsidy,"[47] in large part because of fears about racial mixing. A Texas congressman asked, "Why humiliate the Indian boys and girls, our wards and dependents, by educating them in the same schools with Negro children?" The House Committee on Indian Affairs urged that the government "elevate the red race to the level of the white race and not degrade and humiliate him by sinking him to the low plane of the Negro race."[48] Indians, however defeated and marginalized, retained a certain glamour which was not shared by freed slaves and their descendants.

Pratt, who was responsible for the Indians at Hampton until he moved to Carlisle, opposed the segregation that Armstrong imposed, separating the Indians from black students at Hampton. "If Indians were not to associate with and learn from the more assimilated black students," Pratt believed, "then it did not make much sense to have Indians students become associated with black students in the public mind by attending school together because of the widespread prejudice against blacks."[49]

In his autobiography, Pratt recalled conversations with Armstrong many years earlier in which, "I told the General my dissatisfaction with systems to educate the Negro and Indian in exclusively race schools and especially with educating the two races together. Participation in the best things of our civilization through being environed by them was the essential factor for transforming the Indian."[50]

Pratt had served with Cherokee scouts, whose "intelligence, civilization, and common sense was a revelation, because I had concluded that as an army officer I was there to deal with atrocious aborigines,"[51] against the hostile tribes of the southern Plains. He was later assigned to guard a group of young Indian men from these same tribes. This turned into a career as an educator of Indians. Pratt "liked Indians, but he had little use for Indian cultures."[52] He may be said to have "epitomized the liberal dilemma: he was deeply sympathetic to Indians but regarded reservation life as a morally repugnant form of segregation. . . . Convinced that physical separation was responsible for the Indians' failure to become more like white Americans, Pratt relentlessly condemned what he called 'this whole reservating and segregating process'. . . . Egalitarian in the style of his time, Pratt declared that the Indian 'is born a blank, like all the rest of us. There is no resistless clog placed upon us by birth. We are not born with language, nor are we born with ideas of either civilization or savagery."⁵³

What Pratt objected to about the reservation system was that it kept Indians idle and dependant upon supplies of food and clothing provided by the federal government, while preserving the tribal system that prevented Indians from becoming a part of the wider and extremely dynamic society. The "reservation system worked at 'colonizing' Indians, whereas Carlisle [Indian School] worked at 'individualizing' them. . . . In the reservation school, civilization could only be presented to the children as a theoretical concept; they could not experience it firsthand. In such schools, Pratt argued, Indian children could never be prepared for competition with 'the more skillful, aggressive, and productive race'."⁵⁴ Thus, a major component of Pratt's work with Indian youth at Carlisle was to place them with farming families, to learn firsthand how white Americans lived and worked. As he wrote in letters in 1881,

> All educational work for the Indians is good; I believe that the system of removing them from their tribes and placing them under continuous training in the midst of civilization is far better than any other method. In an Indian school at an Agency the civilizing influences are limited to the instructors with perhaps a few examples of agency employees, with a tremendous pull against what they may do in the persons of the fathers and mothers and all the members of the tribe. . . . Day schools on the reserves are generally impracticable and a positive injury, because they beget expectations of quick and large development that cannot be realized. But there could be a system of industrial boarding schools on the reservations from which the most competent should be taken for final training in the schools in the midst of civilization.⁵⁵

Pratt directed the school at Carlisle from 1879 to 1904, becoming in the process the best-known advocate of the assimilation of Indians into the majority society. The school enrolled in the first academic year, 1879–1880, more than 200 youth representing about a dozen tribes, and by 1887, eight years after the conversion of the army barracks into a residential school for Indians, Carlisle had 617 students. By Pratt's last year as superintendent, there were more than 1,200 students. During his 24 years as its superintendent, Carlisle Indian School educated 4,903 Indian boys and girls from 77 tribes.⁵⁶ A teacher-training ("normal") program was added in 1889, consisting of a three-year course following graduation from eighth grade. Similarly, a two-year normal course was established at Chilocco boarding school in Oklahoma in 1906 for students who had completed the eighth grade and wanted to prepare to become primary-school teachers.⁵⁷

The "outing" system, pioneered at Carlisle, of placing Indian youth with nearby white families—mostly farmers and their wives needing extra help in exchange for providing room and board and the example of American family life—involved 200 students who attended local public schools by 1893.[58] Pratt wrote in his autobiography that "the outing feature of the Carlisle School was its right arm. . . . It enforced participation, the supreme Americanizer. Preventing participation stops Americanization. The native Americans have been, without exception, most harshly and by most devious demoralizing devices excluded from participation in our American family."[59] Pratt delighted in reprinting the positive comments made by local farmers or their wives who had hosted Indian students for a season or longer. Commissioner Francis Leupp, who in other respects disagreed strongly with Pratt, agreed that "whatever brings the Indian into closer touch with whites who are earning their living by hard work, is of prime importance as an educating influence. . . . As the remoter corners of the country fill up, the Indian will have to mix with the whites, whether for good or ill; would he be any better fitted for this a hundred years hence than now, if we kept him socially isolated till then?"[60]

Attempts were made to adopt this system of "outing" for residential schools in the West, where it was much less successful and led to abuse and exploitation of Indian pupils. In 1892, the Superintendent of Indian schools warned that "[w]ith too many the common idea is that the Indian is a creature to be cheated, debauched, and kicked out of decent society. Young Indians from the schools can not be safely located among such people."[61]

The establishment of Carlisle Indian School and then a series of others—12 were opened between 1889 and 1892—occurred at a favorable moment, when there was considerable optimism about what could be achieved in a relatively short time by removing Indian children from their homes and immersing them in the skills and the behavioral standards of contemporary North American society. The same year, 1879, that Pratt began the program at Carlisle, the *Annual Report* of the Board of Indian Commissioners estimated there were 500 teachers in 64 mostly denominationally run boarding schools and 292 day schools teaching 13,343 students, out of an estimated 46,000 school-age Indian children, and reported that "the progress of the pupils in industrial boarding schools is far greater than in day schools. The children being removed from the idle and corrupting habits of savage homes are more easily led to adopt the customs of civilized life and inspired with a desire to learn."[62] A decade later, the Board of Indian Commissioners, echoing a common theme at the time, reported that "unless we can incorporate the red man into the white man's civilization, he will disappear." However, "Ten years of thorough training of all Indian children in industrial schools will take a large portion of them off our hands, and in twenty years there would be but few Indians needing the care and support of the government."[63]

The number of off-reservation industrial residential schools operated by the Bureau of Indian Affairs increased to 25 by the end of the nineteenth century, including several that offered preparation as teachers to Indian youth who had completed the regular eight grades. It should be noted that it was at that period by no means uncommon in North American society for teachers of the elementary grades to be trained as part of a high school program. The residential schools for Indians did not, in general, provide the full high school curriculum, in part because relatively few of their Indian students were prepared to take advantage of what was at the time a largely academic secondary program. The schools offered vocational programs, often of poor quality and perceived by the participants and their parents as more concerned with using their free labor to sustain inadequately funded schools than with giving them skills that would be useful to them in the future. In justification of this practice—also characteristic of the Hampton/Tuskegee model of educating black youth—it was believed by those designing and managing such programs that developing the "habits of industry" were, if anything, even more important than developing individual skills. The prevailing idleness of many Indian adults on the reservations seemed to require that their children be taught such habits through regular employment in the tasks required to maintain the schools.

In Canada, there was a similar confidence in the potential benefits of removing Indian children from the corrupting influence of their families and tribal communities and subjecting them to the discipline of physical labor as well as classroom learning. Egerton Ryerson, Superintendent of Education for Upper Canada (Ontario), had urged in 1847 that the new schools for Indian youth "be called industrial schools; they are not then schools of manual labour; they are schools of learning and religion; and industry is the great element of efficiency in each of these."[64] There were a number of such initiatives; for example, an Anglican clergyman working with Indians, using funding from voluntary contributions, including collections in Church of England Sunday schools across Ontario, started a boarding school serving Indian youth aged 12 to 15. Like dozens of others started in this period, it sought to prepare its pupils for futures as workers and tradespeople in the wider Canadian society; "we want them," the founder explained, "to become apprenticed out to white people and become in fact Canadians." To that end, "we make a great point of insisting on the boys talking English as, for their advancement in civilization, this is, of all things, the most necessary."[65]

The industrial school model, with its combination of academic and vocational training, was first attempted in Canada in the 1840s at the Mohawk Institute and the Mount Algin Institute in Upper Canada (now Ontario). Their objective, wrote Egerton Ryerson, was "to give a plain English [that is, not including Latin] education adapted to the working farmer and mechanic." Since "nothing can be done to improve and elevate [the Indian's] character and condition without the aid of religious feeling . . . the animating and controlling spirit of each industrial school establishment should . . . be a religious one."[66]

Over subsequent decades the more common models of Indian education in Canada were day schools—usually with a single teacher and haphazard attendance—and church-operated boarding schools located on or near Indian reserves. The residential industrial school model, as it emerged in the 1880s, was more ambitious, and was generally located at a considerable distance from Indian reserves with the intention of keeping pupils away from their families and tribes for as much of the year as possible.[67] The origin of this initiative is generally attributed to a study trip undertaken by a member of the Canadian Parliament in 1879 to investigate the American policy of "aggressive civilization" at the newly established Carlisle Indian School and other institutions.

In the Canadian government's *Annual Report* on Indian Affairs, in 1890, a suggestion was made worthy of Plato, of the French Jacobins, or of the Bolsheviks in the 1920s: "It would be highly desirable, if it were practicable, . . . to obtain entire possession of all Indian children after they attain to the age of seven or eight years, and keep them at schools of the industrial type until they have had a thorough course of instruction. . . . [T]he solution of the problem designated 'the Indian question' would probably be effected sooner than it is under the present system" of on-reservation day schools.[68]

Once Indian children were safely in residential schools, government officials discouraged giving them vacations at home, since (as one wrote in 1891, recommending against a request for holidays from the Anglican bishop with oversight over Rupert's Land Indian Industrial School), "such return to their old associations . . . invariably interferes with the progress secured through uninterrupted residence in the schools."[69] A Canadian government report in 1896 concluded that Indian "parents' migratory life style, their dislike of corporal punishment for children, and their indifference to the occupational prospects of educated youths impeded the assimilation policy and programs."[70] Residential schools seemed the only solution, although in many parts of Canada there were no such schools available, "and numerous Indian groups across the country petitioned unsuccessfully in the early twentieth century for creation of residential schools."[71]

Over time, the role and the character of residential schools changed in response to the twists and turns of government policy, but also to changes in society and especially among Indians. In contrast with the Indian youth recruited by Pratt from the Dakota reservations, totally unfamiliar with modern life, by the twentieth century many youth were arriving at residential schools speaking English as their first language. Several of the alumni of the Chilocco Indian School in Oklahoma interviewed by Lomawaima about their experiences in the 1920s and 1930s mentioned that, although of Indian or mixed ancestry, they had had little contact with Indians before arriving in the school, and only two of 53 alumni had entered the school speaking a native language.[72] In Canada, in some cases, "[n]ative students gained some knowledge of Indian languages and cultures at school that they had not previous possessed."[73]

Nor was the use of English outside the classroom all the result of compulsion; a growing number of engaging activities at these and other top-of-the-line residential schools created new interests for Indian youth, and developed in them loyalties beyond their tribes.

> By the turn of the century, for example, Haskell Institute offered students membership in the YMCA, the YWCA, the school orchestra, several instrumental and vocal groups, the marching band, the Thespian society, three literary societies, and two debating clubs as well as the opportunity to compete in track, baseball, basketball, and football.[74]

The famous Carlisle Indians football team, with its victories over leading college teams, was a focal point of pride for students at other residential schools as well; this was a pan-Indian pride.[75] Evidence suggests that "many students, quite independent of parental influence, not only reached a grudging accommodation with the boarding school but came to see it as a positive experience," though "even those who cooperated often did so on their own terms."[76]

Thus, few Indian youth abandoned altogether their tribal distinctives or their emotional links with particular traditions and extended families. They did not become white Americans or Canadians, but neither did they remain mired in the narrowness of reservation life. Many of those who spent years in residential schools used their experience to reinterpret tribal traditions and identity; "time and time again Indian people proved both more receptive to learning and more resilient in culturally contextualizing that learning than policy makers ever imagined." Recent scholarship had reexamined the earlier understanding—still apparently predominant in Canada—that saw Indian youth as simply the helpless victims of the residential school experience; the fact that "Indian people used the schools to suit their needs and purposes . . . raises the often-overlooked notion of agency." Despite unhappiness, despite the neglect or abuse that some experienced, "conversations in the Kiowa community suggest that life at a place like Rainy Mountain [Boarding School] was more than an exercise in resistance, oppression, and misery."[77] Similarly, despite the well-publicized apologies of Protestant and Catholic leaders in Canada for "the pain, suffering and alienation that so many experienced" in the residential schools that their churches had sponsored,

> [f]or a sizable group of former students, the legacy of residential school was not bitter at all. It would be misleading to leave the impression that all or even most staff were oppressive or slipshod in their care of schoolchildren, just as it would be erroneous to suggest that all former residential schoolchildren carried bad memories away with them when they left school. . . . What is sometimes disturbing is that at least some former pupils with positive memories tried unsuccessfully to place their positive recollections before the public via the press and electronic media, only to be rebuffed or ignored.[78]

In contrast with the recent condemnation of residential schools for Indians, in the years after World War I they were regarded as the best means of promoting full adaptation to American life; by the late 1920s nearly half of all Indian youth in boarding school were attending off-reservation schools. While the off-reservation residential schools had long been considered the elite alternative for Indian youth, it was only then that several of them achieved the status of high schools.[79]

CHAPTER 9

Problems of Residential Schools

There have always been some voices lifted against the residential school system for Indians, and its deliberate effort to weaken the ties between Indian youth and their communities and families. As early as 1771, the English Society for the Propagation of the Gospel in Foreign Parts contended that it was "a mistaken Notion that Seminaries at a Distance from the Indians and only among Christians are fittest for the Education of Indian Youths. . . . [T]he Indian Country is evidently the properest Place to fix such a Seminary for this Purpose, where the Parents can frequently see their Children, by which all Uneasiness would be removed from both. . . . It would also be pleasing to the Indians in general. They would look upon it as a Mark of our Regard and Confidence in them."[1] The last remark, in particular, expresses a sensitivity to the message conveyed by the residential school system that was not much heard over the following centuries.

Many problems have been reported in connection with residential schools for Indians. Some of those can be traced to poor management and, in many cases, inadequate funding. Government grants to denominational schools in Canada did not cover the full cost of educating—and often feeding and housing—their Indian pupils; they were a per-pupil grant and all additional costs had to be raised by the churches from the contributions of their members. This put great pressure on those operating the schools to extract as much productive labor as possible out of their Indian pupils, a strategy that was justified as a key part of the educational program. The parsimonious funding formula adopted by the government

> would also stimulate the desire to turn out from the workshops articles which would bring some revenue to the school, and to win from the earth larger supplies of vegetables, accomplishing at the same time the main end & object of their existence as Industrial Schools and the financial advantage of such

returns of money and crops. Under the conditions there might be more time spent in the workshop and garden than at the desk.²

This practice continued until the 1950s. Milloy concludes that "Church charges that the costs they were facing and the deficits were the result of government system-wide underfunding were well founded."³ He shows in detail how parsimonious the Canadian federal government was toward the many residential schools—79 of them in 1939, enrolling more than 9000 Indian pupils—operated by Anglican, Catholic, Presbyterian, and United Church (a merging of Methodist, Congregational, and some Presbyterian churches in 1925) authorities. The amount provided for Indian pupils in Canada and in the United States was often far less than that spent on the schooling of non-Indian pupils. "There never was invested in this project the financial or human resources required to ensure that the system achieved its 'civilizing' ends or that children were cared for properly." As late as 1938, the Canadian government grant amounted to about $180 per pupil per year in the Indian residential schools, compared, for example, with $642 per pupil in the Manitoba School for the Deaf."⁴

The hunger, inadequate clothing, and crowded living conditions reported in many accounts of residential schools, and the farm and domestic labor that the pupils were often required to perform, were not generally the result of malevolence by those running the schools, but of very limited resources. In a sense it was precisely the zeal of the churches to serve the Indians that led to an overextended and underfunded system: "[T]he rapid, uncontrolled and irreversible spread of the system across the land, driven by the churches' missionary zeal, not only pushed the system past the limit of available financial resources, but also quickly outstripped the logic of the system's proposed industrial curriculum."⁵

In Canada, which did not experience the strong political opposition to Catholic schooling characteristic of the United States in the second half of the nineteenth century, it was natural to rely on the churches to operate residential schools. The annual report of the Canadian Department of Indian Affairs for 1898 conceded, with respect to schools for Indians, "its inability to conduct such institutions as economically as can be done by denominations, and consequently it has endeavoured to have their management placed in the hands of the respective churches."⁶ Expenses of church-operated schools were lower because they could often rely on volunteer or semi-volunteer teachers with religious motivations (including, most notably, members of Catholic or Anglican teaching orders), and also because the churches supplemented through voluntary donations the meager funding provided by the government. In 1900, for example, the federal government funding to Indian boarding schools in British Columbia amounted to $41 per pupil a year—not enough to cover even the food and housing—while the churches provided $53 per pupil. The same year, parents of white students at another school in the province paid $160 a year in tuition.[7] In 1941, the per capita cost of the Canadian residential schools was $176, compared with $335 spent on each residential pupil in the United States; "consequently in practically all the Canadian schools the difference must be made up by grants from such missionary agencies as Sunday schools, Bible classes, and women's auxiliaries."[8]

It is no wonder that there were many complaints that Indian youth were inadequately fed and housed, and overworked to support the operations of the residential schools they attended. In the 1920s, an eminent anthropologist charged that the quality of education in many Indian schools across Canada was "exceedingly poor," but he insisted that "[i]t is not the missions that shirked their responsibility, but the federal government, and behind that government the people of Canada."[9]

There were also problems with the location of many of the schools, which "were built in the wrong places. Schools were opened in areas where only a traditional lifestyle was possible," and the training offered by a school, even one with a vocational focus, did not prepare youth to pursue that lifestyle successfully. Those who attended such schools were "disadvantaged by the inappropriate education they received and the separation from 'those pursuits which are taught them by their parents when they are young' and to which they would have to return as young adults."[10]

Many of the staff of residential schools, especially those operated by the churches, were strongly dedicated to the work, but they were not necessarily especially competent; there was, in Canada, a suspicion "that the schools were a dumping ground for less-competent church staff." The salaries provided, a government official pointed out in 1909, were not competitive with those available in the public schools, and the location of most residential schools was isolated. The work was often stressful, the situation claustrophobic. "Many principals and matrons . . . raised their [own] children in the same deplorable conditions suffered by the students."[11]

There were serious problems with mortality, as Indian children and youth from isolated communities where resistance had not developed became infected with tuberculosis and other serious and frequently fatal disease for which treatment at the time was entirely inadequate. It was reported by a Canadian authority in 1913 that "fifty percent of the children who passed through these schools did not live to benefit from the education which they had received therein." A review of Anglican mission work charged that the "appalling number of deaths among the younger children" resulted from removing them from a healthy "out of door life" to crowded and inadequate residential facilities.¹² It would be well to recall, however, that deaths from tuberculosis were also very high back on the reservations, so the residential school should not bear the whole blame.

Other problems arose from what was considered the impractical nature of the instruction provided in the residential schools. Estelle Reel, who in 1898 became the first woman to serve as Superintendent of Indian Education in the United States, was outraged to learn that, at one residential school, several Indian girls were being excused from chores to practice the piano. "I sincerely hope," she wrote, "that the Office will require the superintendents of all Indian schools to see that their large Indian girls become proficient in cooking, sewing and laundry work before allowing them to spend hours in useless practice upon an expensive instrument which in all probability they will never own." Schools for Indians should focus on teaching only what was immediately relevant to the past experience and the future destiny of their pupils.[13]

Most residential schools had problems with runaway pupils. Father Lacombe, principal of one of the group of denominational schools opened in Canada in 1884, admitted that "he had not been able to make the boys like the place. Most of them had either left on their own initiative or had been expelled." The problem, he thought, was that they had been too old and too set in Indian ways to adapt well to the disciplines of residential school life. He recommended that in the future the school should take only children under eight, and that parents be induced to give up their young children "by threatening and deprivation of rations."[14]

As this suggests, there sometimes was understandable resistance from Indian parents to the loss of their children to an institution that was often at too great a distance for visits, and for a number of years. This was poignantly expressed in the petition sent in 1910 from an Indian community in Saskatchewan, asking that a day school be provided as an alternative to residential schooling for the community's children. "We think," the Indians wrote, "we are capable of taking care of our children when not at school. The whiteman loves his children and likes to have them round him in the evenings and on the days in which school is not open. We also love our children with just as warm an affection as the whiteman and we want to keep them round us."[15]

In other cases, it should be noted, Indian parents were eager to have their children enrolled in residential schools, either because of the opportunities that they appeared to offer, or to relieve themselves of the burden of supporting their children in hard times.[16] Luther Standing Bear, at 11 one of the first group of Sioux youth to be recruited to Carlisle Indian School, had been told by his father that, in view of the spread of white settlers into the Dakotas, "the only recourse was to learn the white man's way of doing things, get the same education, and thus be in condition to stand up for his rights."[17] Among the Nisg'a in British Columbia, for example, "those families that were educationally aware persuaded the Indian agent, if they could, to enrol their children in residential schools. By the start of the Second World War, many Nisga'a families were sending children to residential schools as early as grade 1."[18] In Oklahoma, "the willingness of the Kiowas and Comanches to enroll their children [in the residential school]," Ellis notes, "compels us to reconsider the history of Indian schools. Conventional wisdom holds that tribes jealously resisted the schools and used any means available to keep their children out of the hands of government teachers." In fact, Kiowa and Comanche parents frequently complained to government agents that there were insufficient schools available on the reservation. "The agency's annual report for 1897 noted that the Kiowas were so anxious to get enough schools built that they had agreed to donate twenty-five thousand dollars from their grazing fees to build an industrial school ..."[19]

Among the Navajo, there was a similar resistance to the community-oriented approach to education that was promoted by white Progressives. After participation in the Second World War opened a wider world to the often-isolated people of the Navajo Reservation, Navajo leader Chee Dodge told Congress, in 1944, "All day schools should be eliminated and more boarding schools established. Eliminate any effort to teach Navajo language in the schools in that Navajos have to learn English to compete with other people in employment." Similarly, tribal Council member Hoskie Cronemeyer criticized the quality of reservation day schools in 1952 and "called for a return to the 'very good' boarding schools of 'thirty or forty years ago,' [for] compulsory education, and [for] speaking only English on the school compound. 'The teaching of Navajo customs [in schools] should be done away with so that only school work will be carried on for our children'."[20] Another Navajo leader, Jacob Morgan, who would be elected Chairman of the Tribal Council several years later, reflected positively on his own experience at Hampton Institute and

> believed in Christianization, regimented learning, and adaptation to the society of the white majority. Having taught in the boarding schools, he favored separating Navajo children from their indigenous culture so that they could be educated to work effectively in the larger society around them. Emerging as the leader of the opposition, Morgan argued persuasively against the community-centered and pluralistic values of Collier [New Deal Commissioner of Indian Affairs] and the progressive educators: "It is a general feeling of the Navajos today, especially the returned students of the tribe, that when you speak about closing the boarding schools you are simply slapping the boys and girls in the face because that is where they got their start. If it was not

for boarding schools we would not have been here today. Or if we had never attended any school at all we would not be able to know about these things." In 1934, as the plan for day schools was moving forward, Morgan worked with members of other tribes to establish the American Indian Federation, a pan-Indian organization opposed to the New Deal reforms.[21]

On the other hand, administrators of residential schools frequently had to deal with runaways—one of the advantages of the eastern location of Carlisle was that it was too far to escape back to the reservations—and sometimes accused the parents of encouraging such truancy. This was by no means a new problem; one of the women religious in New France had written, in 1668,

> We find docility and intelligence [in Indian youth], but when we are least expecting it they climb over our enclosure and go to run the woods with their relatives, where they find more pleasure than in all the amenities of our French houses. Savage nature is made that way; they cannot be constrained, and if they are they become melancholy and their melancholy makes them sick, besides, the Savages love their children extraordinarily and when they know that they are sad they will do everything to get them back, and we have to give them back to them.[22]

The same complaint of attempts to keep Indian youth in schools would be expressed hundreds of times over the following centuries.

In the twentieth century, however, when school regimes were less strict, resources more adequate, and reservations less isolated from the surrounding culture, many "students grew to love the boarding schools, and in their letters and books they refer to the schools as their homes. . . . When these children went home, some Indians met them with anger, disgust, and disdain. According to some student accounts, tribal members made fun of them for their lack of language skills, dress, ideas, deportment, religious beliefs, and outspoken behavior. This cultural divide sometimes made students more closely aligned with the schools." Thus, "some students left the schools hating and resenting the experience," and it is those voices that have attracted most attention among academics and advocates for native cultures, "while others became very loyal to their alma mater, sending friends, relatives, and their own children to the Indian boarding schools. Many students took a position somewhere in between the two poles, and their experiences and memories are layered and complex."[23]

K. Tsianina Lomawaima noted, in her study of the residential school attended by her father, that "intellectually curious children and adolescents wanted to go to school, especially high school, or they wanted to escape excessive discipline or responsibilities at home. Older sisters fed up with child care or older boys fed up with farm labor might apply without their parents' knowledge."²⁴ "I had enough of hoeing weeds and tending sheep," reported a Hopi boy. "Helping my father was hard work and I thought it was better to be educated."²⁵

It is certainly the case that the boarding school experience is and has always been painful to many youth, including those attending elite independent schools in England or the United States, and there were features of the Indian residential schools—cultural dislocation, language change, physical labor—that made them especially difficult for many, but surely some of the indictments are excessive.

An additional and very grave problem that has emerged (at least to general awareness) in recent decades in Canada was a pattern of physical and sexual abuse in residential schools, in some cases by members of the clergy.

Caught between Two Worlds?

Unfortunately, the results produced by the residential schools, at least in the nineteenth and early twentieth centuries, were in most cases unsatisfactory. Many Indian youth returned to their reservations unable to find a use there for the knowledge and skills that they had acquired, and unfitted for the tasks and the social relations of tribal life. "The ex-pupils of our Indian schools," reported a Canadian Presbyterian leader in 1923, "have such faulty education that very few of them are capable of interpreting Cree into English, or vice versa."²⁶

This was not a new problem. Catholic missionaries in New France, frustrated with their lack of success in seeking to educate Indian youth in situ, sent several of them to France for schooling. A Montagnais boy who studied French and Latin in France between 1620 and 1625 found it of little personal profit.

> When he returned to his native country he had forgotten much of his Montagnais tongue and had missed all the instruction in woodcraft, hunting, fishing, and so forth, necessary to survival among his own people. The Jesuits took him under their wing, had him instructed in his Montagnais tongue, and employed him for a brief period as a language teacher. . . . [The Jesuit] *Relations* commented that "this poor wretch has become a barbarian like the others"; in fact, he had become an alcoholic, would enter into at least five unsuccessful marriages. . . . It was reported that he had finally starved to death in the northern forests—a further indication of his inability to fit back into a traditional way of life.²⁷

Similarly, a missionary among the Cherokee, in 1827, wrote to his sponsoring mission board, "Can we rationally expect . . . youths after being tolerably well educated, would stem the current of iniquity that would come in upon them on returning to their heathenish parents? Can they adhere to the moral instructions given them and remain chaste and virtuous when they would daily be obliged to hear the most impure, the most obscene conversations and witness the most polluting customs?"[28]

It was assumed, by those who promoted and sustained the use of off-reservation residential schools, that young men graduates would marry young women graduates, and together form modern households as farmers or artisans and give leadership to a transformation of reservation life. Unfortunately, for many this was not the outcome of their years of isolation from their families and from tribal life. While Richard Pratt strongly urged that they be discouraged from returning to reservation life and all its limitations and the influence of companions who had not been to school, many Indian youth found it difficult to make their way in the majority society. In Canada, the government "concluded in 1889, in the case of 'the majority [of graduates], for the present at least, there appears to be no alternative' but to return to the reserves."[29]

And yet, returning to the reservation, many found themselves unable to function in terms of the expectations and the opportunities available there. The government agent on a Canadian reserve wrote, in 1903, that "[a]ny lad who had never left the reserve, is at the age of 18, far better off than a lad who has been in school for years, and what is more is very much more self-reliant and able to make his living as easy again as any of these school lads."[30] This phenomenon had been noted repeatedly. In 1886, a U.S. congressman charged that "returned students almost invariably relapsed into barbarism." Another observer found a vivid image to describe the situation of Indian youth: "We catch him like a wild animal, and, when properly domesticated, throw him back into the jungle to survive." After all, wrote another, "after his graduation . . . he returns to a social condition in which civilization must necessarily perish—a stagnant social condition—a condition in which nothing that he has learned can be of any use to him."[31]

For that reason, Pratt of the Carlisle Indian School constantly urged his alumni: "I advise you to flee the reservation. . . . Go out into the business of life of the country where personal rights and the light of civilization will constantly invite and help you on to higher, nobler, better things. Flee away from that which drags you down. Go where you will be free, where you will not be bound hand and foot to your past, but where you can rise and become individuals."[32] But that was not so easy in a society in which racial prejudice shaped so many aspects of life and work opportunities.

In 1901, the American Commissioner of Indian Affairs criticized the residential schools for giving Indian youth a luxurious life for some years—the critics, of course, would contest that!—and then returning him to a reservation "which by contrast must seem squalid indeed—to the parents whom his education must make it difficult to honor, and left to make his way against the ignorance and bigotry of his tribe. Is it any wonder he fails? Is it surprising if he lapses into barbarism? Not having earned his education [by paying for it], it is not appreciated."[33] As we've seen, in 1908 the Canadian Minister of the Interior, resisting Anglican requests to fund schools in the Far North, declared, "I will not undertake in a general way to educate the Indians of the Yukon. In my judgement they can, if left as Indians, earn a better living. . . . To teach an Indian child that his parents are degraded beyond measure and that whatever they did or thought was wrong could only result in the child becoming, as the ex-pupils of the industrial schools have become, admittedly and unquestionably a very much less desirable element of society than their parents who never saw the schools."[34]

A major problem was that most reservations had such underdeveloped economies that few roles existed within which Indian youth who had passed through residential schools could make use of the skills they had acquired. The former Commissioner of Indian Affairs wrote, in 1910, of the tragic situation of the former residential school student:

> Take a boy away from the free open-air life of an Indian camp, house him for years in a steam heated boarding-school in a different climate, change all his habits as to food, clothing, occupation and rest, and you risk—what? Either undermining his physique so that he sickens at the school, or softening it so that when he returns to the rougher life he cannot keep up the pace. Morally, too, he has a hard struggle to sustain himself, for he has no social background at home against which to project his new acquirements. The old people laugh at his un-Indian ways; most of the young people, even those who have had some teaching near home, feel estranged from him; his diploma finds him nothing to do; and he despises the old life while in no condition to get away from it.[35]

The lack of preparation for the employment available was confirmed by a survey of returned students in 1916–1917, which found that "[a]ll the industrial training . . . is next to worthless. He is a carpenter in a land without lumber, a painter with nothing to paint, a tailor where clothes are fashioned from flour sacks, a shoemaker among moccasin wearers. The [government] agent, he learns, is unable to employ him at the agency. And so the retrogression process begins."[36] In Ontario, critics charged that the graduates of residential schools "became marginalized beings, lacking the necessary skills of both White and Indian cultures, confused over their identity, and left to their own devices after their failed school experience."[37]

Similarly, a Canadian parliamentary hearing on residential schools after World War II was told that "a child who returns from a Residential school at the age of 16 or 17 is invariably unable to fit into the life of the reserve."[38]

The failure of the project to assimilate the Indians was not exclusively the fault of residential schools, which did not prepare Indian youth to be at home in white-dominated society; to a greater extent, surely, it was also the failure of that society to accept Indians on equal terms, no matter how well-prepared they might have been. The American Commissioner of Indian Affairs in 1890 quoted an observer that there was "little employment for educated Indians, and there is a general prejudice, among both Indian and white employees, against the young men who have returned from Eastern schools."[39] In her study of the experience of Indian girls at an Anglican school in British Columbia that also enrolled white girls—though the two groups were kept separate—Jean Barman suggests that "the principal opposition to assimilation did not come from Indians but rather from the dominant society. First came the demand for physical separation in the classroom, then more general unwillingness to allow educated young Indians into the work force."[40]

There were more optimistic accounts, such as that of the government agent in the Rosebud Agency in South Dakota, in 1917, who reported that when former residential school students reached middle age and began to be tribal leaders, the schooling that they had received made them more effective. "Returned students acted as intermediaries between tribal and white society. This could often be an uncomfortable position, but it was a very necessary one." Nor did their performance in that role suggest that they had been brainwashed by their "white" schooling; "The historian Wilbert Ahern (1983) concluded that returned students used their education to become 'defenders of community interests' more often than advocates of government policies."[41] Similarly, a government agent among the Hopi insisted that "a returned student only failed to the extent that 'he is not what the taxpayer expected him to be. He is not what the faddist and sentimentalist tried to make him'," and the major study of American residential schools concludes that "[b]ecause of their familiarity with the white 'outside,' returned students were uniquely situated to mediate between Indian and white worlds, uniquely situated to assist tribal elders, 'progressives' and traditionals alike, in their negotiation of the cultural borderlands just beyond the reservation line."[42]

During the "Indian New Deal" of the 1930s, those setting federal policy for the education of Indian youth were optimistic that a balance could be found that would make them competent as well as culturally prepared to function effectively in the mainstream society, while preserving tribal distinctiveness and full engagement in the tribal community. Federal Commissioner of Indian Affairs John Collier wrote that "[a]ssimilation and preservation and intensification of heritage are not hostile choices, excluding one another, but are interdependent through and through." Similarly, his Director of Indian Education urged teachers to help preserve the "original background of native culture when it exists" but also "to introduce . . . an economic and cultural understanding of . . . white neighbors and associates" that would facilitate an adjustment to life after school.[43]

In fact, apart from the Navajo (with their exceptionally large reservation) and a few other Indian peoples, there was little protection in isolation from the majority society. "Even where tribal life lingers," a missionary leader wrote in 1944, "white civilization is pressing close, the growth of new towns adjoining reservations, with the ever present cinema and other attractions, the commercializing of Indian ceremonies, the rodeos and the fairs, the automobiles and the radios, the improved highways and the convenient 'five and ten' emporiums—all have a share in the process of acculturation. In short, the radius of the Indian's circle is greater, his horizon wider. . . . He cannot isolate himself if he would."[44] The only question was whether he could make a success of his relationship with majority society.

As the Canadian and American governments expanded their interventions in reservation life, a growing number of jobs became available as translators, teachers, and other staff of schools, clinics, agricultural development projects, and other government programs. When Shawnee Thomas Wildcat Alford returned to his reservation from Hampton Institute in 1882, he was received "coldly and with suspicion" because of his style of dress and Christian beliefs. At first he was employed by a missionary as an interpreter, then was able to obtain a teaching job at a government day school for Indians. A year later he was made principal of the government boarding school on the Shawnee reservation, "full of ideas for teaching, eager to try out some of the newer methods I had learned at Hampton." While he expected that parents would discourage his pupils from learning "civilized manners," he discovered that they "adapted themselves to the new environment even before they could speak the language."[45] Such experiences, though no doubt exceptional, challenge the common assertion that residential school education unfitted Indians for life on their reservation.

Government employment, or employment by missionary organizations, were indeed the primary economic opportunities on reservations. "By 1899 returned students had captured 45 percent of some 2,562 positions in the Indian School service. And while most of these were at the level of cooks, shoemakers, laundresses, and seamstresses, it is also noteworthy that 16 percent of the teaching positions . . . were occupied by returned students."[46]

A persistent problem, however, was that the skills and knowledge taught in residential schools often seemed to have little bearing on either the previous lives of their pupils, or their future prospects. A staff member of a residential school in Oklahoma, in around 1900, noted that "[f]ew of the pupils had any desire to learn to read, for there was nothing to read in their homes nor in the camp; there seemed little incentive to learn English, for there was no opportunity to use it; there seemed to be nothing gained through knowing that 'c-a-t' spells cat; arithmetic offered no attraction; not one was interested in knowing the name of the capital of New York."[47]

Residential schools have had a powerful impact on those Indian youth who have passed through them. Whether that impact was positive or negative in their overall lives probably had more to do with the personal characteristics of the individual and his home and tribal background, and with the community to which he returned, than it had to do with the school itself. Youth from the more traditional Indian peoples, like the Navajo, returned to the reservation "only to find themselves handicapped for taking part in Navajo life because they did not know the techniques and customs of their own people."[48] In effect, they had not been available during their adolescent years to receive the education required for full participation in Navajo society. Sociologist Alan Peshkin's study found that Pueblo youth take the tribal education centered on traditional practices and the *kiva* more seriously than the education provided to them through formal schooling, even when that schooling is Indian-administered and concerned to be culturally sensitive, because the former is more directly relevant to the lives that they imagine themselves living.

Criticism of residential schools has become a standard trope in the rhetoric of Indian activists, with an emphasis upon forced assimilation, denigration of native culture, and suppression of Indian languages. The critics "condemn the deleterious effects of White man's education of Indian people over a century and a half," a Canadian scholar points out, "but make no effort to document the true nature of that education. However dismal the record of church-run Indian schools in the nineteenth and twentieth centuries, it remains a fact that most of today's Indian-rights leaders are products of those very schools,"[49] which "educated young Indians about one another and politicized them about their place in the larger society."[50]

In fact, the truth about the residential school experience is much less simple than much of the rhetoric would suggest. They did not leave all of their alumni stranded between two worlds, nor did they always force a choice between those worlds.

> Indian children who lived through their boarding school days were transformed. Many learned to speak, read, and write English, and they shared this

and other knowledge with people back home. Students learned new subjects and trades, further developing themselves in new ways. But most Indians did not turn their backs on First Nations people or discard their cultural identities as Indians."[51]

Much of the dislocation attributed to residential schools may, in fact, be inherent in the tensions associated with an institution whose purpose, whether stated or not, was to allow and encourage pupils to move beyond their inherited circumstances, including deeply meaningful ways of understanding the world that were in conflict with those promoted by formal Western schooling. Peshkin's in-depth study of an Indian-controlled high school that sought in many ways to be relevant to Pueblo life noted a basic disconnect between Pueblo youth and the high school they attended. Even though the school was determined to celebrate Pueblo culture, Peshkin found that "it is far from clear what, in Pueblo terms, schooling enables children to be good for. . . . An Indian High School staff worker remarked that the students she sees at school are just kids in their limited roles as students, whereas the same students at home are important, playing roles that contribute to community life."[52]

Unlike among middle-class Americans, "Pueblos have never absorbed schooling into the lifeblood of their tribal culture, fitting it comfortably into place as one among many integrated elements of their cultural complex. As an unassimilated good, school's benefits are shrouded in uncertainty, so that the logic of striving for and attaining these benefits is not persuasive. . . . 'What's the use of succeeding?' because if I do get anywhere, my tribe may no longer accept me, I may no longer fit in well, I may no longer feel as comfortably attached, and I may have complicated my life by the introduction of a continually competing alternative to the requirements of tribal participation. Thus are schools ambiguous to Pueblo communities, and they will remain ambiguous until their ends and means are somehow integrated with Pueblo tribal life, until then, Indian students undergo institutional and cultural dissonance."[53]

Peshkin is concerned to emphasize that he is describing something much deeper than the cultural discontinuity that is often cited as a cause of underachievement by members of minority groups and for which various multicultural pedagogies are prescribed. "It is life ways that I see at issue. Schools of the outside world promote accomplishment in that world. When they do, they are at odds with the ideals of Pueblo culture as currently conceived. It is not how to succeed in school but how to be accomplished in both worlds that remains a mystery. Who one can become in personal and vocational terms as a result of school success is not yet authorized by

Pueblo tradition, not yet integrated in Pueblo social structures. So the charge of acting white is social control at its best: If you act white, you are not acting Indian. If you can't act white, then what is school good for? If you don't act Indian, you abandon your people. If you don't act Indian, then who are you? If you act both white and Indian, you invite both personal and communal strain and discomfort." The fundamental reality is that "the school, as an institution of becoming, and the [Pueblo] *kiva*, as an institution of remaining, are antagonistic, as are the cultures from which these parallel institutions arise. Some people do manage well with each institution and its cultural context, the result of luck or giftedness or resilience. They do not necessarily know how they achieved their success; most Indian High School students are unable to emulate them."[54]

Residential Schools Out of Fashion

By early in the twentieth century, the Canadian and American governments were seeking to reduce their commitments to residential schools. These commitments had in any case not been adequate to provide a supportive and challenging boarding school experience for Indian youth whose families in most cases had no traditions of formal schooling. In Canada, for example, "the state failed to provide the resources to give the experiment a chance of success. The Methodist Church was unable to find men and women of sufficient moral fiber and determination to persist with the unrewarding task.[55]

In part, this was as a result of demand on the part of newly vocal tribal leadership. For example, in 1931, a resolution was adopted by the League of Indians of Western Canada "requesting that the Department of Indian Affairs establish local reserve schools, since children in residential institutions were making such slow progress."[56] There were, it is true, appeals to keep particular residential schools open, as when Kiowa leaders in Oklahoma asked the government to reconsider its decision, in 1920, to close the Rainy Mountain Boarding School. "To discontinue the institution would mean the removal of the very backbone of the tribe," they wrote. "The best Indian pupil in every respect . . . is the one who has been in attendance at a Government school long enough to learn to speak English, understand the necessity of cleanliness, good health, right living, and the general habits of the whites."[57] Their request was unsuccessful, even though it was echoed by whites who did not want Indian pupils attending their local public schools.[58]

The Carlisle Indian School was closed in 1918, when the facilities were turned back over to the Army as it expanded for World War I. Hoxie comments that "despite its harsh conditions and regimented way of life, Carlisle had represented a national commitment to Indian 'uplift' and a link to the idealism of the Christian reformers who had helped found it in 1879. Its closing shifted attention to local schools with modest goals and little federal oversight,"[59] as we will see. A study in the late 1960s found that "many Indian leaders are favorably disposed toward BIA boarding schools. . . . Several Indian leaders in addition to the Navajo Tribal Council have spoken out in favor of boarding schools."[60] In 1997, it was reported that the Santa Fe Indian School, a residential school, "has a long waiting list of parents who seek a program that meets the needs of Native children. Ironically, . . . Native families were largely responsible for keeping the boarding school system alive, even when the United States government and philanthropic reformers de-emphasized residential schools in favor of reservation day schools" around 1900.[61]

The optimism that a few years of schooling in an off-reservation school would produce young men and women fully prepared to make their way in North American society had faded by then as a result of widespread reports of returned students "going back to the blanket," but also because of the growth of scientific racism as well as a sentimental interest in the more traditional aspects of Indian culture. Pratt had been furious when, at the Columbian Exposition in Chicago in 1893, the Bureau of Indian Affairs organized an exhibit featuring Indians engaging in traditional activities, "calculated to keep the nation's attention and the Indian's energies fixed upon his valueless past, through the spectacular aboriginal housing, dressing, and curio employments it instituted." The Carlisle Indian School had its own exhibit, "Into Civilization and Citizenship," which "aimed and showed how to make acceptable productive citizens out of Indians and so end the need and expense of Bureau control through its system of exalting Indianisms." But, he wrote 30 years later, the BIA and the ethnologists had had their way, "and now the annual cost to the country in overseeing our Indians is double what it then was, and the course pursued has promoted rather than ended Indian dependence on the Bureau."[62] By then, however, there were only a few "radical abolitionists" (of the BIA) who still called for an end to government oversight of the Indians.

With the advance of anthropological knowledge and popular interest in its findings, and growing evidence that Indian youth who passed through off-reservation residential schools were not in general fulfilling the expectations held out for them, these schools were gradually closed; some boarding schools located on reservations were converted to day schools, despite concerns that all of their efforts would be wasted on youth who returned at night to homes where traditional Indian ways prevailed. For example, a Congressional committee report in 1944 warned that

> the Indian Bureau is tending to place too much emphasis on the day school located in the Indian reservation as compared with the opportunities afforded

Indian children in off-reservation boarding schools where they can acquire an education in healthful and cultural surroundings without the handicap of having to spend their out-of-school hours in tepees, shacks with dirt floors and no windows, in tents, in wickiups, in hogans, or in surroundings where English is never spoken, where there is a complete lack of furniture, and where there is sometimes an active antagonism or an abysmal indifference to the virtues of education.[63]

If Indian children and youth were to come to appreciate the "white man's way of life," they should be in off-reservation residential schools.[64]

During the 1920s and 1930s, and even more after the Second World War, many residential schools became an alternative for troubled Indian youth, or for those whose home life was disrupted—one is described as "a child-care provider of last resort for Indian families."[65] Indian youth who had been expelled from local public high schools for use of drugs or alcohol, for fighting or theft, were and are still sometimes sent to residential Indian schools, which become "the site for difficult students, a 'dumping ground' for juvenile offenders."[66] Similarly, after the Second World War, residential schools in Canada became depositories for children whose families were deemed unable to care for them adequately, "giving a new purpose to the schools as elements of an expanding post-war welfare system." In British Columbia, in 1961, half of the pupils in residential schools were there "because home conditions [had] been judged inadequate."[67]

Under those circumstances, it could not be expected that the schools would continue to train the future Indian leadership, as had been the case previously. Instead, they became a means of institutionalizing Indian youth for whom, in many cases, neither family nor tribe had a means of providing adequate care. In addition, the wide dispersal of population on some reservations made it difficult, even with improved roads, to get children to day schools and home each day, created a continuing need for residential schools. A comprehensive study of Indian education completed in 1971 concluded that these schools continued to fulfill necessary functions "as regards child welfare, Indian employment, and the school's availability as an educational center for children who have no alternatives due to isolation and dissatisfaction with, or expulsion from, their local schools."[68]

CHAPTER 10

Self-Help and Self-Governance

Although Indian peoples had managed their own affairs to some extent even after forced into dependent relationships with the American and Canadian governments, the 1920s saw a new emphasis on self-determination. Indian leaders were encouraged by white sympathizers who romanticized Indian traditions in ways which, to some Indians at least, seemed to invalidate the painful adjustments they and their children were making in an effort to achieve economic security. The policy of the federal government placed a new emphasis on expecting Indians—whether as individuals or as tribes—to take responsibility for themselves rather than continue in a dependent situation.

In 1917, the Commissioner of Indian Affairs announced that the American government intended to discontinue the guardianship of those Indians who were considered competent to manage their own affairs.[1] As soon as possible, any Indians who—on the basis of education and economic prospects—were ready for it should be made independent of government supervision and placed on the same basis as any other Americans. Once again, it was promised that the government could finally get out of the business of dealing with Indians as a special case, as wards of the state.

The Secretary of the Interior, in 1926, asked what would later become the Brookings Institution to study "the economic and social condition of the American Indians"; the highly influential report, issued in 1928, was instead, significantly, titled *The Problem of Indian Administration*. The so-called "Meriam Report" pointed out that "the fundamental requirement is that the task of the Indian Service be recognized as primarily educational, in the broadest sense of that word," and criticized the fact that "education for the Indian in the past had proceeded largely on the theory that it is necessary to remove the Indian child as far as possible from his home environment; whereas the modern point of view in education and social work lays stress on upbringing in the natural setting of home and family life."[2]

While some Indians might choose "to merge into the social and economic life of the prevailing civilization as developed by the whites," others should be allowed, if they chose, "to live in the presence of that civilization at least in accordance with a minimum standard of health and decency." Respecting this principle, "the survey staff would not recommend the disastrous attempt to force . . . Indians . . . to be what they do not want to be. . . . Such efforts may break down the good in the old without replacing it with compensating good from the new."[3]

The report did not call for a policy of keeping Indians in a condition of untainted cultural integrity, but stressed "the desires of individual Indians." Some would choose to assimilate, others would not, and government policy should respect both choices. The authors warned against efforts by some well-meaning whites to "metaphorically speaking, . . . enclose these Indians in a glass case to preserve them as museum specimens for future generations to study and enjoy, because of the value of their culture and its picturesqueness." After all, "Indians cannot be set apart away from contact with the whites. The glass policy is impracticable." Those Indians who wished to enjoy the benefits of modern life had every right to do so: "These Indians are as much entitled to direct their lives according to their desires as are the conservative Indians. It would be as unjust and as unwise to attempt to force them back to the old or to withhold guidance in the achievement of the new ends they seek as it would be to attempt to force the ones who love the old into the new."[4]

The Meriam Report called for day schools on reservations to replace or supplement boarding schools, which should themselves be reformed. Rather than seeking to provide a single national curriculum to youth drawn from very different tribes, as had been the practice at Carlisle and subsequent boarding schools, there should be an effort to draw for instructional purposes from "local Indian life, or at least [from] within the scope of the child's experience." After all, "Indian tribes and individuals vary so greatly, that a standard content and method of education . . . would be worse than futile."[5] We can see here the influence of the new ideas advanced by Progressive educators about starting from the interests and experiences of pupils.

The authors pointed out that "[i]t is doubtful if any state nowadays in compiling a course of study . . . would do what the national government has attempted to do, that is to adopt a uniform course of study for the entire Indian Service and require it to be carried out in detail. The Indian school course of study is clearly not adaptable to different tribes and different individuals; it is built mainly in imitation of a somewhat older type of public school curricula now recognized as unsatisfactory even for white schools, instead of being created out of the lives of Indian people, as it should be; and it is administered by a poorly equipped teaching force under inadequate professional direction."[6]

Not for the first time, the Meriam Report held out the prospect that what it called the "Indian problem" could be solved within a generation, if the nation were willing to make generous expenditures on a reformed approach to the education of Indian children. This could, the authors promised, lead to "winding up the national administration of Indian affairs. The people of the United States have the opportunity, if they will, to write the closing chapters of the history of the relationship of the national government and the Indians."[7]

This Meriam report, while insisting on keeping open the choice for individual Indians to transition into the majority society, marked a further shift in the purpose of schooling for Indian youth away from the nineteenth century model, one which assumed that they would continue to live to a considerable extent within a distinct tribal culture rather than be assimilated fully into White America.

How did this shift come about? One factor was surely the growing influence of explanations of group characteristics that rested on the newly fashionable concept of culture in contrast with the racial determinism of 20 years before, a concept popularized by Margaret Mead and Ruth Benedict on the basis of their research and that of Franz Boas. Another factor was the increasingly positive attitude among the white majority toward certain aspects of Indian culture. This was manifested at the elite level by the movement of a number of artists, writers, and patrons of the arts to Taos, Santa Fe, and other communities where Southwestern art and mores (and climate) could be experienced as an alternative to what to many in the wake of the First World War seemed an exhausted and failed High Culture.

The attractiveness of Indian mores, selectively perceived, to that generation of intellectuals is reflected in Aldous Huxley's *Brave New World* and in the fashion of Pueblo pottery and Navajo rugs. Consistent with this romantic identification with Indian culture, the doyenne of the Taos colony, Mabel Dodge, wrote in 1922 that the Pueblos were threatened with losing their "whole culture" and could be saved only by "taking them away from the government and by creating a new school system for them."[8] The missionaries were considered a menace as well; novelist Mary Austin wrote that if they had their way, "the Indian will have no future but to be made into 'a lower middle class . . . imitation white man'."[9] Horrors!

By the following year, "a loose coalition of artists and writers in New Mexico had begun to organize itself into a powerful political force. Through their publicity skills and access to major newspapers and periodicals, they began to turn public opinion against the BIA and its long-standing policy of cultural assimilation."[10] A group of self-identified white supporters of Indians—taking a very different line from that of the Lake Mohonk reformers a generation before—issued a "Magna Carta for Indians," which urged the Indian Office to promote "instead of suppressing" Indian commitment to "group loyalties and communal responsibilities," with a focus not only on traditional vocational training but also on "the development of Indian arts and crafts." In addition, Indians should enjoy "religious and social freedom in all matters not directly contrary to public morals."[11] Efforts by missionaries to promote Christianity among the Indians should no longer be encouraged.

At another level, for the previous several decades, the great popularity of "Wild West" shows and novels, and later films, on Western themes had made the Plains Indians, if usually menacing, at least very interesting and sometimes sympathetic. There was, in fact, "more to the popular view of Indians than pity. Harsh racial judgments coexisted with fascination and sympathy . . . in the early twentieth century tribal mythology and handicrafts gained in popularity even as the Indian was being indicted for childishness and ignorance."[12] Two decades later, white intellectuals were finding all sorts of wisdom in "primitive" peoples.

A leader of the various denominational missionary efforts that had worked among the Indians for some decades saw these "sentimentalists" as seeking to "preserve the Indian permanently as a museum piece," and considered them as "no better than others who regarded Native Americans as 'hopelessly degenerate.' Both would withhold 'education and civilizing influences' from the Indians—the one to justify white encroachment on Indian lands, the other to satisfy a 'romantic fancy'." Encouraging Indians to keep their "old life as it was hundreds of years ago," he wrote, might as well lead to abandoning education and vocational training and the opportunity for owning property.[13]

After the Second World War, the emphasis of federal policy for the education of Indian youth changed again, with a renewed emphasis on developing their capacity to find a place in the modern economy and in mainstream society. The Joint Indian Affairs Committee of Congress charged that the "present Indian education program tends to operate too much in the direction of perpetuating the Indian as a special status individual rather than preparing him for independent citizenship."[14]

Whereas there had seemed few prospects for Indians moving to urban areas during the Depression of the 1930s, the war-time economy had drawn some 40,000 off of reservations in the United States to fill positions most of which had never been held by Indians before. More than 24,000 Indians had served in the armed forces, and had thereby been exposed to a range of non-Indian contacts and experiences that prepared them for life beyond the reservations.[15] As a very influential white educator of Navajos told a researcher, "Up 'til World War II, you couldn't fill Navajo schools, partly because you couldn't see what good going to school would do. It didn't lead to any kind of worthwhile work at all. . . . During World War II, a lot of people went into the services, but even more people worked off-reservation and saw that, for better or worse, you were at a real disadvantage without an education. So there was a real *demand* for schools."[16]

In a development parallel to those among Mexican-American and African-American veterans, these experiences had also helped to create expectations of better treatment by American society and new skills for organization and advocacy. The National Congress of American Indians was founded in 1944, and soon was joined by a variety of more specialized organizations to advance the interests of Indians. For the first time, Indians were taking the lead in formulating and promoting their agenda, based on a sense of common Indian—as contrasted with or supplementing tribal—identity. This pan-Indian activism was in an uneasy co-existence with "tribal nationalism, which . . . has surged in the face of ethnic renewal and Indian activists' continued assertion of indigenous rights to collective self-determination."[17]

The agenda was not altogether clear, however. While, on the one hand, there was a new insistence on ethnic pride, there was also an over-riding concern for better schools that would open opportunities for Indian children in the wider economy and society. As a Navajo leader told Congress in 1946, "We . . . ask that . . . means be provided for people without sufficient livestock to make their living in some other manner. . . . We need the schools so that our children can compete with other children."[18]

Separatism and Self-Government

Both in the United States and in Canada there had always been those who urged that the identification of Indians with their tribes was holding them back from enjoyment of the benefits of civilization and prosperity, while others insisted that only a restoration of a substantial measure of sovereignty would enable Indians to solve their many problems. Canada's first Prime Minister, Sir John A. Macdonald (1867–1873), told Parliament that a national goal was "to do away with the tribal system and assimilate the Indian people in all respects with the inhabitants of the Dominion, as speedily as they are fit to change."[19] This was the intention, in the United States, of the General Allotment Act of 1887 (known as the Dawes Act), which reformers believed "held out the possibility of smashing the tribal bond and setting Indians on the road to civilization."[20] This law promoted individual allotment of land that had been held in common by tribes, on the premise that this would promote among tribesmen the habits and attitudes of independent farmers, and thus promote assimilation of Indians to the then-prevailing norms of American life. This was followed, in the Indian Territory, by the Curtis Act in 1898, which abolished the tribal governments under which the Five Civilized Nations had managed their own Affairs, and subjected them to territorial (soon state) and local government.

Commonly, the extension of government authority (or what came to be called "wardship") over Indian individuals and tribes was justified as protecting them from the encroachments of whites while they acquired the education and other qualities that would enable them to stand up for themselves. As we have seen in several cases, some Indian groups rejected both subordination to government supervision and also integration into local communities, seeking to manage their own affairs. Some of their advocates argued that assigning Indian children to local public schools "was a breach of the treaties, which placed education exclusively under First Nations customary jurisdiction. . . . Physical integration in provincial schools may be justified as good for society, but it cannot be justified as good for Indian children and students."[21]

In the Far North of Canada and in Alaska, until fairly recently, "aboriginal people continued to support themselves largely by hunting, fishing, and selling furs," and remained largely autonomous.

> In hard times—to give only two examples, a period of famine in northern Alberta in the 1880s and a lethal epidemic of influenza in the Mackenzie Valley in the 1920s—the Hudson's Bay Company, Northwest Mounted Police, missionaries, and Indian Affairs officials distributed relief in the form of food, clothing, and medicine; but aboriginal communities in the North generally remained independent and self-supporting.[22]

This was far from being the case on the reservations onto which, farther south, most Indians were confined from the middle of the nineteenth century. It was not uncommon for tribes to be forced to move several times, to less and less desirable land, as the pressures of a growing white population turned their traditional hunting areas into more productive farmland. The land that Indians were left with was often good for very little, and made the ideal of self-sustaining economies unrealistic. It seemed to most "friends of the Indian" during the nineteenth century that there was no realistic alternative for Indian youth seeking a better life than to integrate into the national economy to the extent possible. Characteristically, Richard Henry Pratt wrote to a former student, in 1893, "stick to your reservations, hang together, demand rations and support from the Government, and you probably never will be citizens."[23]

There were exceptions, Indian peoples who through a fortunate location or who through their own efforts made their allotted reservations prosperous. "When the Hobbema Cree settled on their reserves [in Canada] around 1880, they had virtually nothing. Fifty years later, they had a viable agricultural community with houses, cultivated fields, livestock, roads, schools, churches, and money in the bank. Strikingly, the level of [government] subsidy had become very low by the 1920s."[24] Similarly, the Cherokee and other "civilized nations" responded successfully to their forced transfer from the forests of the Southeast to the very different plains of Indian Territory, and the Navajo in recent years managed to prosper to some extent from the natural resources of their reservation.

Demands for self-government and an end to government wardship (though not government benefits) were increasingly heard from Indian leaders in the United States and Canada after the Second World War. The way for this had been prepared in the United States by legislation, known as the Wheeler-Howard Act, proposed by the Roosevelt Administration and enacted, in much-reduced form, in 1934. As described by its opponents, the bill "prescribed a return to tribal life and to the status of incompetency from which the Indian had been trying emerge. Under the provisions of this bill no Indian was ever to receive full title to his acreage. Indeed, the original proposal was to take the land from those who had received title in trust, and put it again into tribal and governmental ownership."[25] From the point of view of John Collier and other supporters, however, the proposal was intended to restore the integrity of reservation lands that had been distributed to individual Indians and often were leased out to white farmers, and to promote tribal self-government in the common interest.[26] The context of this proposal was a widespread belief in elite circles that market-based individualism had demonstrated its failure with the 1929 Crash and subsequent worldwide Depression, and that collective solutions—including the shared ownership of property—were the solution. Indian reservations seemed the ideal laboratories within which to try out solutions that the wider society was unready to accept. The dependence of tribal governments on the federal authorities made them much less able to resist than could local and state governments of the majority society.

The immediate problem that the bill was intended to address was that distribution of reservation land to individual Indians ("allotment") had not had the anticipated effect of promoting enlightened self-interest and economic independence on their part; in most cases, "individual Indians lost their lands: some sold for quick cash, others forfeited their lands to mortgage debt or tax liabilities, and still others were the victims of swindling Indian agents and land-hungry whites." In order to protect Indians, there had been a constant growth of government bureaucracy and intervention in the affairs of individual Indians. Collier and his allies saw return of land to the tribes and creation of strong tribal governments as the solution. "Over time, as Collier envisioned it, tribal corporations would take over all the health, education, welfare, land management, and law and order responsibilities that the federal government was providing."[27] Indians could not be swindled out of personal property that they did not possess!

For the opponents, however, tribal self-government would be a pious fiction so long as the tribes were almost completely dependent on the government for support. "The whole effect of recent legislation," an opponent wrote in 1944, "is to draw the net more tightly about those known as Indians, to segregate them more and more from their white brothers."[28] The only way to real independence was for Indians to participate fully in the American economy, with all its risks and challenges.

Although the number of Indian pupils in local public schools continued to grow in Canada and the United States, by the 1960s such integration had already lost its attractiveness as a policy option; indeed, this occurred just as integration of black pupils in public schools across the United States was gaining effective momentum. Increasingly, among Indian tribes in both countries, the demand grew for tribal control of schools, which inevitably required a pulling back from participation in local public schools, even with Indian representation on local elected school boards. Indian leaders were beginning to stress separateness, just as, in the United States, the emphasis on Black Power was drowning out the demand for racial integration. A cynical view would be that their continued credibility as spokespersons for other Indians depended upon their remaining separate and unassimilated.

In response to the growing demand for Indian control of Indian schools, and the theme in President Johnson's War on Poverty of promoting "maximum feasible participation of the poor," the Bureau of Indian Affairs began a pilot program called "Project Tribe" that contracted out the management of a few schools to Indian groups; one of which, discussed below, was the Rough Rock Demonstration School on the Navajo Reservation in Arizona.[29]

A decisive step in this process, in Canada, was the confrontation that occurred at the Blue Quills Indian School, a Catholic institution, in 1970. The government had decided, in 1955, that pupils in the upper grades would be bussed into the local town to attend a Catholic public high school. As it became clear that this was only the first step toward closing the Indian school and assigning all the pupils to integrated public schools, Catholic leaders expressed their opposition, insisting that Indians represented "a culturally distinct human community with an educational problem and process of its own." These could not be served adequately in a regular school that lacked teachers who knew how to teach Indians, and which could not train for Indian leadership.[30] Catholic educators also argued that "integrated schools, which naturally prepared graduates for working and living in non-Native Canada, threatened to deprive the reserves of their best and their brightest."[31]

The proposal to close Blue Quills and other Indian schools reflected the trend of national policy toward Canada's Indian population, abandoning group solutions for integration on an individual basis into Canadian society. A decision, consistent with this policy direction, that Blue Quills would be closed and all of its pupils assigned to integrated schools led to a widely reported confrontation in the summer of 1970, when local Indians occupied the school and others came from across Canada to lend their support. Indian leaders insisted that their treaty rights were being violated by shifting jurisdiction for the education of Indian children from federal authorities to those of the province and thus of the local school board.[32] After some weeks, the federal authorities backed down and announced that Blue Quills could be operated as an Indian-controlled school, setting a precedent that was soon followed by other tribes.

This retreat by the government in the case of Blue Quills School presaged its retreat in the face of opposition by Indian leadership to the Trudeau administration's "White Paper" calling for complete integration of Indians (see below). The National Indian Brotherhood's *Indian Control of Indian Education* charged that "integration in the past twenty years has simply meant the closing down of Indian schools and transferring Indian students to schools away from their Reserves, often against the wishes of Indian parents. . . . [N]either Indian parents and children, nor the white community: parents, children, and schools, were prepared for integration, or able to cope with the many problems which were created."[33]

Under the new policies, by 1975–1976, 53 Canadian Indian communities had taken control of their schools, and by the mid-1980s, 22.8 percent of Indian pupils nationwide were attending schools operated by 187 (out of 577 nationwide) Indian bands; the number of Indian-controlled schools increased to 329 by 1991–1992.[34] Despite this impressive growth, nearly half of Indian children in Canada attended provincial public schools or private schools, and nearly 30 percent attended schools operated by the federal government.[35] Thus, though the band-operated schools received the most policy attention, in fact half of the Indian pupils were already attending integrated schools, with mixed results.

Public hearings were held, starting in 1992, by the Canadian Royal Commission on Aboriginal Peoples, resulting in a call for "more aboriginal control of education, more aboriginal teachers, more cross-cultural training and education programs, and more Native language, culture, and history in schools,"[36] all within the context of demands for the recognition of autonomous nationhood by the various Indian peoples. If the recommendations of the Royal Commission, issued in many volumes in 1996, were followed, one Canadian political scientist predicted that

> Canada will be redefined as a multinational state embracing an archipelago of aboriginal nations that own a third of Canada's land mass, are immune from federal and provincial taxation, are supported by transfer payments from citizens who do pay taxes, are able to opt out of federal and provincial legislation, and engage in "nation to nation" diplomacy with whatever is left of Canada. . . . Although aboriginal leaders might achieve rewarding political careers, most aboriginal people would remain poor and dependent, marginalized on reserves and other territorial enclaves. This would be a lose-lose situation in which both Canada and aboriginal peoples would both become worse off than they should be.[37]

Imposed Dependency

In many cases, tribes have not been able to develop successful economies on the reservations allotted to them, and have fallen into continued dependence on government subsidies and provision of the basic services that more typical communities provide from property tax and other revenues. An anthropologist who studied the social dynamics of a large reserve in Manitoba found that political competition and alliances among small groups of Indians led to "fluid and temporary" coalitions, with distribution of government benefits "the main purpose of politics." This is consistent with several studies of Rough Rock on the Navajo Reservation. One of the results is that the "scope of aboriginal self-government on reserves means that the local public sector is enormously overdeveloped in comparison to other Canadian communities of similar size." For example, the "Stoney reserve has three chiefs and twelve councillors, all drawing full-time salaries." Funding for the activities of government on hundreds of Canadian reserves comes primarily from the federal government, since "generally . . . Indians on reserve do not tax themselves and are not taxed by any other government."[38]

One result of the seduction of life on the dole is that, to a greater extent than other Americans or Canadians, Indians continue to live in rural areas that offer few prospects for employment other than from government, and thus reduce the incentives for Indian youth to persist in their schooling. When the Rough Rock Demonstration Project began in the late 1960s, few of the Navajo in the area had ever held paid jobs. A Canadian political scientist argues that mistaken government policy over many decades has created a pattern of multigenerational dependency with profoundly negative effects.

> Just as the transition from buffalo-hunting to agriculture was slowed by the provision of rations necessary to avoid mass starvation, the transition from rural to urban life was slowed, in an even more damaging way, by the welfare state. The extension of the welfare state to Canadian Indians just as their rural economies were breaking down has proved to be one of the greatest policy disasters in Canadian history. . . . The result of these changes has been a staggering level of welfare dependency. By the time the Canada Assistance Plan was passed in 1966, about 36 per cent of reserve residents were receiving welfare assistance each year. That figure continued to grow, reaching 42 per cent by 1992, compared with a national utilization rate of less than 10 percent for other Canadians in the same year. The on-reserve rate of welfare dependence was reported to be 45 per cent in 1998, and Indian Affairs has estimated that it might rise to 57 per cent by 2010.[39]

The prospects for self-government in a meaningful sense by Indian tribes or bands depends upon their remaining resident together on reservations, but this in turn may (in the absence, at least, of the casino opportunities available to those located reasonably near urban centers) make it difficult to participate in the national and regional economies of Canada and the United States. After all, "if the band offers a place to live, if the government pays for every bit of health care, if some government jobs are available and there is a tradition of sharing the benefits with family members, and if all of this is tax-free, is it surprising that so many people stay on the reserves even if no real jobs are available there?"[40] As with reservations in the United States, most Canadian reserves do not have strong enough economies to support the people who live on them; generally, reserve income is produced off-reserve by non-Indians through the taxes they pay. It can in fact be asked, "Is there any validity to the definition of self-government if it simply means that people living on a reserve have the privilege of spending money generated by someone else?"[41]

In the late nineteenth century, the prevailing opinion among American and Canadian white elites was that expressed by Theodore Roosevelt in *The Winning of the West* (1889): "[W]e undoubtedly ought to break up the great Indian reservations, disregard the tribal governments, allot the land in severalty (with, however, only a limited power of alienation), and treat the Indians as we do other citizens, with certain exceptions, for their sakes as well as ours."[42]

Such views were consistent with the criticism of government officials responsible for Indian Affairs as having a self-interest in keeping Indians dependent upon themselves. Richard Henry Pratt criticized the Bureau of Indian Affairs for decades, and in fact lost his long-time position at Carlisle because of a speech calling for its abolition. Some prominent Indians like Carlos Montezuma also expressed resentment at government paternalism, and argued that as long as Indians were the only American group with a special bureaucracy overseeing them, they would be "singled out, given a special legal status, and subjected to prejudiced treatment from the American public." More and more Indian alumni of residential schools returned to their reservations ready to give leadership and were frustrated by the close oversight by government agents, since the "government's expenditures in Indian education and welfare gave it the presumptive authority to regulate virtually every aspect of Native life to achieve the most efficient use of federal funds."[43]

The National Study of American Indian Education, in the late 1960s, found that in some cases Indians were reluctant to accept responsibility for their schools because of a concern that this would lead to conflict within the tribe. An Apache advisory school board member reported that those he consulted about the possibility of running the local school under contract with the Bureau of Indian Affairs wanted it to remain under BIA management. "The feelings of the people were that if the contracting took place, politics probably would enter the picture and relatives of the politicians would take over the various positions."[44]

By confining Indians to reservations where, in many cases, there were few prospects of economic development and then supporting their idleness (meagerly) with food and clothing, the government created generations of dependents. An experienced missionary wrote in 1944, "[T]he placing of practically an entire people on rations was the first experiment with the dole, unfortunately not the last. The paternalism thus fostered has laid the cold blight of dependency on the Indian people. It is expressed in the phrase often heard on the reservations, 'Why work? Uncle Sam won't let us starve'."[45]

The more successful tribes were able to organize for the purpose of obtaining various government benefits, including—in the United States—the right to operate gambling establishments with associated resorts. About a third of the tribes in the United States now take advantage of their special status to operate casinos, some of which have produced tremendous revenues for the tribes but also for non-Indian entrepreneurs. These efforts have become increasingly sophisticated, and one must question for how long those who serve as spokespersons for the interests of impoverished tribes will retain credibility. In Canada, "the activists in the aboriginal political movement, unless they are band chief, tend to live in towns and cities, where they work as lawyers, professors, administrators, and consultants." Despite their own mastery of the skills required for successful participation in the society and economy, it is in their interest to encourage other Indians "to withdraw into themselves, into their own 'First Nations,' under their own 'self-governments,' on their own 'traditional lands,' within their own 'aboriginal economies.' . . . Under the policy of withdrawal," Flanagan charges,

> the political and professional elites will do well for themselves as they manage the aboriginal enclaves, but the majority will be worse off than ever. In order to become self-supporting and get beyond the social pathologies that are ruining their communities, aboriginal people need to acquire the skills and attitudes that bring success in a liberal society, political democracy, and market economy. Call it assimilation, call it integration, call it adaptation, call it whatever you want: it has to happen.[46]

Even when schools are under the control of Indian school boards, those find themselves under pressure to provide their students with the skills and knowledge required to do well on tests which have been normed on the national, overwhelmingly non-Indian, student population. Without such preparation, the life-prospects of Indian youth would be sharply reduced, and yet inevitably it makes it more difficult to educate from a distinctively Indian perspective. "Increasingly, Indigenous schools face the dilemma of 'doing' Indigenous education while complying with high-stakes tests that devalue local knowledge and jeopardize children's life opportunities by threatening to deny them a high school degree."[47] In recent years, the Navajo board of the Rough Rock schools has adopted goals much like those of any other school, and without the impassioned emphasis on Navajo language and culture that characterized the beginnings of the school 40 years ago.

In response to such demands, the focus of government efforts shifted again, from cultural maintenance, to assimilation and integration into the economic mainstream. "Set the American Indians Free" demanded a 1945 article in the *Reader's Digest*; "American Indian soldiers who had fought for their country should therein be given the opportunity to become totally assimilated in the mainstream culture."[48] It became government policy to terminate the dependent status of Indians and treat them like any other citizens. As so often before, however, this policy direction lasted only about 20 years.

In November 1969, a Subcommittee on Indian Education of the U.S. Senate issued its report, after several years of hearings and reports. Chaired originally by Senator Robert Kennedy, it was chaired, after his assassination, by his brother Senator Edward Kennedy. The report did not mince its words: "We have concluded that our national policies for educating American Indians are a failure of major proportions." The "Kennedy Report" found that of the 160,000 Indian children in all types of schools—public, private, mission, and Federal—one-third were in federally-operated institutions." The government operated 226 schools in 17 states, of which 77 were boarding schools. There were 34,605 Indian children enrolled in Bureau of Indian Affairs residential schools, 15,450 in BIA day schools, and 3,854 housed in dormitories while attending public schools at BIA expense.[49]

The results were unsatisfactory. "Forty thousand Navajo Indians, nearly a third of the entire tribe, are functionally illiterate in English . . . more than one out of every five Indian men have less than 5 years of schooling . . . only 3 percent of Indian students who enroll in college graduate; the national average is 32 percent." It seemed, the Committee found, as though the Indian Service operated largely for the benefit of its civil service employees. "In 1953 the BIA began a crash program to improve education for Navajo children. Between then and 1967, supervisory positions in BIA headquarters increased 113 percent; supervisory positions in BIA schools increased 144 percent; administrative and clerical positions in the BIA schools increased 94 percent. Yet, teaching positions increased only 20 percent."[50] Bureaucracy, rather than effective services to Indian pupils, was the main product of the BIA.

The report found that Progressive Education ideas had had the effect of lowering expectations for what Indian pupils should be expected to accomplish. "When asked to name the most important things the schools should do for the students, only about one-tenth of the teachers mentioned academic achievement as an important goal. Teachers stressed the educational objectives of personality development, socialization, and citizenship."[51] It is interesting to note that, in a survey by the National Center for Education Statistics, 40 years later, the principals of Bureau of Indian Affairs schools were substantially less likely to stress "academic excellence" (55.9 versus 69.6 percent) and "work habits/self discipline" (49.6 versus 59.8 percent) than those of non-BIA public schools with less than 25 percent Indian pupils, and more likely to stress "personal growth" (40.6 versus 32.4 percent) and "multicultural awareness" (28.9 versus 11.2 percent).[52] Soft objectives and low expectations seem to be a continuing pattern for those who educate Indian pupils.

Perhaps the most significant conclusion of the Kennedy Report was the importance of "increased Indian participation and control of their own education programs."[53] This would soon result in a redirection of policy from the assimilating focus of the previous two decades; a similar redirection occurred at just the same time in Canada, where a study commissioned by the government had proposed, in 1967, abandoning group solutions for individually "integrating Indians into Canadian society."[54] This served as the basis for a new policy direction of the Canadian government in 1969, after the election of Pierre Trudeau's Liberals. Parliament was told that the separate legal status of Indians "and the policies which have flowed from it have kept the Indian people apart from and behind other Canadians."[55] The new approach was "premised on the achievement of individual Indian equality at the expense of cultural survival. . . . Indians would receive the same services, including education, available to members of the dominant society. The Department of Indian Affairs would be abolished and the reserve system dismantled . . ."[56] Responsibility for Indians would be transferred from the federal authorities to the provinces, treaty obligations would be shelved, and the legal category of "status Indian" would be abandoned, with Indians henceforth considered ordinary Canadian citizens.[57]

The Trudeau administration's "White Paper" calling for complete integration of Indians—parallel to the Eisenhower administration's similar policy proposals in the United States a decade earlier—was quickly countered by Indian leadership, whose reaction was overwhelmingly negative; it was a "thinly disguised program of extermination through assimilation."[58] (Of course, there would perhaps be no need for Indian leadership once integration was achieved . . .). In 1972, the National Indian Brotherhood issued a position paper, *Indian Control of Indian Education*, appealing to "two educational principles recognized in Canadian society: Parental Responsibility and Local Control of Education," and asserting that these rights had continuously been denied to the Indians of Canada.[59]

The paper charged, as we have seen, that "integration in the past twenty years has simply meant the closing down of Indian schools and transferring Indian students to schools away from their Reserves, often against the wishes of Indian parents. . . . [N]either Indian parents and children, nor the white community: parents, children, and schools, were prepared for integration, or able to cope with the many problems which were created."[60] "What we want for our children," they wrote, "can be summarized very briefly: to reinforce their Indian identity; [and] to provide a good living in modern society. We are the best judges of the kind of school programs which can contribute to these goals without causing damage to the child. We must, therefore, reclaim our right to direct the education of our children."[61] In an ethnic essentialism common at that period, the paper asserted that "only Indian peoples can develop a suitable philosophy of education based on Indian values adapted to modern living."[62] This would mean not only Indian control over schools on reserves but also "a special effort to train Indian teachers and for revision of the curricula in Indian schools to eliminate the white man's derogatory image of native peoples and to pass on the values of tribal culture to the next generation."[63]

The recommendations were accepted, at least in principle, in 1973 by Jean Chrétien, then Minister of Indian Affairs and Northern Development, but in practice, "Indian Control" was implemented slowly and with many difficulties. Indian activists charged that "the Department of Indian Affairs, while accepting the 1972 policy of Indian control, had redefined 'control' to mean 'a degree of participation'."[64]

For Indian activists, this was not enough; they insisted that they represented sovereign "nations" whose rights had been suppressed but never surrendered. In 1981, the Declaration of the First Nations insisted that "[w]e have never given up our sovereignty. . . . We retain the right to determine the type of education most suitable for our children."[65] After all, as activists like to insist, "Western education is hostile in its structure, its curriculum, its context, and its personnel.[66]

One result of the new thinking in the United States about control of schools by Indians themselves was passage of the Indian Education Act in 1972, providing additional resources and a new administrative structure to promote the education of Indians, both in public schools and in government-controlled schools. Perhaps more significant, however, was the Indian Self-Determination and Education Assistance Act of 1975, which paved the way for Indian-controlled schools. Three years later, Congress enacted the Tribally Controlled Community College Assistance Act, which has resulted in a proliferation of Indian-controlled colleges, and then the Tribally Controlled Schools Act in 1988. Also in 1988, when a report was prepared by the BIA on its schools, they enrolled fewer than 10 percent of all Indian pupils in the United States. Enrolment in schools operated by Indian tribes under contract with the BIA had increased from 2,299 in 1973 to 11,202 in 1988, while enrolment in BIA schools had decreased from 35,532 to 26,715 pupils.[67]

In contrast with the previous underfunding of schools serving Indian pupils, the 1988 report found that average expenditure on Indian pupils in BIA schools was $7,917, compared with $4,051 average per pupil expenditure for public schools in general, and the staff-to-pupil ratio in BIA schools was 4.4 to one, compared with 9.6 to one in public schools.

CHAPTER 11

Indian Languages and Cultures

The most endangered aspect of the culture and distinctiveness of an Indian people, and the most difficult to preserve, is the language spoken by at least the older generation of its members. No other issue, it is safe to say, has so divided Indian leadership as whether and in what forms traditional cultures should be maintained, and to what length Indian parents and educators should go to maintain the proficient use of Indian languages. While cultural elements may be maintained in the form of familial and communal practices with relatively little effort, the worldviews or *mentalités* that give them deep meaning are more fragile, and only disciplined effort can maintain a minority language when daily activities impose that of the majority. Nevertheless, languages have enormous symbolic meaning. As sociolinguist Joshua Fishman has written,

> To abandon the language may be viewed as an abandonment not only of the traditional doings and knowings, but as an abandonment of personal ancestral kin and cultural ancestral heroes *per se*. Similarly, guaranteeing or fostering the specific language's acquisition and use is often viewed as fostering one's own personal (in addition to the culture's) triumph over death and obliteration via living on in one's own children and grandchildren. Life and death imagery is pervasive in ethnolinguistic consciousness the world over.[1]

This heavily symbolic significance of language arises especially in situations in which members of a minority culture see their coherence and identity as under threat from a majority culture that seems to press in from every side; language is the most powerful marker of the boundaries of such a group, since it enables in-group communication from which those outside the group are barred. The phenomenon is of course not limited to the native peoples of the United States and Canada—think of the powerful meanings attached to the use and preservation of Basque, Catalan, and Gallego in

Spain, the efforts to revive Welsh in Great Britain, the persistence of Yiddish among Hasidic Jews in the United States, and of course the elaborate protections for French in Quebec.

Such a "socio-linguistic" perspective must be qualified by a recognition that it is not universally the case, and that the significance of a language can change over time. In Ireland, for example, the use of Celtic Irish had a strong symbolic meaning during the late nineteenth and early twentieth centuries, when the struggle for independence from England (and thus from the English language) was at its height, but more recently with that struggle a distant memory use of Irish has tended to fade away despite extensive government efforts to encourage its use. Thus an activist for maintenance of "endangered languages" concedes that "not all cultures . . . seem to have the same regard for language as a potent symbol of ethnic identity. . . . Because of its complexity and pervasiveness in society, of course, language is widely acknowledged as the behaviour with the greatest potential to act as a badge . . . but it is not the only way that culture can be transmitted. Culture does not come to a complete stop, when any one of its elements changes or ceases to exist, even when that is language."[2]

For the Indians of Canada and the United States, becoming proficient in spoken and written English (and in French in Quebec) has been an essential step to participation in the economy beyond that of the tribe, and to effective advocacy for the interests of their peoples. It has also, in many cases, been a step toward the abandonment of the ancestral language. "There appears to be a correspondence between bilingualism and subsequent language loss. As there is an increased need for bilingualism for employment or economic advancement . . . the new language takes dominance."[3] But is that process irreversible? This is the question that many tribes have been wrestling with.

The "native peoples" of the United States and Canada are reported to have spoken more than 600 different languages at the time of European settlement.[4] More than half of these languages have already disappeared, and it seems likely that only a few have long-term prospects. Linguists two decades ago identified 210 surviving native languages in the United States and Canada, of which only 34 were spoken by the young as well as the older generations. In the early 1990s, the U.S. Census identified 136 different groups of Indian languages. "Of these, 47 were spoken in the home by fewer than 100 persons; an additional 22 were spoken by fewer than 200. And this is probably a conservative estimate of linguistic erosion, because the Census has no way of knowing how well or how often these people actually use the language." Others count 155 indigenous languages in the United States, 135 of which are said to be dying; "[A]ll of California's 31 Indian languages are moribund; of these, 22 are spoken only by small groups of elders."⁵ Another study estimated that "for 125 of 175 indigenous languages still spoken in the USA, the speakers represent the 'grandparental generation and up', including 55 languages (31%) spoken only by the very elderly."⁶

In Canada, there are currently 53 Indian or Inuit languages but only three of them—Ojibway, Cree, and Inuktikut—"are perceived to be enduring, though not necessarily flourishing. . . . Most speakers of the Aboriginal language are bilingual and the mainstream language is used exclusively in some situations."⁷

Of Indian eighth grade pupils in the United States who participated in the National Assessment of Educational Progress in 2003, 51 percent reported that no language but English was spoken in their homes, while 22 percent reported that another language was spoken at least half the time. Only 11 percent of Indian pupils, in 2000, qualified for special services for pupils with limited proficiency in English, compared with 36 percent of Latino and 23 percent of Asian pupils.⁸ More than half of the Indian eighth graders reported that they attended 'tribal ceremonies and gatherings' less than once a year or never, and only 24 percent said that they did so several times a year, indicating a low level of involvement with their tribes that would in turn tend to reduce the relevance of its language.⁹

Christian churches have often been an important link in maintaining native languages. In the missionary-managed schools among Indians during the nineteenth century, "classes were typically conducted in the vernacular [Indian language] to promote understanding of biblical teachings, although most mission schools eventually added English-language instruction."¹⁰ In Canada, the (Anglican) Church Missionary Society required its missionaries to learn the indigenous languages.¹¹

At Rock Point on the Navajo Reservation, "across different church activities, the . . . language for oral and written functions was Navajo, and community participation was highly collaborative. Religious messages came from community people who used the Navajo language exclusively during sacred and pedagogical activities, and who used Christian and native concepts alongside one another. . . . The end result was a process of empowerment, scaffolded by values for self-determination and nativized Christianity and structured by forms and functions of Navajo print." The pastor, a non-Navajo, had made extensive use of Navajo lay leaders to conduct the services, including preaching, out of a conviction that "if any message was to get through to the people, it would have to come [in Navajo] from one of them."¹²

By 1944, all or parts of the Bible had been translated into 46 North American Indian languages; in most cases, this required developing a writing system for a language that previously was in an exclusively oral form, and in turn opened the way to other written materials in the language.[13]

Religious use can preserve a language that is no longer used in other contexts, as in the case of Old Church Slavonic. It is reported that, in Canada, some Indian bands "sing from hymnbooks written in a dialect no one speaks or has ever spoken outside the church."[14]

This use of native languages for Christian religious purposes is by no means a new phenomenon. As we have seen, the efforts, in the seventeenth and eighteenth centuries, by Catholic missionaries to provide schooling for Indians in New France had only limited results, even when the natives were gathered into reserves where they could be protected from the corrupting effects of contact with whites and subjected to systematic instruction. The Indian children "seem to have learned little, if any, French, and it was the missionaries who continued to learn the Amerindian languages and to translate catechisms and missals into the Native tongues."[15]

This practice continued among Protestant missionaries on the western frontier of Canada and the United States. "As the result of an innovation by James Evans, a Wesleyan Methodist missionary and fluent speaker of the Ojibwa Indian language, thousands of Algonquian and Athapaskan Indians were literate only a decade later, without any schooling at all. By 1841, after his arrival at Norway House, in present-day northern Manitoba, Evans had devised the system more commonly known today as syllabics."[16]

It was in fact characteristic of Protestant as well as Catholic missionary efforts worldwide to seek to employ the native languages of those whose conversion and nurturing in faith was intended. Before and during the period of government-sponsored assimilation efforts at the high tide of Western colonialism in Africa and South Asia during the second half of the nineteenth century, the educational programs of Christian churches among native peoples were considerably more respectful of their languages, if not always of their cultures. Effective evangelization had always been associated, since the first Pentecost, with preaching in whatever language would communicate effectively with the target group. In many cases, as with the Goths and Slavs in early medieval Europe, the first written form of the language was developed in order to provide portions of the Bible and religious instruction materials.

This practice continued among the Maori of New Zealand, where "over a thousand items were printed in Maori between 1815 and 1900; in 1872, Bishop Colenso wrote a text book for teaching Maoris to read English remarking in the preface (which was written in Maori) that seeing they could already read their own language so well, they should have no difficulty in learning to read a second one."[17] In the early years of European settlement in New Zealand, "mission schools were established and proved enormously popular. Instruction was provided in the Maori language, and . . . a cautious estimate would be that by the early 1840s a little over half the adult population of 90,000 could read or write a little in their own language."[18]

It was Catholic missionaries to the Micmac Indians in what became the Maritime Provinces of Canada, beginning in the seventeenth century and continuing into the twentieth, who created successive systems of writing their language and produced the first printed materials, including not only religious materials but also a grammar of the language.[19] In 1843, the Mohawk Indians asked Anglican Bishop John Strachan to provide two schools, one where Mohawk would be used for instruction and a second using English. "They even offered to pay for the cost of printing Indian books for use in the school."[20]

In their outreach to the Sioux, the American Board of Commissioners for Foreign Missions and the Presbyterian Board of Foreign Missions published a monthly called *IAPI OAYE* (The Word Carrier), mostly in the Dakota language. At mission schools, initial instruction was in the vernacular since the missionary organization believed that was more likely to promote understanding of the Bible and of Christian teachings. Defending instruction in the Dakota language, a missionary to the Sioux wrote that the goal of education at his mission school was "to impart ideas, and not words." He and other missionary teachers said they had learned from experience that the "quickest way to teach them English is to give them a start and set them to thinking by the study of their own language first." At the mission school established at the Yankton Agency in 1869, the students were first taught to read and write in their own language: "We expect every scholar who understands no English to complete this primary course first. Most Indian children are able to do this in six months. Then we introduce them to the English language." In order to provide this bilingual instruction, the Santee Normal Training School was established with denominational support in the 1870s to train Dakota teachers, who were then employed to teach the younger pupils.[21]

As a result of such efforts, Choctaw historian Clara Sue Kidwell suggested that "[t]he most lasting result of missionary activity among the Choctaw in Mississippi was the preservation of the Choctaw language."[22] Although the half-breed elite leadership of the Cherokee Nation decided that its schools would be conducted entirely in English, white missionaries persuaded the ruling council to fund the publication of bilingual textbooks to further the education of full-breeds who spoke only Cherokee.[23]

Even in recent years it has been the case, as linguist Bernard Spolsky has pointed out, that "Navajo literacy was supported only by some churches and by a few Navajo-controlled bilingual schools."[24] In Canada, where denominational boarding schools had traditionally used Indian languages for religious instruction while using English or French for secular instruction, it was relatively easy for them to respond to the growing interest in maintenance of Cree or Chipewyan by simply expanding its use.[25]

In addition to making use of native languages for evangelization and instruction, missionaries often showed respect for native cultural practices, or at least those that did not conflict too obviously with what were considered Christian moral standards. This was not always the case, of course. Writing to the funding agency for missions among the Indians, in England in 1710, Cotton Mather asserted as an established fact that "[i]t is very sure the best thing we can do for our Indians is to Anglicize them in all agreeable instances; and in that of languages and cultures, as well as others. They can scarce retain their language, without a tincture of other savage inclinations, which do but ill suit, either with honor, or with the design of Christianity."[26] But, on balance, it was religious rather than secular motivations that defended Indian languages, since religious conversion—unlike economic adaption—did not require adoption of English or French. A nineteenth-century Anglican missionary in Ontario who was active in creating schools for Indian children condemned efforts to "un-Indianize the Indian, and make him in every sense a white man. . . . Why should we expect that Indians alone should be ready quietly to give up all old customs and traditions and language, and adopt those of the aggressor upon their soil?"[27]

Attempts to Replace Indian Languages

Government policy-makers were often less sympathetic than were church leaders toward native languages, and came into conflict with efforts by missionary groups, which they judged insufficiently committed to assimilation of the Indians among whom they worked. Government commissioners from Toronto visiting a Jesuit school for Indians in 1858 rebuked them for offering secular as well as religious instruction through the native language.[28] An American government agent insisted, in 1867, that "a great evil befell the Cherokee Nation when Sequoyah invented the Cherokee alphabet," and "the sooner the Cherokee alphabet and Cherokee language cease to be used, the better."[29] The same year, the first report of the "Peace Commission" appointed by the U.S. Congress in response to a number of violent incidents between Indians and whites, included among its conclusions that differences of language were standing in the way of peaceful relations:

> [B]y educating the children of these tribes in the English language these differences would have disappeared, and civilization would have followed at

once. . . . Through sameness of language is produced sameness of sentiment and thought; customs and habits are moulded and assimilated in the same way, and thus in process of time the differences producing trouble would have been gradually obliterated. . . . In the difference of language lies two-thirds of our trouble."[30]

The solution? "Schools should be established, which children should be required to attend; their barbarous dialect should be blotted out and the English language substituted."[31] This would make it possible, it was believed, to break down the tribal identities based on distinct languages and cultures, and so to "fuse them into one homogeneous mass."[32]

Government agents on reservations often criticized the use of native languages in the mission schools. An agent among the Sioux in 1878 "was fiery in his objection to the pedagogical approach of these missionaries," complaining that "the study of English is too much neglected, and it is very rarely spoken by the children." Two years later, another agent wrote, "I cannot too strongly condemn the practice of teaching in the Indian language. . . . It is believed by nearly every one of experience that it is both time and money thrown away. The day-schools should be in charge of competent, practical, self-reliant, white teachers, who would devote all their energies to teaching in the English language, and in English only."[33]

Although this emphasis on English was criticized by popular author Lydia Maria Child in her *Appeal for the Indians* as reflecting "our haughty Anglo-Saxon ideas,"[34] there can be no question that it reflected the predominance of "enlightened" opinion outside of the churches. Based on similar reasoning, Maori was banned from New Zealand schools in 1870.

Nor was this emphasis on English limited to white policy-makers; as we have seen, when the governing Council of the Cherokee Nation decided, in 1840, to establish a system of public schools for their new territory in what later became Oklahoma, they "required that the schools be taught in English, which placed a serious obstacle before the vast majority of children, who spoke only Cherokee. Ultimately, the children of mixed ancestry obtained the greatest benefit from the schools." One of the results was that most full-blood pupils—mocked by their classmates from English-speaking homes and unsupported by teachers who spoke no Cherokee—dropped out of school.[35]

In the United States, the Indian Bureau required, in 1880, that "all instruction must be in English" both in its own schools and also in mission schools operated with public funding,[36] and an official report in 1881 stated that "so long as the American people now demand that Indians shall become white men within one generation . . . [they] must be compelled to adopt the English language, must be so placed that attendance at school shall be regular . . . and must breathe the atmosphere as a civilized instead of a . . . barbarous community."[37]

The requirement was reiterated in 1883, when a mission school teaching in both Dakota and English was officially informed that the "English language only must be taught the Indian youth placed there for educational and industrial training at the expense of the Government. If Dakota or any other language is taught such children, they will be taken away and their support by the Government will be withdrawn from the school."[38]

The most determined opponent, among American government officials, of the use of native languages was Indian Commissioner John D. C. Atkins (in office from 1885 to 1888) who wrote, in 1887, that the language "which is good enough for a white man or a black man ought to be good enough for a red man," and suggested that teaching an Indian youth in "his own barbarous dialect" was a positive detriment to him. After all, "the first step to be taken toward civilization, toward teaching the Indians the mischief and folly of continuing in their barbarous practices, is to teach them the English language." Accordingly, he issued orders to government agents on reservations and to the representatives of missionary groups that all schools for Indians—not only government schools but also those operated under contract by church groups—use exclusively English as the medium of instruction. The missionary organizations, which had been using Indian languages to preach the Gospel as well as to teach secular subjects, objected strongly. In a partial compromise, the Indian Office issued a clarification the following year, specifying that

> 1. No textbooks in the vernacular [that is, in an Indian language] will be allowed in any school where children are placed under contract, or where the Government contributes to the support of the school; no oral instruction in the vernacular will be allowed at such schools. The entire curriculum must be in the English language.
> 2. The vernacular may be used in missionary schools, only for oral instruction in morals and religion, where it is deemed to be an auxiliary to the English language in conveying such instruction; and only native Indian teachers will be permitted to otherwise teach in any Indian vernacular; and these native teachers will only be allowed so to teach in schools not supported in whole or in part by the Government, and at remote points, where there are no Government or contract schools where the English language is taught. . . .
> 3. A limited theological class of Indian young men may be trained in the vernacular at any purely missionary school, supported exclusively by missionary societies, the object being to prepare them for the ministry, whose subsequent work shall be confined to preaching.[39]

He justified this stringent policy by the example of Germany in its recently acquired provinces of Alsace and Lorraine, "forbidding the teaching of the French language in either public or private schools." After all, "No unity or community feeling can be established among different peoples unless they are brought to speak the same language,"[40] and so "no school will be permitted on the reservation in which the English language is not exclusively taught. . . . It is believed that if any Indian vernacular is allowed to be taught by the missionaries in schools on Indian reservations, it will prejudice the youthful pupil as well as his untutored and uncivilized or semi-civilized parent against the English language, and, to some extent at least, against Government schools in which the English language exclusively has always been taught."[41]

Episcopal Bishop William Hare, founder of a boarding school on the Yankton Reservation protested that the government had gone too far, issuing a "tyrannical and officious" order banning the use of Indian languages in schools. Similarly, the July 1887 issue of *IAPI OAYE* announced in apocalyptical terms, "*It has come!* The government has begun its work of breaking up missionary work among Indians," and in the next issue the readers were warned that the government's intention was "NO MORE INDIAN SCHOOLS! NO MORE INDIAN BIBLES! NO MORE MISSIONS! These are the logical results of the present policy of the Indian Bureau, as shown in its astounding rules against the use of the Indian language." The missionary position received support from an editorial in the *New York Times*, which argued that "it is outside the province of the United States Government to interfere in a matter like this. Even Indians have some rights, and among them is the right to the use of their own national tongue. For the Government to offer them the advantages of schools on condition that they give up their language is not an act of kindness, but a piece of stupid tyranny."[42]

The missionaries comforted themselves that, "as a result of being told they could not study in their own language, . . . Dakotas gained a deeper appreciation for the Dakota Bible. The crisis also inadvertently contributed to a renewed pride in Dakota literacy: Dakotas increased their demand for books written in Dakota and resolved to perpetuate the language."[43]

Meeting extensive criticism of this restriction on the activities of missionaries even in institutions not supported by government, Atkins responded that use of Indian languages in church-funded schools could prejudice Indian parents against government schools that used English exclusively. He was supported by Captain Pratt of the Carlisle Indian School and others, including the government agent on the Cheyenne River Agency, who declared that "to teach the rising generation of the Sioux in their native tongue is simply to teach the perpetuation of something that can be of no benefit whatever to them."[44]

A similar position was taken by the Canadian government. The *Annual Report* of the Department of Indian Affairs for 1895 emphasized that, without English, Indians would be "permanently disabled" and the process of assimilation to Canadian society would be frustrated. "So long as he keeps his native tongue, so long will he remain a community apart."[45] The task was much more difficult than teaching correct English to children who spoke English at home, and was in fact also more difficult than teaching English to the children of immigrants, who were strongly motivated to learn the language of their adopted homeland. Indian children, by contrast, were perceived as clinging stubbornly to the language of their tribe and refusing to adapt. Milloy concludes that "[t]hough children were removed from their parents and communities, divorced from direct involvement in their own culture for many years, English and French, and thus western culture, remained quite 'unnatural to them'."[46]

Both in the United States and in Canada, government pressure was placed on mission schools that insisted upon continuing to use the native language together with English.[47] In Canada,

> both [Roman Catholic] Oblates and Anglican Church Missionary Society teachers, who were instructed by their superiors to learn the languages of their charges, frequently found themselves under pressure from Indian Affairs to use only English. The same was true of early Methodist missionaries in Alberta who learned one or more Indian languages for proselytizing and then found themselves obliged by the government to insist on the use only of English in the schools they ran.[48]

The American government even challenged the right of tribes to use their own funds to assist these schools, but "Indians were vehement defenders of sectarian schools threatened by closure,"[49] and several national denominations provided funding, sometimes raised through special collections among their members, to support this work. Thus the effect of denominational schools on loss of native languages (and cultures) was less drastic than that of government-operated schools.

In some denominational schools, like the Blue Quills Catholic Residential School in northeastern Alberta, the native language (in this case, Cree or Chipewyan) was used for religious instruction, though English was the language of instruction for the secular subjects required by government. Use of a Native language outside the classroom was tolerated by the staff, and students were seldom punished for speaking in their Native tongue. It is reported that some "students from the Enoch reserve near Edmonton came to Blue Quills speaking only English and learned Cree at the school. For children who arrived speaking only Cree, some teachers tried to accommodate them."[50] At the largest of the Canadian residential schools, Qu'Appelle, the Catholic Oblate teachers "ignored government instructions to use only English, and used Cree and Sioux materials, as well as allowing pupils to use their languages."[51]

In general, however, schools were—as intended—one of the major forces, though by no means the only one, promoting the shift of language use on the part of younger generations of Indians. Not uncommonly, parents themselves saw the primary function of school attendance for their children to be development of a level of proficiency in English that the parents themselves did not possess. Thus a teacher in a Mohawk-controlled school reported to researchers that "[h]er family spoke only Mohawk at home when she was younger. In fact, her older siblings spoke no English when they went to school. . . . Her use of Mohawk had diminished because she learned that 'you didn't go to school to speak Mohawk.' It was 'taboo' and 'something they were trying to get you away from'."[52]

The Changing Attitude toward Indian Languages

A new factor in the policy debates, beginning in the 1920s (though there were isolated voices earlier), was a growing support for preservation of Indian language and cultures. Initially, much of the interest in "letting the Indian remain an Indian" was expressed by non-Indians, since those Indians who expressed themselves on the issue were generally strong supporters of adaptation to the majority society and economy; before the emergence of a rewarding social role as advocate for Indian distinctiveness, fair treatment and equal opportunity were primary concerns of Indian leaders.

Over time, a new generation of Indian leadership emerged for whom affirmation of their people's distinctiveness was decisively important as a basis for group solidarity and demands upon the wider society. These leaders had generally developed the skills that made them able to articulate such demands in residential schools where they often developed a sense of pan-Indian identity, rooted not so much in a particular tradition as in the worldwide development of resistance to white hegemony, whether on the part of W. E. B. DuBois, of Gandhi, or of Charles Eastman, a Sioux who graduated from Boston University Medical School. This was, of course, a period when the "self-determination of peoples"—defined largely on linguistic terms—was a cause beloved of Progressives.

In the general culture, as well, there was less concern for assimilating Indians as a popular view developed which wished Indians to remain as they were . . . at least until they vanished entirely.

Literature and photography, for example, presented an increasingly romanticized, nostalgic view of Indians. Pulp westerns, dime novels, and arcade movie reels all highlighted Indians as a vanishing race. Wild West shows promised scintillating re-creations of Indian life and the Old West that locked Indians into the frontier that, by the 1890s, was declared closed, if not dead. When Hollywood joined the fray the metamorphosis was complete.[53]

Whereas a common attraction for visitors at events like the Columbian Exposition (Chicago 1893) had been a classroom of Indian children demonstrating the progress of civilization, "interest in the government's Indian school exhibits declined with such stunning rapidity that by the 1910s the public clamored to see troupes of dancing Indians trucked in from the reservations but could not have cared less about hearing Indian school children recite scripture."[54]

The way had been prepared for this assertion of distinctiveness as something to be retained by Indians by other elements of Progressivism. After all, the insistence of Francis Leupp that "the commonest mistake made . . . in dealing with the Indian . . . is the assumption that he is simply a white man with a red skin,"[55] can be read as (and was) a denial that Indians had the potential to join white society on equal terms, but it was also intended as a recognition of cultural distinctiveness.

Initially, at least, even with the strong influence of Progressive Education and its emphasis on starting instruction from and relating it constantly to the experience of children outside the classroom, this did not extend to using Indian languages for instruction in BIA schools, though that had long been the practice in many missionary schools. The Director of Indian Education wrote in 1932 that "[we] do not attempt to use the local language as the medium of instruction" since "the practical difficulties are probably insurmountable." Many of the roughly 230 Indian languages at use in the United States at that time had never been given a written form suitable for instruction, and even Navajo was given a written form only in the 1930s.[56] But gradually, the climate was changing in a way that would make development of the mother tongue of Indian pupils seem to be an essential element of their education.

Already in 1908, the enormously influential psychologist G. Stanley Hall, president of Clark University, told the annual meeting of the National

Education Association that Indian students should be provided primary education in their own languages. Why not, Hall asked, "make him a good Indian rather than a cheap imitation of the white man?"[57] After all, "primitive" societies were perhaps more attentive to what Hall and other Progressive thinkers considered the "nature and needs of childhood," which was poorly served by schools' overemphasis on "book-learning." On the other hand, because Hall considered Indians a "lower race," he doubted their capacity to master the demands of American civilization; surely they would be happier remaining within their customary way of life.[58]

In this spirit, Estelle Reel, the Superintendent of Indian schools from 1898 to 1910, called for a child-centered approach to teaching Indian children, while expressing doubts that much could be expected of them in terms of academic outcomes. As she wrote in her 1900 annual report, "[T]he theory of cramming the Indian child with mere book knowledge has been and for generations will be a failure."[59] Better to lower expectations and make school relevant to Indian life as it had been and was, rather than to some imagined future that Pratt, Morgan, and others had urged.

Like Hall and Reel, John Dewey placed a strong emphasis on learning through experience, a word that Dewey uses 485 times in what he considered his most important book on education, *Democracy and Education* (1916). "Experience," he insisted, is the touchstone by which book-learning must always be judged. "One has only to call to mind," he writes, "what is sometimes treated in schools as acquisition of knowledge to realize how lacking it is in any fruitful connection with the ongoing experience of the students—how largely it seems to be believed that the mere appropriation of subject matter that happens to be stored in books constitutes knowledge. No matter how true what is learned to those who found it out and in whose experience it functioned, there is nothing which makes it knowledge to the pupils. It might as well be something about Mars or about some fanciful country unless it fructifies in the individual's own life."[60]

When, more than half a century later, the cofounder of the Rock Point bilingual program (discussed below) said that all education should be "based on experience" and rooted in Navajo culture,[61] she was, perhaps unconsciously, echoing this central article of Progressive Education faith.

This emphasis on experience and on relating instruction to the whole life of the pupil inevitably came to mean, in the case of Indian pupils, a rejection of the deliberately decontextualized curriculum of the Indian boarding school, with its forbidding of Indian languages and its ignoring of Indian culture and reservation life. The findings of anthropologists and other social scientists—followed with great interest in elite circles—lent support to making the education of Indian pupils adapted to their distinctive qualities, now defined for the first time in positive terms. When the standard curriculum for federal Indian schools was modified in 1918, the Commissioner of Indian Affairs stressed, "We must . . . take into account the development of those abilities with which he is peculiarly endowed and which have come to him as a racial heritage . . . religion, art, deftness of hand, and his sensitive, esthetic temperament." The "nonessentials" such as geography, history, and arithmetic could be eliminated from the curriculum.[62] Despite requests from Indian communities for accredited academic high schools, "Federal educators . . . defined locally relevant education to fit entrenched notions of Indians' lesser abilities and circumscribed opportunities, stressing vocational training."[63] Of course, this was a formula for "separate development" parallel to the "Bantu education" provided in South Africa some decades later, and to some of the excesses of "Afro-Centric Education" in the United States, and with the same effect of shutting children of a minority group out of the mainstream of opportunity in the name of cultural sensitivity.

In the new jargon about pedagogy, the old standard curriculum for Indian schools was an example of the rejected "teacher-imposed curriculum" that failed to "meet the pupil where he is." The BIA began to encourage its Indian schools to cultivate native arts and crafts—sometimes on the grounds of economic utility—and to use Indian legends and traditions as instructional material. Although as late as 1952 the director of the American Studies Program at the Smithsonian Institution would pass an Indian school whose motto was, "Tradition is the Enemy of Progress,"[64] it is safe to say that this conviction had gone out of fashion several decades earlier.

Since of course there was no single culture common to the different tribes, the effort to base curriculum on Indian traditions had an undermining effect on the very premise of a Uniform Course of Study that could be provided to Indian youth from various tribes in off-reservation boarding schools. At least it was possible to remove subject matter that, from a Progressive point of view, was alien to the experience of Indian youth, such as "English classics, algebra, geometry, and ancient history."[65] Inevitably, though, this effort to be "relevant" widened the gap between what Indian pupils learned in school and what was being learned by the children of the white majority, thus potentially deepening the isolation of Indians and limiting their access to higher education and to jobs in the national economy. This was a small price to pay from the perspective of those who attached a romantic significance to "Indian ways," but it did not necessarily respond to what Indian parents and their children expected from school.

An emphasis on teaching Indian arts and crafts in schools serving Indian children was a logical application of Progressive Education pedagogy but, as a former BIA official lamented in 1944,

> The three R's were relegated to the rear while Indian arts, legends, and traditions were fostered. The use of the Indian's own language instead of English was represented as a feature of the "self-expression" toward which the system was directed, and this trend would have been pushed farther had it not been that the teacher seldom, if ever, could tell what the pupils were expressing in the Tewa or Paiute or Apache tongue.[66]

As Szasz points out, this approach was ultimately shallow; after all, a "course in silverwork or in Indian history did not answer the child's question: Who am I?" She concludes that "the prodigious effort . . . to develop a cross-cultural education program in the federal boarding schools was a failure. The program in the [reservation] day schools was more successful simply because of daily cultural reinforcement in the home and community."[67] Both represented a surrender of the old confidence that education would be a way out of the isolation of reservation life.

The primary author of the education section of the very influential Meriam Report of 1928 was a leader in the Progressive Education movement,[68] and, as we have seen, that report was opposed to "the theory that it is necessary to remove the Indian child as far as possible from his home environment; whereas the modern point of view in education and social work lays stress on upbringing in the natural setting of home and family life."[69]

The interest in the pedagogies associated with Progressive Education within the BIA did not originate with the Meriam Report; Francis Leupp, by then the former Commissioner of Indian Affairs wrote, in 1910, "My heart warmed toward an eminent educator who once told me that if he could have the training of our Indian children he would make his teachers spend the first two years lying on the ground in the midst of the little ones, and, making a play of study, convey to them from the natural objects right at hand certain fundamental principles of all knowledge."[70]

The influence of Progressive Education was reinforced during the New Deal, when John Collier served as Commissioner of Indian Affairs, especially after Willard Beatty was appointed, in 1936, to serve as Director of Indian Education. Beatty, who continued in that position until 1952, had become well-known for his earlier work as Superintendent of Schools in two suburban communities committed to Progressive Education. He was President of the Progressive Education Association from 1933 until 1937, and sought PEA help in training teachers of Indian schools in Progressive teaching methods. The opportunity to shape the schooling of Indian children along Progressive lines without dealing with the resistance of local school boards or parents seemed heaven-sent. "If there really is a new way in education," predicted W. Carson Ryan in 1932, "certain Indian groups offer the best possible place to apply it," and the same year the Progressive Education Association devoted an entire issue of its journal to pedagogical experiments on Indian reservations.[71]

Thus, the federal government's Indian schools were, in the 1930s, a notable center of Progressive Education methods, with an emphasis on activity-based instruction based on Indian cultures. That was, at least, the intention of the leadership in Washington, though many teachers and school directors resisted the new pedagogy. As John Collier's son would recall, "[M]y father could not, or would not, communicate his ideals to individual agents and teachers."[72] The half-hearted response of teachers faced with the actual realties of classrooms and pupil needs is exemplified by the account of a retired teacher that she "received an Indian Service directive encouraging teachers to take Progressive Education courses at Milwaukee State Teachers College in 1933 . . . 'I found this method of teaching interesting and challenging but also difficult to use in teaching my students enough of the basics. I felt that sometimes the students were shortchanged by the use of this method alone, and I supplemented it with materials correlated to the state course of study'."[73]

With the increasing reliance upon local public schools to educate Indian children, the effort to apply Progressive methods became even more hampered by the lack of understanding of—or opposition to—such methods among local educators. In his 1934 *Annual Report* as Commissioner of Indian Affairs, Collier expressed his concern that Indian pupils were likely to be in poorly funded and otherwise inadequate rural public schools, struggling with the effects of the Depression. They were thus likely to eliminate courses in "health and physical education, shop work, home economics, art, music," which Collier described (in best Progressive style) as the "real fundamentals" necessary for what he called a "modern type of education."[74]

The emphasis on Progressive Education pedagogy was only one aspect of a broader change of thinking that came to dominate federal policy toward Indians during the so-called Indian New Deal, under Collier's leadership. Collier had been drawn into advocacy for Indian interests in 1922 when the influential General Federation of Women's Clubs, concerned about pending legislation that they judged unfair to the Pueblo Indians of New Mexico, commissioned him to investigate the situation on their behalf. Collier subsequently became a lobbyist for Indian interests and perhaps the most prominent representative of an elite attitude that found much to value in

Indian traditions as an alternative to contemporary American and European culture in the wake of the First World War. As his son wrote after Collier's death, "[I]f he was devoted to the tribal Indian, he was as vehemently opposed to civilized modernity. I believe my father saw civilization in destruction through one historical default after another. He saw modernity as a disaster that was defeating man's perfectability. He saw the Indian as the last remnant of natural perfection, a model that must be preserved for human rejuvenation."[75] Thus, government policy should oppose rather than promote the "modernization" of Indians.

Collier had been a social worker and a strong believer in redemption of society through community, as an alternative to the "shattering, aggressive drive" of modern life. He was a leader in the efforts, early in the twentieth century, to turn public schools in New York City into community centers intended to unite all the residents of immigrant neighborhoods in common activities; later he promoted the same social intervention in California. In 1919, "he would discover among Pueblo Indians of New Mexico the kind of community life he had unsuccessfully labored to create for the past eleven years"[76] in urban settings. Collier initiated what came to be called the Indian New Deal, finding its legislative expression in the Indian Reorganization Act of 1934, which brought a halt the process begun by the Dawes Act of 1887.

The Dawes Act had sought to promote the assimilation of Indians to American life by ending communal ownership of reservation land and turning some of it into the private property of individual Indians (allotments) while making what was left over available for purchase by whites. The effect of this federal policy was not, as anticipated, to turn Indians into independent family farmers, but to further impoverish many tribes. Hamlin Garland, in his popular novel *The Captain of the Gray-Horse Troop* (1902) about a white army officer protecting a fictional Indian people, has a sympathetic character say that

> Any attempt to make the Tetong conform to the isolated, dreary, lonesome life of the Western farmer will fail. The redman is a social being—he is pathetically dependent on his tribe. He has always lived a communal life, with the voices of his fellows always in his ears. . . . Now the Dawes theorists think they can take this man, who has no newspaper, no books, no letters, and set him apart from his fellows in a wretched hovel on the bare plain, miles from a neighbor, there to improve his farm and become a citizen. This mechanical theory has failed in every case; nominally, the Sioux, the Piegans, are living this abhorrent life; actually, they are always visiting. The loneliness is unendurable, and so they will not cultivate gardens or keep live-stock, which would force them to keep at home.[77]

The white hero of Garland's novel, proclaiming that "if I could, I would civilize only to the extent of making life easier and happier" for the Indians under his care, worked to persuade them to adopt an agricultural economy on their communal land, and the last scene of the book describes a harvest festival that includes "fifty of his young warriors carrying shining hoes upright, as of old they carried their lances," and a procession of schoolchildren, each with "a book and a slate, and their faces were very intent and serious as they paced by on their way from the old to the new."[78] Such happy endings are easy in fiction. . . .

The allotment process had diminished tribal lands by two-thirds in less than 50 years, and came to be seen by many Progressives as conclusive evidence that efforts to persuade Indians to assimilate to white society were doomed to fail. Consistent with his conviction that modern life and culture were in catastrophic shape, Collier "reversed the doctrine of assimilation that had guided federal policy since the 1880s, and committed the federal government firmly to the strengthening of the tribes."[79] "So convinced was Collier of the righteousness of his cause and the purity of his motivation," we are told, "that he found it impossible to accept compromise or to tolerate opposition. Anyone who dared to challenge his authority or question his methods [as Commissioner of Indian Affairs] was written off as corrupt, the representative of vested interests, or, at best, misguided. This black-and-white approach to the solution of complex problems . . . turned all his battles into crusades of right against wrong, of justice against injustice."[80]

This reflex of self-righteousness would become all too common on the part of non-Indians who saw themselves as guardians of the authentic interests of Indians, even leading, as we will see in the case of the Rough Rock Demonstration School, to overruling of decisions of an elected Navajo board because they were considered, by a white administrator, inconsistent with Navajo culture.

Inevitably, the emphasis on traditional elements of Indian culture, including religion, was perceived as an unwelcome invitation to go "back to the blanket" by many Indians who had already, often over several generations, "invested themselves in adaptive strategies such as Western education, church membership, the holding of private property, and American citizenship. For them, Collier's programs threatened to erode the gains they had made."[81] One of Collier's chief opponents in missionary circles charged, in 1944, that

> romanticists who seek to maintain the *status quo* of pre-Columbian days seem to be indulging in a naïveté that closes their eyes to the blatant anachronism

of their position, particularly when the Indians themselves do not desire to be different "for the sake of being different" nor to any perceptible degree resist the influences now making for social unity and harmonious cultural development. The educated Indian of today does not accept the false theory that, if a group possesses some peculiar cultural heritage or some treasure from the past, the thing to do is to withdraw from others in order to preserve it.[82]

Lindquist quoted a Choctaw-Chickasaw leader who wrote, in 1938, that "[a]daptability had ever marked Indian history—and ever will. To pine for the old tribal days is to fly from reality. . . . It is a mark of weakness, not strength; of cowardice, not courage. The Indian always had some defense against his enemies, but there was no one to protect him from his oversentimental friends."[83]

Cultural pessimism about modernity and a Progressive understanding of education came together when Collier was appointed Commissioner of Indian Affairs in 1933, a few weeks after Franklin Roosevelt became President. Collier was convinced that "Western civilization was on the verge of collapse," and that, "[u]nless it adopted some of the primary values of Indian culture—living in and through a community, living in harmony with nature, and stressing spiritual rather than material values—the white race might not survive."[84] Collier wrote that "[i]t is the ancient tribal, village, communal organization which must conquer the modern world." A natural result of this attraction to the traditional character of Indian communities was that, according to the supervisor of Navajo Reservation schools during Collier's time in office, the Commissioner "had a great reluctance about building roads in Indian country, or providing universal education, or providing other services that he felt would destroy 'Indian culture'."[85]

It has been suggested that the growing dependence of the BIA (which more than doubled its staff during the 1930s) on anthropologists and other social scientists under Collier's leadership, while ostensibly intended to bring a greater sensitivity to the making and implementation of government policies, was also manipulative, penetrating deeper into Indian life and consciousness than had been the case previously. Knowledge of Indian culture was seen as making it possible to persuade Indians to accept the measures determined by government experts as being in the best interest of the Indians, whether it suited their natural inclinations or not.

> New Deal policies increased the scope and authority of the government's bureaucracy for managing Indians. Despite its rhetoric of liberation, the Indian New Deal strengthened indirect controls through administrative consolidation, conservation programs, and localized community education where none had existed before, thus reaching more deeply than ever into the

social and family structure of the tribes. Concomitantly, the New Deal's subsidized employment and mandates for regional economic development accelerated the disintegration of traditional subsistence economies on the reservations and helped to incorporate Indians as wage workers into regional economies that they entered at a disadvantage, lacking appropriate skills and education. . . . The humane vision of the reformer, the empathy of the social scientist, the compassion of the educator were embedded in a larger framework of public purpose whose strictures were often quite at variance with the felt meanings carried into the field by idealistic participants. A regimen of coerced sacrifice accompanied the rhetoric of mutual adjustment, and behind the hopes for voluntary compliance stood legislated mandates of economic development. If Indian affairs were a laboratory of ethnic relations, a staging point for the "new way" in education, they were at least as much a testing ground for New Deal programs.[86]

It seems clear in retrospect that many of those like Collier who prescribed for the Indian were doing so on the basis of their own romantic concepts of the unspoiled primitive and of the utopian possibilities of communal economies protected from the individualism that they saw as having made contemporary life unbearably shallow. Already a decade before he was given government responsibility, Collier was insisting that the focus of Indian education should change, and thereby help to change the entire country, through "remaking the school system both primary and secondary, basing it more largely on esthetics and on arts-and-crafts, on rural industry, etc., and carrying it out so as to strengthen rather than mutilate the tribal relationships. We have a wonderful chance here to develop 'socialized schools' which would have an influence on the whole school system of the country. . . . [T]o keep alive the Pueblo civilization with its cultural elements and its romantic point of view. To make it possible for these archaic communities to live on, and to modernize themselves economically (on a cooperative, communal basis) while yet going forward with their spiritual life."[87]

As this indicates, there was also a religious dimension, a sort of anticipation of New Age spirituality, in Collier's approach to Indian culture. The supervisor of Navajo schools described him as "a man of mysticism and paradox." Collier himself said that he had "experienced the Indian religion to the center of my being as a shaper of my life." Adoption of the Indian "reverence for the web of life," Collier believed, "could redeem the Western world from a 'bleak winter' of self-seeking materialism and dissolve the unfortunate marriage of Christianity and nineteenth-century individualism." The Christian Reformed Board of Missions protested, in 1947, that Collier "openly encouraged the Indians to cling to their 'beautiful' religion. The Navaho [sic] council was told: 'We white people have nothing to give to you

Indians. . . . Our culture is a disintegrating thing. Yours is an integrated culture. You must do your best to preserve it.'" The missionaries complained, "We always tried to keep our Christian Indians away from the pagan ceremonials, now they were brought there in government trucks."[88] While earlier administrations had sought to suppress the use of peyote for religious purposes, Collier insisted that it was as legitimate as bread and wine and that "to discriminate against its use would be to oppose one denomination of the Christian church"; when a tribal council in South Dakota adopted a resolution opposing the introduction of peyote on its reservation, this was vetoed by the federal government on the basis of infringement of religious freedom.[89]

In some cases, Indian religious ceremonies had became an attraction for tourists, as much performance as worship, charged some critics of Collier's encouragement of them, but he insisted that they "contained all the components of the most exalted human spirituality." The most outspoken critics of the new government approach to the revival of Indian traditions were Christian Indians—in the minority, but a substantial minority—who charged, like one Navajo leader, that they were transforming his reservation into "a 'monkey show' for gawking tourists and anthropologists."[90]

It is in fact a striking aspect of the attempts to recover—and to some degree re-invent—Indian identity that they often place an emphasis on native religions, sometimes in ways that imply their considerable superiority to Christianity. The leaders of the Navajo program at Rock Point described below, for example, were all members of the Native American Church, a trans-tribal religious movement centered around the use of peyote. The account of a Mi'kmaq school in Canada reports that "a typical day begins with prayers in Mi'kmaq. . . . The students then go to their classes. The first half hour in P-2 classes focuses on oral Mi'kmaq dialogues, prayers, or stories . . ."[91]

American public school leaders who strictly ban reading materials presenting any aspect of Christianity often find Indian religion unobjectionable, as was illustrated in the *Roberts* case in which a principal ordered that books presenting stories from the Old Testament of the Bible be removed from a fifth grade classroom, while making no objection to a presentation on Navajo religious beliefs.[92] Should this be taken, by Indians, as a positive sign, or as an indication that their culture and the beliefs that some of them continue to hold are considered a curiosity that no one could take seriously?

CHAPTER 12

Navajo, Cree, and Mohawk

Entirely naturally, schools have been at the center of both the learning of the majority language and—more recently—attempting to preserve or revive the ancestral language. The most widely publicized efforts to do so occurred on the Navajo reservation, where until recent decades there was a high rate of illiteracy and of continued use of the Navajo language. Similar efforts have been made in Canada, where the remoteness of Indian bands in the north have to some extent protected the use of Cree and Mohawk.

Example: Navajo

The Indian peoples for whom the ancestral language has been adapted to the demands of contemporary life, and is spoken on a daily basis, are in general those, like the Navajo, whose numbers and geographical remoteness have sheltered them to some degree from external influences. The Navajo, occupants of the largest reservation in the United States and the second-largest Indian people after the Cherokee (the 2000 U.S. Census reports that there are some 276,000 Navajo), have traditionally lived physically scattered lives in small family groups, tending their sheep. As late as the 1940s, most Navajo spoke little English, if at all; in 1935, only 15 percent of Navajo children were in school. Research in the late 1960s found, unsurprisingly, that "the farther children live away from Reservation population centers and/or paved or all-weather roads, the more likely they are to speak Navajo at home."[1]

Even among these isolated people, however, there has increasingly been a strong orientation toward acquiring proficiency in English, not as a rejection of the native culture but because of the instrumental importance of the majority language. Kluckhohn and Leighton found among Navajo parents before the Second World War a strong concern that their children be able to speak and write English.

The availability of schooling began to change during the Depression, when Public Works Administration funds were used to build 40 day schools on the reservation, while also creating construction jobs for the fathers of their pupils. These schools, according to John Collier, were to be community centers, addressing "the fundamental economic and social problems of the Navajo. Child education will not be their dominant function, but rather the creation and focusing of group thought and group activity on the pressing problems of erosion control, stock reduction, grazing management . . ."[2] Unfortunately, these day schools never reached capacity; they were too difficult for Navajo children to get to from their scattered and transitory encampments, over the dirt roads on the reservation, subject to frequent washouts and other obstructions. Another problem was that, consistent with the latest Progressive thinking about child development, pupils "took naps after lunch and, in Navajo logic, were being taught to be lazy."[3] A former BIA official noted that "the Navajo did not welcome the type of education that consisted of miniature *hogan* building and amateur weaving, both of which the child learned at home from a skilled practitioner."[4]

In addition, unpopular Federal programs created such resentment that many parents refused to send their children to school as "one of the few ways people could resist coercive policies such as stock reduction."[5] After ten years of experience, in 1951, the federal authorities concluded that day schools could not meet the educational needs of the Navajo Reservation.[6]

As a result of isolation and the inadequacy of schooling, "as recently as a generation ago, nearly all Navajo people spoke Navajo. Navajo was the . . . language of oral communication between Navajos at social gatherings, ceremonies, trading posts, chapter meetings, and work; in fields, canyons, and school hallways; on playgrounds and trips to town; and across generations within nearly all family contexts.[7] The written form of the Navajo language "was developed, in large part, to meet the acute need of explaining, to thousands of illiterate older Indians who knew no English, the government program worked out in their behalf."[8]

Efforts to use Navajo and other native languages as a vehicle for at least initial education and transition to English gained temporary government support in the 1930s, when bilingual readers were produced in Navajo, Hopi, and Sioux, and Spanish-English materials were produced for Pueblo and Papago children.[9] In 1940, the reading and writing of Navajo was introduced on a pilot basis in some reservation schools, though there was a stronger emphasis upon teaching adult Navajo-speakers to read and write their language in order to work with outsiders on health and economic development projects.[10] Such efforts were largely abandoned once the

United States was distracted from domestic issues by the Second World War, but interest revived in the 1960s.

After the war the returning veterans and defense workers were familiar with the advantages of proficiency in a wider means of communication, and determined that their children should seek to acquire more formal education than had been the case in the past. The National Study of American Indian Education, in the late 1960s, noted that over 60 percent of the Navajo living on the reservation were unemployed, and that the tribal scholarships given to study at off-reservation colleges had not produced the intended results because of a 90 percent college non-completion rate. As a result, although education was the primary employer on the reservation, over 90 percent of the teachers were non-Navajo.[11]

There was, along with this desire for more effective participation in the wider economy through education, a growing concern that the Navajo language, which up to that point had been widely spoken, was under threat. Improved communication and access to media, jobs in the national and regional economies, a growing number of non-Navajo businesses on the reservation, intermarriage with non-Navajos, and a variety of other factors led to increased use of English. In the late 1950s, a study of the Rough Rock area, found the beginnings of a generation gap in language use that would gradually wear away at the transmission of Navajo. "Although many men had no formal education, 'they had acquired the speech skill in their work situations with non-Navajo speakers and thus were placed in the category of English speakers'. . . . Of young people aged 14–19, 109 girls and young women (80%) and 103 boys and young men (62%) were identified as speakers of English. Of adults aged 30 to 64, only 26 women (20%) and 62 men (38%) were so identified."[12] The young women and men of the 1950s, predominantly English-speakers, were the parents of the 1960s and 1970s, and the grandparents of the 1980s and 1990s. If even their grandparents use English, it is unlikely that children will grow up using Navajo comfortably.

Despite the limited success of "community-oriented" schools during the Depression, the idea was not altogether abandoned, and it revived with the War on Poverty of the mid-1960s. Rough Rock Demonstration (later, "Community") School was the first school operated by Navajos under a charter agreement with the BIA, anticipating by two decades the "charter school" movement in public education. It was natural that community control of Indian schools would start on what is much the largest and most populous of the reservations, one on which thousands of adults and youth still did not, in the 1960s, read or write English. The Navajo Reservation had not been affected by the periodic government efforts to distribute reservation land through allotment to individual owners, and thus it had not been splintered through sale of land to whites; nor had mineral wealth been individually divided. By 1965 the Navajo Nation had some $100 million in its treasury, so it could to a considerable extent adopt and support initiatives apart from those of the BIA.[13]

In one of the early efforts to extend President Lyndon Johnson's War on Poverty to Indians, the Office of Economic Opportunity (OEO) committed to fund a three-year project in Navajo-controlled schooling proposed by Robert Roessel, already a well-known (non-Indian) "poverty warrior," starting in 1965. After an unsuccessful year at another site on the reservation, the BIA offered a newly constructed school with boarding facilities at Rough Rock, in a remote part of the Reservation. BIA agreed to fund the regular costs of school operation (initially $307,000 a year), and the OEO funds (initially $335,999) were used for a variety of non-curricular purposes: staff working "in the development of school-culture and school and community relations; in guidance and counseling; in adult education, recreation, arts and crafts; and in TESL (Teaching English as a Second Language). They also provided for a librarian, a speech and hearing specialist, a nurse, dormitory and room parents, and one-half the administrative costs."[14] Instruction would be in both Navajo and English, and Navajo adults would be employed to teach a variety of aspects of their culture, in a largely unstructured curriculum. Because of the isolation of families in the area, Rough Rock was a boarding school for most of its pupils.

The goals set for this demonstration project reflected the lingering influence of Progressive Education themes: "(1) the community should be stronger, more cohesive, more aggressive, more independent; (2) pupils should demonstrate a higher level of social-psychological functioning—especially feeling better about themselves and their culture; and (3) pupils should be capable, cognitively and affectively, of succeeding in both worlds—Navaho and Anglo."[15]

With the massive infusion of federal funding, the school became the chief local employer[16] and, fatefully, more a "cash cow" for the community than a focused academic institution. "In the first year the school had 91 employees, including 45 Navajos of whom 38 were local, plus 15 Vista volunteers and 8 dorm parents. . . . In April 1967 the staff included 10 teachers with 20 aides . . . 370 children and 250 regularly scheduled adults. . . . Some teachers would not teach for a whole week because of the 'difficulty in scheduling and finding time for all the subjects in the school'. . . . The math teacher complained about the 'lack of time for teaching.'"[17]

One of the Navajo community leaders reported, 30 years later, that "[p]eople were enthused about the school. . . . The school was created to learn everything possible. A great amount of [income] was distributed. . . . The intentions there at the time the school began were more for economic development. And now it's different . . . I guess time has changed." "For many people," a history of the Rough Rock project noted, "the school provided their first wage employment. Local knowledge was rewarded financially and by the social status conferred by school jobs." Within a few years, "Thanks to school jobs and school-initiated opportunities for professional development, family incomes had risen five-fold."[18] As a way to improve incomes in a desperately poor area, by defining skills that the residents already possessed as essential, the Rough Rock strategy was highly successful.

For example, a project funded by the National Institutes of Health at Rough Rock sought to train more practitioners of traditional Navajo healing; "the Navajo Mental Health Project funded months- and years-long apprenticeships during which aspiring healers trained under locally recognized ritual specialists."[19] No white medical specialist could compete for such employment.

Primary among the local skills that were rewarded was the ability to speak Navajo. The community that it served was one of the more isolated and economically depressed on the Navajo Reservation and, consistent with the research suggesting a direct relationship between physical isolation and limited exposure to English, when the project started in 1966 only one child among 38 in the two beginners classes was assessed as able to speak English.[20] The usual pedagogical approach in government day schools on reservations (but not necessarily in mission schools like the one already operating for some years at Rough Rock, which taught partially in Navajo) would have been to teach those children in English. The latest thinking on the schooling of language minority pupils, however, was that they should be taught in their home language, and so the lower grades in the new Rough Rock school used Navajo extensively though not exclusively. Several of the teachers recruited to the new school were literate in Navajo, in fact, because they had themselves been pupils at the mission school, operated by Quakers. "At the mission school," one of them reported, "we were taught in English, but there was a time when we did written Navajo, and we read in Navajo'."[21]

It is not clear whether instructing the younger pupils primarily through the Navajo language corresponded to the desire of the parents, though the use of Navajo in many aspects of the school's program was welcome because it offered so many opportunities for employment based on proficiency in the language spoken by adults in the local community. As linguist Bernard Spolsky has observed, "It was not an immediate aim of the school to change the sociolinguistic situation, it would probably not be unacceptable to the community if the program produced graduates who were bilingual in Navajo and English but, like the community as a whole, monoliterate in English."[22] But the project began at a time when instruction of linguistic minority children through their home languages was a new and exciting idea, and had allegedly proven itself with Finnish children in Sweden as clearly superior to their instruction through the language of the school.[23]

Rough Rock was an immediate hit in progressive circles during the late 1960s, when it seemed a perfect illustration of leading themes in the War on Poverty, "Community Action" and "Maximum Feasible Participation of the Poor." The first evaluators, in 1969, reported that it had "become a widely recognized symbol of the avant-garde in American Indian education."[24] With its broad scope of community-oriented services, and its control by an elected board of local Navajos, Rough Rock became a "poster child" for the new strategies. "Each month, an estimated 100 to 500 visitors—anthropologists, educators, psychiatrists, film crews, politicians, and others—passed through Rough Rock's classrooms . . . leading the school board to hire a full-time public relations officer."[25]

The honeymoon did not last long. At the end of the three-year period of the initial grant, an OEO-mandated evaluation of the Rough Rock project by education professor Donald Erickson of the University of Chicago and doctoral student Henrietta Schwartz found that, while the community-oriented activities of the school had been well-received (not least because many members of the community were employed to carry them out), the traditional instructional program had been very weak, and "Rough Rock failed to demonstrate any superiority to other [Navajo Reservation] schools in the study."[26]

The most damaging charge, however, did not bear upon the academic performance of the pupils in the Rough Rock school—after all, that had been a secondary concern of the OEO funding—but upon the model that the project seemed to offer for community control of Indian schooling, and especially its employment practices. "Few people would doubt, demonstration or not," the report pointed out, "that using federal funds to create rotating employment opportunities for at least 50 per cent of family breadwinners . . . would contribute considerably to the well being of an impoverished community. [However], funds of this magnitude are not likely to be available to the vast majority of disadvantaged communities in the United States . . ."[27]

It seemed to the evaluators as though jobs, rather than education, were what the Rough Rock Demonstration was about, and they were probably correct. As one local Navajo recalled years later, "[T]he main thing for the first day and several weeks after, people wanted jobs. The whole thing was open. People were in and out . . . they wanted to apply for jobs." The board members were paid at the discretion of the white administrator who in theory reported to them, and their stipends, according to the evaluation, "made the board members very wealthy" by community standards. They also spent most of their time on personnel matters, hiring and firing local people, many of whom, inevitably, were their relatives and friends, but spent little time on other matters affecting the school. The 1969 evaluation concluded that "Rough Rock's patronage system is badly out of control," and that "the school's impact on community optimism and well being was effected mainly through the employment program," but the evaluators saw "little by way of an economic base that would be left if the funds were removed."[28]

In defense of the emphasis on the employment policies followed by the Rough Rock board, with constant turnover of positions, a later study of 35 years of the Rough Rock project argued that the "evaluators' criticism . . . ignores board members' and their constituents' expectations that school resources, particularly jobs, be distributed *throughout* the community."[29]

But was Rough Rock a good example of "community control"? According to the evaluators, the board members complained about not being consulted by the charismatic director, Robert Roessel, telling the evaluators that teachers were fired without their approval and that funds were diverted to purposes for which they had not been budgeted. "On numerous occasions, members of the board complained about widespread pupil absences and argued for stricter attendance policies. The old procedures were not scrapped. The white director argued that it was contrary to Navajo culture to give the school more control over the lives of pupils." In the school's instructional program, Roessel supported an "ultra-traditional Navajo culture, at the expense of preparation to compete in more modern contexts," and to this end ruled out a number of techniques for teaching English as a second language, without discussion with either the elected Navajo board or with the teachers, as "an affront to Navaho culture." Navajo language courses had been put together hurriedly with little support from the "lavishly funded 'Navajo Curriculum Center'," which concentrated its efforts on producing a few handsomely produced books of Navajo stories, but not practical classroom materials.[30]

The principal of the elementary school, reflecting the same attitude, was critical of the way that teachers sought to demand that pupils pay attention to them as "an Anglo ego-building advice," but the evaluators noted that "Navaho teachers and aides . . . demanded attention from their pupils."[31] Erickson, whose expertise and interests were in education rather than community development, observed that the school had "no prescribed curriculum," with the result that "teachers had to start from scratch each year, not knowing what the child had mastered before" with "much random behavior, boredom, and disruption" in the classrooms.[32]

Rough Rock had become a much-visited showcase for "maximum feasible participation of the poor," but the report found that

> the handful of "community education meetings" staged during the first two years were usually arranged to coincide with visits by important people. . . . It was not widely known among Rough Rock's Navajo teachers, let alone among the uneducated local people, that board meetings were open to the public. . . . [W]e identified five complaints, widely discussed by local Navajos, which the board had either totally ignored or disregarded after discussion: that board members favored their close relatives blatantly when hiring local people to work at the school; that too much emphasis was placed upon courses in Navajo language and culture at the expense of skills the children would later need to secure employment; that materials were covered repetitiously year after year, teachers being unaware of what had been taught earlier; that disciplinary procedures were inadequate; and that some members of the dormitory staff insulted and mistreated the children.[33]

Perhaps, Erickson concluded sardonically, "Rough Rock unintentionally demonstrates a new, effective method for giving leeway to an administrator: divert the board's attention to peripheral functions. . . . [T]he board . . . commissioned a hand-trembler and a star-gazer to ferret out the facts of a theft. It decided that a wall painting [in the school] must contain more errors, lest ceremonial secrets be revealed."[34] But the board did not make the important decisions about what the school should be seeking to accomplish for its pupils.

Thus, an ultimately more serious charge was that the school was failing in its responsibility to prepare Navajo children for the lives that they would be living in the late twentieth century. Interviews with students as part of the study found that "practically *no one* was interested in traditional Navajo occupations." Even the local teachers of Navajo language and culture, the school's proudest boast, told the researchers that they were concerned "that the children's language handicap and other learning problems would be complicated as a result of the time devoted to these subjects. . . . Will the school produce a museum-piece community, quaintly traditional but economically impotent, when virtually none of its patrons desires that outcome?" the evaluators asked, insisting that "the 'both-and' slogan is hardly an adequate guideline on those many occasions when the two cultures are contradictory, when one *cannot* simply 'do both'."[35] The evaluators found that "a surprising number of unlettered parents complained that the school was devoting too much attention to Navaho culture and not enough to the academic subjects." Christian Navajos, in particular, told evaluators that "they preferred a school that did not emphasize traditional Navaho culture as Rough Rock was doing."[36]

Nor did the employment of Navajo staff necessarily lead to more effective engagement with Navajo students. Erickson was especially critical of the situation in the dormitories, where the board, in order to spread employment as widely as possible, had decided upon short-term appointments and frequent turnover. The evaluators "observed that, while dormitory workers spent much time watching television, many children sat around for long periods staring into space."[37]

Perhaps the most remarkable result of the Erickson Report was the fury that it aroused among the modern-day "friends of the Indian"—no longer prominent members of evangelical churches as in the late nineteenth century, but anthropologists, linguists, "policy warriors," and Indian activists. The community board governing the school voted to forbid other external evaluations, though a few years later they were forced to back down because of grant requirements.[38] An observer of the heated controversy warned that "[i]f the reception of the Erickson report is any indication, we are about to witness the same process of covering up the facts and abusing honest researchers that has so long characterized the field of public education."[39]

One of the defenders of the Rough Rock program in an issue of *School Review* devoted to the controversy conceded that "the organization of Rough Rock is casual and, in many instances, inefficient," but pointed out as an excuse that "Navajos are noted for their casualness and abhorrence of bureaucratic forms." In the Erickson Report, "The board was criticized for not involving itself with curriculum and budget matters. Yet Navajos are traditionally unconcerned with money. And in the area of curriculum, the board (wisely, I think) has left to the administrator those matters which are his specialty. In a poor rural area, jobs and resources are in constant demand. What are the most logical areas for the board to concern itself with? The allocation of jobs and resources." He concluded, in dismissing the evaluation, that "Erickson . . . is suffering from that form of psychological trauma called culture shock—caused by a reaction to the strangeness of another culture which usually results in a violent and indiscriminate rejection of everything which is part of that culture."[40]

This defense was dismissed scornfully by Gloria Emerson, a Navajo graduate of Harvard Graduate School of Education and an education specialist for the Office of Navajo Educational Opportunity, who had visited Rough Rock in 1967 and 1968. She declared that the project was "bent on selling an image to whites, to Navajo communities, to bureaucrats, and, most important, to funding sources." The defenders "make the error of . . . condoning most administrative deficiencies and calling them Navajo 'cultural ways'." Condemning such a defense as patronizing, she insisted that "if they had seen half the problems of Rough Rock in an Anglo-controlled situation, they would not have hesitated to blister it as an 'ego-tripping' showcase. . . . Didn't it occur to [them] that Navajos also have their standards? . . . When the 'utopia' showed signs of growing pains, white scholars rushed to defend it. Non-Navajos are responsible for puffing up Rough Rock."[41]

In a rejoinder to the critics, Erickson expressed his concern "that a relatively small group of white leaders, mostly anthropologists, has been establishing itself as the unquestioned authority on what American Indians need. Doubtless they mean well. But they often seem unwilling to tolerate criticism or, as [Vine] Deloria asserts, to give the Red Man a voice in his own future." In the case of Rough Rock, "[i]t was simply assumed, so far as I could determine, that white experts on the Navajo knew what ought to be done. The Navajo school board . . . was not being asked, judging by any evidence I could uncover, to participate in those decisions of unrivaled moment" about how to strike the right balance between preserving traditional Navajo ways, including language, and preparing pupils for a wider world. While the administration of the school and its defenders insisted that they were doing both, "the 'both-and' slogan is hardly an adequate guideline on those many occasions when the two cultures are contradictory, when one *cannot* simply 'do both' . . . I see no reason at all," Erickson urged, "why the board should not begin discussing *immediately* the future local parents envision for their children."[42]

In an article presenting the conclusions of the evaluation for a popular audience, Erickson noted that some educators were "demanding that Rough Rock's methods, as yet not proven superior by any firm data at all, be universally adopted. My belief is that the schools would be much better if local Indians were given real control, rather than the 'paper' control they exercised at Rough Rock at the time of our study."[43]

Subsequent evaluations confirmed the finding of the Erickson Report about the academic weakness of the Rough Rock school; in fact, "the school accumulated the lowest evaluation of any BIA school in the area." In addition, the community-oriented activities that had been largely responsible for creating widespread interest in Rough Rock largely faded away as OEO funding was phased out, "for routine BIA funding paid only for academic teachers and school administrators. Unfortunately, it was these Navajo life activities that had brought the community into the school and had paid wages for these enriching contributions. To cut them back meant also a cutback in direct community action in the school, and this directly reduced Rough Rock energy."[44]

There was also continual instability. Between 1966 and 1983, turnover averaged 50 percent a year among the Navajo language and culture faculty, and about 33 percent among the elementary classroom teachers. In addition, "between 1968 and 1983 students attended, on average, less than three-quarters of the school year, or about 130 days."[45] One study found that "nearly 25% of Rough Rock students were new to the school each year."[46]

By the late 1970s, enrolment in the Rough Rock school "dropped precipitously. Fearing that parents were transferring their children to other schools because of Rough Rock's lack of curriculum guidelines—and knowing that a lower student count meant a reduction in Federal funds—the board hired a curriculum supervisor, a White educator from the Midwest, to overhaul the K-12 curriculum." This led to implementation of a curriculum focused on acquisition of basic skills in English, and "except at the beginners level, in special cultural presentations, and in periodic 30-minute Navajo language lessons, all instruction took place in English."[47]

This was probably an appropriate response, if the school was really committed to responding to the community it served. "I placed my children in school to learn the White man's way," said one elderly Navajo. "When you teach both Navajo and English, you just confuse kids."[48] A study in 1980 conducted a "survey of Rough Rock parents, teachers and students, who were asked to identify local needs and related educational goals. . . . Virtually all of the 100 individuals questioned agreed that Navajo students need the skills and knowledge for full adult participation in the off-reservation economy. They disagreed, however, about the best means to achieve this. Many described the school's primary job as 'teaching the white man's way,' while others stated emphatically that Rough Rock, with its legacy as the first Indian-controlled school, was 'the only place where children today can learn what they need to know about their language and culture'."[49]

Faced with community demands, and with the growing prevalence of English as a home language for Navajo families, "by the 1980s the school had become a place where, at least in classrooms and during staff meetings, English was as likely to be heard as Navajo. This was a major change from the linguistic ecology of the school during its early years," when only one out of 38 beginning students could speak English. As one teacher asked, "Should I be teaching Navajo or teaching the standards?" Another said bluntly: "We don't have time for Navajo." In fact, increasingly, Navajo was no longer the prevailing language of the community. A study in the mid-1990s concluded that "between 50% and 60% of Navajo kindergartners [at Rough Rock] speak Navajo reasonably well . . . [but] . . . their numbers and native language proficiencies are declining each year."[50]

In 1985, 20 years after its launch with great fanfare as the model for community-based Indian education, another evaluation of the Rough Rock school by the BIA found that "scholastic expectancy was low as in earlier academic evaluations. But the most serious failure, surprisingly, was in the very flow of Rough Rock culture: lack of cooperation between school and community, failure to carry through the main charter contract to provide a Navajo self-determined program of education."[51] Ironically, as Collier points out, these were the very deficiencies for which Indian activists had criticized both missionary and BIA schooling.

The strained relationship reached such a low point by 1996 that a new school board was elected and the school's executive director and most central office administrators were forced out. Parents were removing their children wholesale: the elementary enrolment dropped from 199 to 119 in a single year. "So many parents had removed their children from the school at Rough Rock that the board was forced to impose a 4-day school week."[52]

Rough Rock continues today to serve all grades through high school, but it is no longer the focus of excited attention. Its website states that "Rough Rock Community School is a grant school and receives federal supplemental entitlement funding. Entitlement funding is formula funding provided through the Office of Indian Education Program (OIEP) who receive federal appropriation from U.S. Department of Education"; the goals of the Board are those conventional for any school: improve achievement, involve parents more, use technology for instruction. An AmeriCorps program enrolling local youth provides tutoring and assistance to the elderly.[53]

A more successful, though less-publicized, instance of community-based education on the Navajo Reservation was that developed at Rock Point, another isolated area where, initially, "children did not need or use English except for direct communication with the relatively few non-Navajos in the community." In the 1960s, the staff of what was at first a two-room BIA school (gradually expanded with new construction and better pupil transportation) began to introduce English as a Second Language methodology in 1960, and then the development of literacy in Navajo in 1967. In the 1966–1967 academic year, Rock Point had only 45 percent of the per pupil instructional budget enjoyed by Rough Rock, though the gap narrowed to 71 percent in 1968–1969, as War on Poverty funding became less generous.[54]

Forming a strong alliance with the local community, Rock Point leaders were able to obtain a considerable measure of autonomy to design a program that would make extensive use of both languages for instruction. In 1972, the community elected a school board that, in 1973, was able to contract with the BIA to operate the school. Although there was resistance from BIA officials on the Navajo Reservation, they were supported by "key people in the Central Office in Washington who were much more interested in contracting with Indian tribes and communities."[55]

As the Rock Point program developed, each primary classroom was staffed with two teachers, one of whom was to use only Navajo, the other only English. Children would be taught to read first in Navajo. In the upper elementary grades, the classroom teachers taught in English, but pupils went in small groups during the day to classes taught in Navajo, such as Navajo Social Studies and Science-in-Navajo, so that "perhaps a third of these students' class time was in Navajo." At the junior high level, this fell to 10–15 percent of the instructional time, and at the senior high level, to 5–10 percent.[56]

It comes across clearly from the 1969 evaluation of Rough Rock, which used Rock Point as a comparison, that the academic emphasis at the latter school was considerably more consistent. The principal told the evaluators that "these children have so much to catch up on we can't waste a moment of classroom time." This school culture was evident to parents: while only 11.8 percent of the Rock Point parents agreed that their child "plays around too much, doesn't work enough, doesn't learn enough, lacks push or competition," this response was given by 25.9 percent of the Rough Rock parents, more than twice as many. The evaluators found "a sense of controlled urgency at Rock Point. Teachers pushed the children and pushed themselves. Their engagement in a common task seemed to promote high morale in both groups." In the four grade levels at which it was possible to compare academic results at the two schools, "Rock Point emerged as superior. In one case, the extent of the superiority was the equivalent of an entire grade-year." The evaluators concluded that, compared with Rock Point and also with another Navajo boarding school that received no special attention or funding, "Rough Rock was doing less than the other two schools to prepare children to function well in Anglo society."[57]

Rock Point was urgent that pupils become proficient in English, but not at the sacrifice of Navajo language or culture. The evaluators found much less support among the Rock Point teachers than among those at Rough Rock of the idea that they should encourage pupils to become more independent of their parents. In 1988, two decades after the evaluation, 43 percent of the pupils were assessed as Navajo-dominant, 5 percent as English-dominant, and the half somewhere in between.[58]

As at Rough Rock, the Rock Point school hired staff locally as much as possible, and provided on-site college courses for those staff who did not have college degrees; by 1989 about 45 Navajos working at Rock Point had completed college. In contrast with Rough Rock, there was not a high turnover of staff. Of the fifty teachers working at the school in 1989, 21 had been there for 10 years or more.[59]

Without the large initial funding for a wide range of cultural and community-oriented programs, and also without as much publicity, Rock Point managed to build a solid educational program that balanced two languages and two cultures without as much ideological baggage or as much instability as were evident at Rough Rock.

In 1984, the Navajo Tribal Council voted that "[t]he Navajo language is an essential element of the life, culture and identity of the Navajo people. The Navajo nation recognizes the importance of preserving and perpetuating that language to the survival of the Nation. Instruction in the Navajo language shall be made available for all grade levels in all schools serving the Navajo Nation."[60] As we will see in the following chapter, this may have been too late for the thousands of children and their families who had already essentially abandoned use of the language.

Example: Cree and Mohawk

Similar struggles over language and culture occurred in Canada. A government study in 1971 concluded that "unless the schools encourage Indian children to study their own language as a curriculum subject children who reach the high school level and continue their education in various secondary programs might give up their Indian language entirely," and warned that "English seems to be displacing the use of an Indian language in the home."[61] As part of a generous policy toward minority languages (especially those of immigrants), in the mid-1980s, nearly 60 Indian languages were taught in Canadian schools, but generally as a subject rather than as the medium of instruction.[62] Such token efforts are powerless to reverse the language shift that occurs as a result of use of the majority language for instruction as well as in the daily give-and-take of school and community life, and of course in entertainment media.

A study based upon successive Canadian censuses found a steady erosion in the use of most Indian languages between 1981 and 1996; while 60 percent of those over 85 still used their mother tongue, this was true of only 20 percent of children under five. In 1981, 74 percent of women aged 20 to 24 were using an Indian language, but 15 years later only 45 percent of that age group—when women are most likely to be passing on a language to their young children—were doing so.[63]

The "health" of native languages depends upon a variety of factors, including especially the extent to which their speakers are in regular contact with speakers of the majority language. In Canada, Cree has been the language of a number of peoples spread over much of the country, but its continued use varies greatly. "Although the writing system has existed and been used in church hymnals since the 1840s, adults tend to be literate in English (and more recently French) instead of Cree, since most have received their formal schooling in a mainstream language." Researchers found that one elected Cree School Board had prescribed "English (or French) through all grades except kindergarten. This has been the communities' wish. Cree has only been taught as a subject area . . ."[64]

A study on one reservation found the Cree language "in extremely critical condition . . . Among those surveyed, no one under 30 was fluent in the language and only about half of those between 30 and 49 could speak Cree well. There were no Cree speakers among the youth." On another Cree reservation, by contrast, there was "a fairly healthy level of use of the Cree language" as a result of "a relatively isolated location . . . [with] . . . about 1,200 residents . . . some of whom still spend time living on their traditional traplines in winter and near the fishing camps in the summer. . . . It was the main language in virtually all of the homes surveyed, and it was the primary language of the community. There was also a great deal of Cree used at school. The school has been administered by the Lac La Ronge Indian Band since 1976 and has had a bilingual/bicultural program since that time."[65]

Among the James Bay Cree, a survey in 1990 found that about four out of five of the respondents reported that they could speak Cree and used it with their children, but only half that proportion could read and write their ancestral language, and those who could do so have mostly learned it at church. "The majority reported using Cree at home, but English at work and school. Although respondents believed that children were learning Cree, they questioned the quality of the children's vocabulary and their ability to understand elders."[66] Another study found that "often young Cree people, who try to learn to use the language of their ancestors, are mocked by more fluent speakers."[67]

Under such circumstances, conflicts often arise when the older generation views the younger one as not speaking the "proper language," discouraging members of the tribe for whom it is not their first language from attempting to use it. Languages in contact situations inevitably change, adopt new vocabulary and new grammatical forms; those who want minority languages still to be in living use need to accept such changes; after all, as Crystal points out, a "purism on behalf of an endangered language is no less stultifying than a purism on behalf of a dominant language."[68]

It is common, in fact, for anthropologists to find that each generation speaks the ancestral languages in fewer contexts and less elaborately than did its parents. In Saskatchewan, a study noted that "one teacher . . . commented that ten years prior (in the 1970s) the children spoke Cree on the school playground, whereas at the present time (1983), they spoke English."[69]

In September 1970, as a result of the protest about its closing that summer, Blue Quills in Alberta became the first school in Canada officially administered by an Indian band. As a symbol of their independence and reclamation of their culture, the leadership decided that the Cree language would be part of the curriculum.[70] Far to the east, in 1975, the James Bay and Northern Quebec Agreement with the provincial government provided for Cree to be "the teaching language. In a province like Quebec—where the English-French conflict is so intense and the government is intent on ensuring that the French language is pervasive—subsection 16.0.10 is a landmark provision with regards to the relationship between the provincial governments and the Native people in this province and, indeed, throughout Canada."[71]

Others followed, and by 1983–1984 20 percent of Indian children were attending schools operated by the different bands or tribes, particularly in Western Canada.[72] This was in effect a belated validation of the position maintained by the missionary education efforts of the churches, that Indian youth could best be educated in schools exclusively dedicated to them.[73]

In many of these cases, "control" involved a contractual relationship with the Canadian government, which fell considerably short of the degree of autonomy enjoyed by local public school districts. Apparently government officials were by no means confident that Indians could manage their own schools. The first tribe in Canada to gain complete control over their schools were the Nisga'a in British Columbia, who were able to become a local school district in 1974.[74] Nor was the assumption of control over schooling limited to Indians; in 1978, the first Inuit-controlled school board in Canada assumed control over schools in 14 villages in the Far North.[75] Also in the North, in 1975 Cree and Inuit representatives "negotiated the James Bay and Northern Quebec Agreement with the governments of Canada and Quebec. The agreement gave the Cree authority over many aspects of their lives," including schooling. Cree leaders (representing about 10,000 people scattered over 150,000 square miles) became determined that the schools contribute to maintenance of Cree language and culture, and in 1988 they decided that Cree would become the language of instruction at the elementary level.[76]

That was easier voted than implemented. The Cree language was little used in written form even within the James Bay Cree community; it was spoken, although less among the younger generation, and the challenge was to find contexts for which literacy in Cree would be rewarding and necessary. In addition, "Parents and other community members were not convinced; they generally believed it was important to learn in a mainstream language at school."[77]

Among the Mohawk, a long-term association with southern Canadian society and many ties with the mainstream economy of Canada made the affirmation of distinctive Mohawk mores and language an uphill battle. One community where these issues were researched had controlled its schools since the late 1970s, but there were "few young Mohawk speakers left." In an attempt to reverse this situation, "an alternative elementary school was started with an immersion Mohawk program from kindergarten to grade 6. In this school all teachers are Mohawk, and Mohawk is the language of the halls, staff room, and classes, except at the later elementary level when students are taught in English alternating weeks."[78]

The research focused upon two women teachers, both Mohawk, one a fluent speaker of the language and the other not. The most interesting finding was that the teacher fluent in the language was much less self-conscious about her Mohawk identity than was the other. The researchers found that "it would appear that her culture is so firmly but unconsciously embedded in her teaching that it is not something that she names. In other words, she experiences her identity, her distinctness from mainstream society, in a nonproblematic way. She has her own language to communicate and live in and feels no need for further means to distinguish herself from others." As a result, she was not especially interested in stressing to her pupils other aspects of Mohawk culture and identity. For the teacher who did not speak Mohawk, by contrast, "other cultural holdings are necessary in order to feel that she is distinct from the mainstream culture,"[79] and she placed much more emphasis on such non-linguistic elements of Mohawk identity in her teaching.

The researchers concluded that "the variation in beliefs between the two Mohawk teachers led us to conclude that there is not necessarily a set of uniform cultural holdings that can be designated as Mohawk."[80] Tribal control of the schooling of Indian children would not necessarily, under those circumstances, lead to a culturally coherent and revitalizing education. This was demonstrated in the Far North, where in 1989 the Nunavik Educational Task Force "found that self-governance did not automatically lead to more culturally relevant education or higher student academic achievement"[81] for Inuit children.

Such a conclusion is in stark contrast with attempts by some academics to identify an "aboriginal epistemology"[82] and other pan-Indian ways of thinking and of living that could serve as the basis for curriculum and pedagogy manifestly superior to that derived from the majority culture. Although high hopes are being placed on that form of education as "a mechanism of revitalization of Indian culture,"[83] one wonders to what extent the culture to be "revitalized" is in fact the invention of intellectuals projecting onto Indians—as has occurred since Rousseau and before—an idealized opposite of an "over-civilized" European culture.

A characteristic statement of the contention that there is something distinctively spiritual about the Indian perspective on life is an essay in "Redefinition of Indian Education" by the president of Saskatchewan Indian Federated College, a former participant in the doctoral program for Indians at Harvard Graduate School of Education. Eber Hampton argues that "the first standard of Indian education is spirituality. At its centre is respect for the spiritual relationships that exist between all things,"[84] a statement sufficiently vague to mean almost anything (or nothing) and to be affirmed by almost any religious tradition.

Similarly, a study of the "recovery schools" serving Indian youth in some Canadian cities asserts that "Indian culture has at its heart a spiritual worldview which suggests that all things in life are related in a sacred manner and are governed by natural laws. Three fundamental elements that most Indian cultures have in common with respect to their sacred ways are a belief in or knowledge of unseen powers, or what some people call the Great Mystery, . . . knowledge that all things in the universe are dependent on each other . . . [and that] personal worship reinforces the bond between an individual, the community, and the great powers. Worship is a personal commitment to the sources of life." One such school, for example, requires that "[t]eachers at Wandering Spirit Survival School must do more than pass on cultural history. If they are not Anishnawbe [Indian], they must live the Native Way and practice Native spirituality. . . . [T]he Native Way is a worldview, a set of perceptions and attitudes to permeate one's experience of and interaction with the world."[85]

The author concedes that "[u]rban public school boards are often hesitant to allow what they perceive as the teaching of religion in schools. The concern has some validity in survival schools which admit students from a wide variety of religious backgrounds. Parents of Indian children from Christian families may not approve of their children being taught Indian spiritual beliefs and practices. . . . It is because of this issue that Wandering Spirit School is attempting to attract students from families who are committed to Indian spirituality."[86] The premise of such efforts is that youth of Indian ancestry, whether their families hold such beliefs or not, have somehow imprinted in their genes an affinity for a generic "Indian spirituality," which will enable them to flourish in a way that would otherwise be impossible. The school described by McCaskill, now called First Nations School and accepted by the Toronto Board of Education as a "Cultural Survival School," includes among its academic offerings "Native as a Second Language," though which of Ontario's many native languages is not specified.

CHAPTER 13

Continued Decline of Indian Languages

Other schools on the Navajo Reservation imitated the educational model that Rock Point had developed, but in a sense the efforts to promote the Navajo language in schools were a race against time, as public demand grew for improved education in English. At the end of the twentieth century, "only a handful of schools" serving Navajo pupils had adopted instruction through Navajo, though others provided various supplemental instruction in Navajo language and culture; altogether, though, "only 10% of all K-12 Navajo students receive instruction in or about Navajo language and culture." Even in those schools where the language is taught, a study found, "the teachers of Navajo language courses are . . . isolated and unsure how to teach a group of students that have a wide range in Navajo speaking and comprehension abilities. Most often, the teacher utilizes the more fluent students as tutors for more limited students, thereby limiting the more fluent students' progress and development in Navajo."[1]

Although Navajo continues to be spoken more than most Indian languages—the Navajo reservation has an extensive administrative structure that uses the language to some extent—English is used for written communication. "Despite what is probably the largest absolute number, and largest relative percentage, of native-language monolinguals of any tribe in the United States, the written business of the tribe goes on in English."[2] Among Navajo aged 5 to 17 living on the reservation, the proportion who spoke only English rose from 11.8 percent in 1980 to 28.4 percent in 1990,[3] and this trend has gathered strength in subsequent years. A study of Navajo children in Head Start Programs in the early 1990s found that only 18 percent of the three- to five-year olds spoke Navajo.[4] Proficiency tests of pupils in a 99 percent Navajo school on the western edge of the reservation found that only 7 percent could speak Navajo fluently, while 11 percent had limited proficiency, and 82 percent had none at all.[5] At Rough Rock, site of the much-heralded program in the 1960s, researchers working with the bilingual/bicultural program "observed an alarming shift in children's use of and proficiency in Navajo. More and more children come to school each year with only a passive knowledge of the community language."[6]

A study in 1993 by Wayne Holm, the primary force behind the Rock Point bilingual school, surveyed the language abilities of 3,300 kindergartners on the Navajo Reservation. Less than one-third were considered fluent in Navajo, 52 percent had limited Navajo-speaking ability, and 13 percent had no knowledge of the language at all, even to understand without speaking it.[7] The intergenerational language shift represented, according to some, "a crisis of identity. It is a crisis of values, morality, and ways of knowing—of the most basic question of what it means to be Navajo—and whether children will, indeed, be 'lost,' disconnected from the words and worlds of their forebears. . . . [E]ven in Navajo-speaking homes, young children tended to respond to their parents' and grandparents' Navajo *in English*. At the tender age of 4 or 5—in some cases *before they had entered school*—children had internalized the covert and overt silencing messages of an English-dominant society."[8] But is it really the case that preschool children in an isolated community on the reservation were experiencing such powerful "silencing messages" that they abandoned the language spoken by their parents? Or is it not more likely that the parents themselves were speaking English with their children because it had become their primary medium of communication?

The irony for schools like Rough Rock and Rock Point is that their successes in creating new employment and educational opportunities for adults in previously isolated communities "has facilitated many of the social changes that lead to Navajo language loss."[9] By the end of the twentieth century it was reported that "English is predominant in tribal committee meetings, judiciary proceedings, tribal council meetings, and everyday activities of tribal employees" and there was a "trend toward the rapidly decreasing use of Navajo among young children."[10]

The fact is that schools, by themselves, are seldom effective in maintaining an endangered language.

> Languages are not just abstract and abstruse subjects, like arithmetic, spelling, and history, that can be perfectly tamed by their segregated school institutions and taken out for display purposes. . . . Languages do not really attain their proper shape or function in schools. . . . [T]heir true rationale is personal and interpersonal expression and participation within a complex sociocultural-communal communication network. . . . Many of the functions of Navajo

will have to be shared (even among Navajos) with English. This puts Navajo face-to-face with the greatest power-linked language of the modern world. In order to survive this competition, Navajo must also have some functions and statuses that are entirely and exclusively its own, and to which powerful English will simply not be admitted. The school may need to be bilingual, but perhaps the intimate and identity-forming family setting should not be. . . . [P]erhaps the religious rite should not be.[11]

After all, "ultimately, . . . the decision to maintain or renew a threatened language must be made by the speakers of that language, not by outsiders such as linguists or anthropologists, no matter how well-intentioned. Without this ownership by speakers themselves or their descendants, attempts at revitalization are destined to flounder and ultimately fail."[12] In particular, it is important, in this age when almost everyone is forced to make extensive use of literacy, that the native language not be limited to casual use in conversation, but that it be used for reading and writing. As linguist Bernard Spolsky wrote almost three decades ago, when Navajo was more widely used than it is today, "I believe that a decision to develop wider roles for Navajo literacy will be fundamental in the preservation of the language and the culture."[13] Whether that is feasible, even on as large a reservation as the Navajo, remains to be seen. A recent study found that "written Navajo is rarely used in tribal government operations. English is the written language and language of control for state and federal offices serving Navajo populations as well."[14]

Similarly, in Canada, an effort by Cree tribal authorities on a very large—though thinly populated—reservation to promote the use of their ancestral language among the younger generation has run into problems. "The major difficulty foreseen for this program is the lack of written Cree in community life. Although most organizations use Cree for oral communication, almost all written communication is in English. Unless written Cree is emphasized in business and social settings, and is something that adults are seen to do, children will not find their efforts to read and write in Cree to be socially valued."[15]

On the other hand, minority languages may be preserved if they have a strong religious significance, as has been the case of Old German with certain Amish and Mennonite groups, of Yiddish with some Hasidim, and of Pueblo languages. Navajo literacy has in fact been developed and preserved within Christian churches on the reservation, and the same is true of Cree and Micmac on reservations in Canada, and of other Indian languages. Spolsky, in listing sources of Navajo literacy, identified the Christian missions as most significant: "First, there is a Navajo translation of the Bible used in Protestant churches, so that there is a special kind of vernacular-based sacred-text literacy associated with Christianity. Second, there is a small number of schools with bilingual education programs that also teach reading and writing in Navajo."[16] Navajo is also used within the Native American Church, which practices a mixture of Christian and traditional elements through "the sacramental use of the earthly plant known as Peyote with its teachings of love of God and right living."[17]

Navajo continues to retain considerable symbolic importance, even for those who experience their cultures largely through English. The Navajo (now Diné) Community College, founded in 1968, established a program to teach Navajo "to members of the tribe who have lost their ability to speak Navajo," as a rejection of the hegemony of American culture; non-Indian faculty members were also denied a voice in the decision-making process of the college, and served only until Navajo replacements could be found.[18] More recently, its teacher education program has trained a group of Navajo language teachers, and the Navajo Tribe has ordered that Navajo be the language of instruction in its more than 160 Head Start centers.[19] On the other hand, as an advocate for the maintenance and revival of Navajo admits,

> English has become the lingua franca not only because it is the language of money but also because it is the primary tongue of Hollywood, MTV, and the NBA. And with these come glitz, glamor, hype, and all things cool and wannabe. We as educators can rant and rave about how important it is to preserve the language, but to a seven year old child it is the moment that counts, not the blood and tears of their ancestors. In 1978, my first year on the reservation, many Navajo still lacked electricity and running water. Today, if you travel to the most remote corners of the reservation, you will see satellite dishes sprouting from the rooftops. Today, federal legislation protects indigenous languages. American Indians cannot be prohibited from speaking their tribal tongue. They can, however, be persuaded not to speak it or simply lulled into a state of denial or indifference about its death.[20]

The same issues around language have arisen in Canada, both the demand for government-sponsored efforts to support native languages, and the seemingly inexorable decline of those languages. The very influential policy paper of the National Indian Brotherhood in 1972, *Indian Control of Indian Education*, stressed "a great need for formal instruction in the Native languages." A survey of 20 Indian communities, more recently, found that in 18 of them "there was unanimous support among the interviewees for the retention of indigenous languages. Of course, there is no certainty that a discourse supporting language means that the interviewees take an active stance to support the language in their daily life."[21]

In the United States, as well, Indians give lip service to maintenance of their ancestral languages, but often do not use those languages consistently enough with their own children to ensure that they become proficient. Nor, generally, are Indian parents as enthusiastic about instruction through their ancestral (no longer "home" in most cases) languages. A national study in the late 1960s found only four students out of 1200 interviewed who believed that knowledge of their ancestral languages was more important than knowledge of English. The study found that, among Indians in cities,

> Except when older persons are present, Indian languages are generally not spoken at home. However, many middle-aged couples are able to speak their native tongue and in fact do so when they are visiting back home [on the reservation]. When asked why they didn't speak Indian in the home, many were genuinely perplexed. . . . [M]any seem to have never really thought about it. . . . [M]any persons had a definite idea of white-world English and Indian-world Indian. Attempts to start up Indian language classes in the city are by and large unsuccessful. The lack of printed material in a usable form and interpersonal conflicts over correct word forms are major disadvantages.[22]

Even on reservations, "the anthropologist William Leap (1982) could find no tribe that had allowed Native language restoration to outrank teaching English in importance."[23] This is consistent with research on Latino immigrants, who consistently report on surveys that they would like public schools to teach their children Spanish—so long as it does not take any time away from English! Joshua Fishman warns that speakers of "endangered languages must assume control . . . of the intimate spheres of family and community—even though they may never attain control of . . . the status spheres of supra-local power and authority." If endangered languages are displaced in the home, the prospects of survival as real means of communication are limited. What Fishman calls

> an ethnically encumbered interaction (such as the celebration of a festival, a birth, a birthday party or a marriage ceremony) in a language other than the historically associated one, signals a different family culture, as different everyday reality, a different interpretation of and involvement in the tangible past and a different view of the future.[24]

Nor do native communities always welcome efforts by schools to teach their languages, quite apart from the concern that children master English. In the 1930s, when Commissioner Collier was giving strong encouragement to the introduction of elements of Indian culture into government schools, a Hopi teacher found resistance to her introduction of Hopi legends and songs; "parents questioned what she was teaching, saying, 'We send them [our children] to school to learn the white man's way, not Hopi. They can learn the Hopi way at home'."[25] For the Utes, the use of their language by the school was unwelcome, since it seemed to presage a breach in the wall that the language provided between their own life and that of the wider—and generally hostile—society. "Parents feared that written Ute language materials might give any literate person, including non-Utes, access to esoteric dimensions of Ute culture." For this tribe, like many others, "political success meant maintaining its own institutions, not integrating into the county, state and national systems,"[26] much less becoming part of a "multicultural mosaic."

Anthropologist William Leap points out that literacy "in Northern Ute is not a part of the Tribe's ancestral language tradition; written Ute remains in many ways a recent addition to the inventory of language skills to be found on this reservation" and that tribal members "remain skeptical about the idea of reading and writing in the tribal language. Aesthetic and spiritual concerns are being voiced here, but so are some more mundane, practical matters. . . . There is little in the way of reading material in Ute, and no great demand for the production of new written texts. Moreover, each time some parties begin to describe the long-range benefits that may be associated with Ute literacy, other parties point out that the *real* needs in education and employment on this reservation are English centered; hence, they argue, efforts to promote written Ute skills reflect nothing more than a response to faulty priorities." As a result, only 44 percent of Ute adults and 20 percent of Ute children speak the language "adequately or better," and literacy in Ute "is still something largely unfamiliar to many of the individual members of that speech community."[27] Without reinforcement and stabilization through extensive written use, any language has a tendency to retreat into ceremonial and limited domestic use.

Resistance arose in the Talpa School District in northern New Mexico, in the early 1990s, when the school system bilingual program staff were excited about offering instruction in their language to Pueblo pupils, but the Tribal Council "reacted angrily, declaring that no outside entity or person had the right to use their language for any purpose without the council's participation and official consent." "Generally," Martinez observes, "school personnel have not understood how Pueblo people view their own languages, how the languages have been utilized, or how these views have developed. . . . The reason Pueblo adults wish for children to learn their heritage language has nothing to do with the acquisition of English. It is so that the children can participate knowledgeably and appropriately in the maintenance of their traditional culture and religion. . . . For these small communities where everyone's participation matters, all of the children must be prepared to play a role in the future of the community."[28]

The Pueblo example is a useful reminder of the importance that "decisions about language education policy be grounded in sociolinguistic reality. . . . Educators may choose to try to change the situation . . . , but they will be very likely to fail if they ignore the local societal pattern of literacy." Well-meaning attempts to bring minority languages into the classroom may do more harm than good if they fail to "ask who is literate in which language and for what purposes."[29] For the Pueblos, their various different though related languages are essential to participation in religious and community-sustaining traditional activities in a "complex religious cycle. . . . Writing the language would allow indiscriminate access, thus potentially exposing sacred or private information."[30] Under those circumstances, a Pueblo language has no place in the curriculum of a school whose function is seen as preparing youth to function in the "other" world of American society.

Indeed, "a community can easily interpret the proposal of bilingual educators to teach in the home language as an intention not to teach the standard language and so deny the children access to the wider society. Similarly, a major task of school is to provide students with access to and skill in the various kinds of publicly-approved literacy,"[31] which, in American society is English and in Canadian society English or French. One of the alumnae of Chilocco Indian School, explaining why her younger siblings did not follow her to the school, explained, "Well, I don't think that my mother was really too impressed with the way we turned out. We came home singing Indian songs, and doing little Indian dances and she said, I thought I sent you kids up there to be educated, and get civilized. 'Course, we didn't grow up in an Indian environment anyway."[32]

On the other hand, Pueblo communities have been concerned that their children were not becoming proficient in their languages, and in some cases they have set up community-based language programs.

> For the children, programs have been designed to immerse them in their languages for a major part of a day throughout the summer months when they are not in school. . . . So far, only one community has instituted an immersion program within the structure of a public school. . . . Heritage language teachers and their tribal leaders have no illusion that school programs can someday take the place of language learning within the rich and meaningful context of the community. School programs are envisioned more as a way of reinforcing what the children have already learned in the community. . . . [S]everal tribes have chosen to employ the language teachers themselves and then send those teachers to teach in the public schools for a portion of their day.

The function of these programs is quite different from that of first-language classes in Spanish, for example; "educators should not expect Pueblo heritage language classes to reflect, introduce, or reinforce concepts that are being covered in the English language curriculum."[33] No, the Pueblo language classes are intended to pass on an alternative worldview, not the majority worldview in a minority language.

Even though schools may make various gestures toward teaching native languages, the actual effect of receiving more education is often to make it less likely that an individual will use that language. Schooling opens economic opportunities which, in turn, call upon proficiency in the majority language and reduce the proportion of interactions that are within a limited linguistic community. "Education does increase the probability of participation in the labor force and to that extent education may improve the economic situation . . . but at the same time education reduces the probability of language retention."[34]

The Indian Education Act of 1972 provided support not only for programs on and near reservations, but also for efforts to reach and serve Indian children living in cities and in the East. Federal support had already been expanded with the enactment of a program to support various forms of bilingual instruction, in 1968. Though the primary focus was upon the needs of Spanish-speaking children, a variety of pilot programs were implemented in Cherokee and Navajo (1969), Chocktaw, Ute, Yuk, Crow, Cree, and Northern Cheyenne (1970), and Zuñi, Lakota, and Passamaquoddy (1971).[35] Other languages have been added over the years, in some cases only after written forms were developed for the first time. Bernard Spolsky identified 84 American Indian bilingual programs in 1974.[36]

These programs, it should be noted, have mostly been concentrated at the lower grades of schooling, and have been designed more for transition to English than for maintenance of the native language as the primary means of communication. Though "culturally related topics and special heritage classes"[37] are common, they have done little to slow the abandonment of Indian languages in cases where they do not receive strong support from the community outside the school. The situation is especially complicated by the fact that "many reservation schools serve students from multiple Indian nations thus creating the problem of deciding what languages and what cultural traditions should be taught."[38]

Even the enthusiasts for instruction through Navajo are forced to concede that "there was a great variety of attitudes among Indian parents and leaders towards the teaching of Navajo language and culture in the schools, and that many felt these were better taught by parents at home. . . . [O]thers felt that there was insufficient information on what Indian parents really thought on the subject."³⁹ A typical view is that expressed by the first Navajo woman tribal council delegate, who complained in 1947 that

> our White instructors are trying to get our Native language taught in school along with English, and confusing our little children, but will this fulfill their part in our treaty, even if they do succeed in getting our little ones to speak Navajo the broken White Mans way? Will this qualify our children to compete with their White Brothers? The answer is *Positively No*, it only confuses them, and holds them back so they will have to be wards of the Government, and have to hire high paid white men to help them get a mere existence our [*sic*] of this country we live in.⁴⁰

There were, however, compelling reasons of self-interest for promoting and—once established—for defending an educational program employing, with federal government funds, a language that few outsiders were qualified to teach in.

> The decision to establish bilingual education, even a transitional variety for the first three grades, implied the need for a thousand Navajo-speaking teachers. Whatever other educational or linguistic rationales might have been presented, it is clear that bilingual education in this situation offered the possibility of jobs within the community for a sizable number of people. . . . [This] would immediately establish within the community a well-paid middle class whose potential influence on the political development of the Navajo Nation is obvious.⁴¹

More broadly, Spolsky concludes, "in the United States, one of the rationales for bilingual education has been to give previously underrepresented groups control over the resources of the educational systems that affect their children; it serves then as part of the general affirmative action movement,"⁴² since the adult members of the group are uniquely qualified for employment. As we have seen, this was the primary focus of the Rough Rock project. In effect, minority-language teaching and cultural instruction, under these circumstances, are no longer ends in themselves but come to serve purposes that may make it difficult to evaluate them objectively or to assess to what extent they respond to authentic demand.

School-based programs are not, however, by themselves enough to maintain endangered languages. As Spolsky has written more recently, "unless language becomes a central issue in ethnic or religious mobilization and succeeds in gaining political power, language movements are unlikely to be successful. Only an ideologically supported, preferably religious, separatist movement that involves not only language but also a community willing to cut itself off from many of the features of modern life, can also hope to build the kind of separation that will maintain a minority language distinct and safe from the concurrent use of the language dominant in the outside society."[43] The possibility cannot be excluded that such movements would arise among Indians in Canada or the United States, but to date any that have developed have been few and scattered.

It does not appear, despite the best efforts of language advocates and the lip service paid, in American society, to diversity in many forms, that the effort to revive the use of Indian languages is succeeding, apart from exceptional cases. The most recent study by the American government, based upon a very extensive nationwide survey in connection with the 2007 National Assessment of Educational Progress, found that Indian pupils were actually *less* likely than non-Indian pupils to report that they spoke a language other than English at home "all or most of the time," and more than half answered "never." There was a notable difference, as might be expected, between those Indian pupils attending schools operated by the Bureau of Indian Education (BIE), normally on reservations, 35 percent of whom reported speaking another language, and those attending public schools. To the extent that BIE schools may help to maintain ancestral languages, it should be noted that they served only 6–7 percent of the Indian pupils in the national study. More than three-quarters of the teachers of Indian pupils reported that they did not speak the ancestral language of their pupils.[44]

Concerns about access to the educational and employment opportunities available through English seem to have greater significance than continued use of ancestral languages for the actual users of language: the rising generation of young Indians. Is it possible that minority languages, in a highly interrelated society, are a luxury good that those who are still struggling for their place on the economic ladder cannot well afford? It seems possible that the Native American Church could serve as the vehicle for continued use and transmission of Indian languages, but the fact that it is a pan-Indian movement means that its common language is inevitably English. Increasingly Indian children live in cities and attend public schools with non-Indian children, another reason—together with the pervasive influence of electronic media—to doubt that Indian languages will in another generation serve more than a symbolic role, reduced to a few phrases employed in ceremonial contexts or for personal greetings.

It is, of course, not inevitable that Indian languages will die out. The social and economic environment within which a language community raises its children has a tremendous influence on whether those children make the effort to use and continue to develop their ancestral language while becoming proficient in the language of the society and of educational and employment opportunities, but this does not prevent them from choosing to do so. After all, "[i]f speakers take pride in their language, enjoy listening to others using it well, use it themselves whenever they can and as creatively as they can, and provide occasions when the language can be heard, the conditions are favourable for maintenance."[45] While, as we have seen in the case of Navajo and Cree, physical isolation helps to preserve an indigenous language, and economic pressures in a situation of increased contact with the majority society tends to undermine it, the achievement of a measure of economic security can lead to a new and deliberate attention to the promotion of the language for symbolic reasons. Under these circumstances, the ancestral language may become a sort of hobby or luxury good, cultivated for sentimental rather than practical reasons, as studies by Alba and Waters have shown with respect to immigrants to America.

Crystal suggests that "[b]ecause the two languages have different purposes—one for identity, the other for intelligibility—they do not have to be in conflict."[46] While this is certainly true, it assumes that identity rests upon language use, and that it is of sufficient importance that people will make the effort to use it even when they have ready-to-hand another language that they *must* use in other contexts.

When the heritage language does not have the sort of significance that derives from traditional religious practices (as it does with the Pueblos) or with the assertion of a threatened identity (as with French in Canada), it is often abandoned or not passed on consistently to children. Does this necessarily mean the abandonment of a culture and all that goes with it? It is often asserted that "in Native communities . . . the transmission of a distinctive culture still depends upon the maintenance of Native languages in their oral mode. Myths and legends, for example, are seldom, if ever, told in English, and the lessons they contain about history, human relationships, proper behaviour, and universal truths are thus lost on the younger generation."[47]

There are, however, many instances of cultural groups—especially those whose distinctive way of living their culture is centered on a religious tradition or practices that set them apart—who are able to carry over what they most value about their culture to a new language as part of a natural adaptation to life in a society where that language is the ordinary means of communication. Despite the tradition of "language essentialism" stretching back to Johann Herder in the eighteenth century, the "soul of a people" is not lost when it begins to express itself in a new language, provided that it deals successfully with other aspects of the transition. Indeed, the transition of a peasant and family from a rural village in Anatolia to Istanbul or Ankara is probably more culturally disruptive, though they continue to speak Turkish, than is that of a scientist and family from Istanbul to Frankfurt, even though they must adapt to a new language.

The Native American Language Act of 1992 asserted that "the traditional languages of Native Americans are an integral part of their cultures and identities and form the basic medium for the transmission, and thus survival, of Native American cultures, literatures, histories, religions, political institutions, and values."[48] The implication is that those who do not speak their ancestral language (or, given the mixed ancestry of most North American Indians, several ancestral languages) can no longer claim to be authentic Indians, and that those Americans of Indian descent who did not speak those languages—the great majority, by that point—had no share in the cultures and identities of their ancestors. There are Indian language activists who assert precisely that "one cannot be Mohawk without speaking the language, and that the culture dies with the language,"[49] but this would be vehemently denied by hundreds of thousands of Native Americans who continue to identify strongly with their ancestral traditions even though they speak at most a few words or phrases of Micmac or Cheyenne.

Robert Bunge expressed the "language essentialist" view in a lecture in Saskatchewan in 1987:

> There is nothing more important for native young people than to know their native language and the tribal lore and wisdom embodied in that language. It is the very heart of identity. . . . [C]haracter . . . can only arise from an identity and an identity one can be proud of, undergirded by a knowledge of our ancestral wisdom and the language containing that wisdom. The worst aspect of cultural genocide is that, once successfully cut off from one's roots, loss of identity follows, the deepest calamity that can befall a people or an individual.[50]

He described a village he had visited twice, 20 years apart, where "the youth of the village, young adults and teenagers, made a decision to go with the language of the larger society. This is cultural suicide."[51] But it may, in fact, also have been a rational choice, given the importance of proficiency in what Bunge calls "the European tongue of the dominant society."

Experience in many parts of the world, however, demonstrates that "there can be cultural continuity despite language shift. The new culture is not the same as the old, of course, but it is not totally different either."[52] As in the case of immigrant groups, the maintenance of ethnic languages and cultures "are both far greater at an attitudinal level than at an overt behavioral one."[53] Members of ethnic groups, in other words, often claim to be more "ethnic" than their actions demonstrate, and in particular fail to shoulder consistently the heavy burden of using two languages when one will suffice. There is no reason to believe that Indians are different.

To the extent that it is desired, by any group, to maintain and transmit the use of a heritage language, it is probably necessary that this be given a specific function for which the majority language absolutely cannot serve. As noted, this is commonly a religious role, though as the Navajo example demonstrates it may to some extent also be a role in government and other public functions in which it is possible to mandate what language will be used. The bottom line is that "language maintenance will be most efficient, in the long term, if one begins by providing support for the cultural milieu or matrix within which that language is found, and from which people will draw their motivation to use it. Promoting the culture as a whole is the best precondition for enabling a language to grow."[54]

Ideally, from the perspective of those committed to Indian language maintenance, a sufficient number of opportunities would be provided for Indian youth within a separate Indian sector of the economy so that they would not have to acquire the language and other skills and habits necessary for employment in the wider economy. This seems unlikely. There is a nice ring to asserting that "the most viable political and economic position for Indian tribes has been coexistence with American society, not entry into it,"[55] but that holds true only for those tribes, like the Ute, who are supported by royalties from oil and mineral rights without compromising their splendid independence. Those tribes that are now supported by casino and resort income are, of course, deeply engaged with the majority culture as its hosts and cannot hope to remain protected from its influence.

The question remains, whether the traditional culture (and its associated language) of a people making a rapid and successful transition to modernity can itself evolve rapidly enough so that it can become the culture and language through which they orient themselves to a radically transformed situation. Failing that, they will inevitably adopt the language prevalent in the wider society, with perhaps some vestiges of the traditional culture expressed in the new language.

There are, unfortunately, many examples worldwide of "native peoples" who have apparently become stuck halfway through the transition, having abandoned the coherent culture and way of life that once sustained them without successfully mastering those of the dominant society. It may be that the effort to bridge the gap is doomed to fail, and that those who make the transition successfully must accomplish the feat by an intensely painful act of renunciation of the old ways and a mastery of the dominant culture and its associated language. It is not a question of whether they have the *right* to maintain their ancestral traditions (and there are few governments, today, that would deny them that right), but rather of whether those traditions can be more than a marginal aspect of successful participation in the wider society. The national study of Indian education in the late 1960s found that "many tribes are divided among themselves concerning their expectations of the school as a teacher of Indian culture and history."[56]

In the case of the United States and Canada, the fact that tens of thousands of people are "rediscovering" Indian ancestry out of a romantic identification with what has been presented in schools and the media as a less corrupted culture or out of a desire to benefit from schooling and employment preferences available to members of minority groups—or, indeed, because of the new prosperity of those tribes that are operating gambling casinos—is further weakening the case for treating native languages as an essential element of the Indian identity. It seems highly unlikely that much of the dramatic growth in the number of individuals reporting to the U.S. Census that they have Indian ancestry consists of persons who speak Indian languages. The situation is thus sharply different from that of the other fast-growing groups, persons of Mexican and of Asian ancestry, among whom immigrants are constantly replacing those who make the transition to primary use of English.

CHAPTER 14

Indians in Local Public Schools

The policy goal over recent decades with respect to African-American children, Latino children, and every immigrant group has been their integration into the regular public school system serving the area where they live. Official policies had sometimes relegated them to separate public schools, as in the obvious case of black pupils both in the South and even in many cases in the North, and also—though less notoriously—in the case of Latino and Asian pupils in the West. Even when such de jure laws and policies have been absent, achieving integration of schools has had to contend with the opposition of white parents, and with patterns of segregated housing that allowed the phrase "neighborhood school" to become a code for racial separation. Consistently, advocates for integrated schooling have urged that it is essential to the full participation of marginalized groups in the wider society and that the benefits would accrue to children of the majority as well as to those of the minority. This logic was belatedly applied to Indian children and youth as well.

In some cases, almost always for religious reasons, some groups have sought separate schooling for their children. Canadian law since the founding of an independent Canada with the British North America (now Constitution) Act of 1867, and American law since the 1925 Supreme Court decision in *Pierce v. Society of Sisters*, have acknowledged the right of groups to do so, but "liberal" opinion, though in principle friendly to societal pluralism, has often deplored this concession to freedom of conscience. Only through exposure to the "common" public school, Amy Gutmann and others have argued, can children acquire the values and attitudes that prepare them for independent thinking and full civic participation.[1]

This argument was frequently made with respect to Indian children. Richard Henry Pratt of the Carlisle Indian School argued that it was necessary so to disperse them that there could be no question of keeping them separate from white American children. He wrote, in 1889, to the Board of Indian Commissioners,

We must get them into America and keep them in. . . . It is a very peculiar situation that in this country and at this time we have no individual Indians here and there in our communities—none that live with us. The idea is segregation and Indian reservations everywhere. At Carlisle I cannot work the Indians en masse. If I send them in numbers to Sunday school, at once a class of Indians is formed. If I send them out into the country into public schools, . . . forthwith there is segregated a class of Indians. To overcome this hindrance, which is our own act, we must by thorough distribution make it impossible to create a class of Indians. . . . [T]here would be only about one Indian boy or girl to every five or six schools in the United States. . . . Carlisle has over two hundred Indian youth out in families and in the public schools of Pennsylvania. We ought to save them as individuals, invite and urge them out of their savagery and into our civilization one by one, the whole of them. How long would it take to assimilate them if we went about it with all our forces? Not more than from three to five years. . . . It would only make nine Indians to a county throughout the United States.

Pratt predicted that "we may have our contract schools, our church schools, and our government schools till Gabriel blows his horn, and we shall always have Indians and be struggling with the Indian problem."[2]

The Board did not need this urging; already in 1880 they had asked, "If the common school is the glory and boast of our American civilization, why not extend its blessings to the 50,000 benighted children of the red men of our country?"[3] Despite such exhortation, in 1896 there were only 303 Indian students officially enrolled in local school systems in the United States.[4] There were, of course, many others simply attending the off-reservation schools where they happened to be living; even in the eighteenth century "in many places Indian families lived side by side with the whites, as they were induced to embrace the white man's way of life and civilization. When the Indians were close at hand, one could go out and buy game from them or sell them household manufactures."[5]

As Szasz notes, the failure of most of the efforts to create schools explicitly for Indians during the seventeenth and eighteenth centuries did not mean that no Indian children received formal schooling; she finds evidence that in areas where Indians continued to live, their children sometimes attended school with white children. For example, a resident of Farmington, Connecticut, in the middle of the eighteenth century recalled that there were about as many Indian and white children in the school and that the groups were evenly matched in their games and battles. Szasz points out that "[w]henever a schoolmaster included one of two Indians among his students, he was engaged in an attempt to educate the Indians, but since it seldom occurred to him to record his effort, it has largely escaped our scrutiny." She suggests that "this informal schooling [of Indian children with white children] probably occurred to a greater extent in the American colonies than has been previously recognized. . . . [I]t offered one clear advantage for the Indian: it allowed for gradual rather than forced acculturation."[6]

A century later, this would be the initial pattern across North America. For example, in California in some districts "where the local white people [did] not have enough children of their own to maintain a school they usually let in enough Indian children to make up the required number."[7] A law was enacted in 1860 denying state funding for the schooling of members of racial minority groups, including Indians, although providing that separate school funds could be established for separate schools. "Even had most Indians been in a position to benefit from public schools, which they were not in 1860, the effect was to handicap the few who might have attended." It was not until the 1920s that California accepted "responsibility for providing schooling to those Indian children living near reservations, and not until 1935 did the legislature give up the option of maintaining separate schools for Indians if local school districts chose to maintain them."[8]

An unusual case is that of the Lumbee Indians of North Carolina, of whom there were about 26,000 reported in the 1970s. Not speaking any Indian language nor preserving extensive customs that can be identified as indigenous, and with no treaty rights extending to them federal protection and support, the Lumbee appear to derive from "remnants of southeastern Atlantic Coast tribes who early in the history of our country drifted into the backwaters and swamps . . . and while intermarrying somewhat with whites and Negroes, kept their social identity as Indians." In 1885 the state legislature provided for separate Indian schools as an alternative to the segregated white and black schools, and a teacher-training normal school was established for them in 1887. As of the early 1970s, the local school system in the area where most Lumbee live offered all three types of schools, each staffed predominantly by teachers of the same race as the pupils. Thus, a major source of income for Indians was jobs in the public school system: the "pattern of separatism gave the Lumbees a monopoly on a group of jobs that paid regularly, were secure, and which rewarded individuals who achieved higher education."[9]

In British Columbia, Indian children were enrolled in the common schools during the early years of white settlement, welcomed because "in many outlying settlements Aboriginal children were necessary to secure the minimum enrolment necessary for a public school's establishment and survival." When the provincial Superintendent of Education was asked, in 1886, by some parents of white children whether Indian children should be in their classrooms, he replied that "[t]here is no authority given in the

School Act to refuse them admittance. Since the inception of the present School system they have been admitted on an equality with other pupils." Within the next several years, however, it became increasingly difficult for Indian children to be accepted into their local schools. As white settlement increased, the Indian children were less necessary to keep up school enrolments, and white parents began to object to their presence. The Superintendent of Education ruled in 1891 that "the matter of attendance of Indian children is left entirely in the hands of the [local] Board of Trustees," and he retreated farther by ruling, in 1893, that "if a single [white] parent objects to the attendance of Indian pupils, they cannot be permitted to attend" the local public school.[10]

At an Anglican private school in British Columbia, founded in the late nineteenth century, Indian girls were enrolled along with white girls; in fact, it could be put the other way, since the school was established as an missionary effort toward Indians, but whites were included subsequently to support the finances of the school. The principal reported in 1895 to the mother superior of the teaching order, back in England, that "[i]n accordance with the wishes of the English parents, the white children and the Indians do not mix." Notably, on the other hand, "While Indian pupils at All Hallows rapidly became physically separate and unequal in work duties, they were recognized through the turn of the century as possessing comparable intellectual capacity. Individual advance depended on individual ability and initiative, and many achieved much." Despite receiving what was, for girls at the time, an unusually good education, however, the subsequent opportunities for the Indian alumnae were limited. "White Canadians did not want young Indians entering their socio-economic order, even at the bottom rung. . . . The principal opposition to assimilation did not come from Aboriginal peoples but rather from the dominant society."[11]

At the same time, the Canadian federal authorities responsible for Indians were expanding their provision of schools; by 1900, there were 14 residential and 28 day schools run by the federal authorities in British Columbia, and in 1920 there were 1,115 Indian children in 17 residential schools, and 1,197 in 46 day schools operated by the federal government within the province.[12] As a result, local school systems were able to disavow any responsibility for the Indian children living in their vicinity.

Integration of Indian children in local public schools was, as we have seen, a priority for Thomas Jefferson Morgan, Commissioner of Indian Affairs for the United States from 1889 to 1893 and a strong believer in the common school as a force for assimilation. In 1891, he announced a new policy of contracting for the education of Indian children in public schools. The purpose, as stated in 1894, was to "render the specific Indian

School unnecessary as speedily as possible, and to substitute for it the American public school. . . . It is in full accord with the desire of the nation to do away with the Indian problem by assimilating the Indians in the body politic of the United States."[13] This would also reduce the cost of maintaining a separate federally operated system of Indian schools. The BIA sought to persuade local school districts to serve Indian children by offering to pay tuition of $10 per quarter for each pupil. "By 1894, three California school systems enrolled 54 pupils under the plan. Community opposition, stimulated by prejudice as well as logistical and financial problems, reduced that number drastically after 1896. By 1903 not a single California school was engaged in a contract with the Office of Indian Affairs. Only twelve existed in the entire nation, and that number was declining rapidly."[14]

In 1895 the new chief of Indian Education—a well-regarded professional educator—announced that the time had passed for the government's policies toward appropriate schooling for Indians to be guided by "the few philanthropic men and women missionaries" who had taken the lead in the previous decades; now they had "gradually stepped aside and the schoolmaster stepped in." The time had come to integrate Indian children into local public schools. He drew up a model contract to be executed between the Indian Office and county school boards: "it required local authorities to give native students the same education they gave the children of tax-paying citizens; and it called on teachers and administrators 'to protect the pupils included in this contract from ridicule, insult and other improper conduct at the hands of their fellow pupils, and to encourage them . . . to perform their duties with the same degree of interest and industry as their fellow pupils, the children of white citizens."[15]

Unfortunately, this effort encountered strong resistance, especially from white parents who objected to their children being in classes with Indian children. In 1860, Northern Paiute Sarah Winnemucca, later herself a teacher, and her sister were removed from the "Sisters' School" in San Jose, California, because "wealthy parents" complained about having their children educated with Indian children.[16]

While in 1895 there were 45 school districts in the United States accepting federal funds to enroll Indian pupils, there were only half as many five years later. Federal officials concluded, in 1900, that "notwithstanding the incentive of $10 per capita offered by the government . . . indifferent results were obtained." Successful integration of Indian and white pupils in local public schools would work only where these "are located in sections favorable to the co-education of the races,"[17] and there were vanishingly few of those. In 1899, spaces in public schools were available under government contracts for only 359 Indian pupils, and only 167 were in attendance; by 1905 there were only 84 Indian pupils under government jurisdiction in six public schools nationwide,[18] though undoubtedly there were other Indian pupils here and there whose families were assimilated into local communities.

Matters improved somewhat after 1904, when Congress passed an act establishing a fund for paying salaries of teachers in integrated schools, which would "be under the joint control of the United States superintendent of schools and tribal school authorities." Congress justified this action by insisting that "the Indian must lose his identity by absorption, and such absorption will be rapid and positive; and he must soon cease to be recognized as a separate and distinct race." By 1909, 3000 Indian students were enrolled in contract public schools in California, Nebraska, South Dakota, and Utah, and another 818 were enrolled in non-contract public schools in 12 states.[19]

Former Commissioner Leupp wrote, probably too optimistically, that "in most neighborhoods with a mixed population the whites have been glad to let Indian children attend the public schools as long as the government would pay the cost of their tuition. In others, white parents have objected to letting Indian children mingle with theirs, not on grounds of race prejudice, but because the homes from which the little Indians come are so often ill-kept, loosely disciplined, and unwholesome, that infection is feared, moral as well as physical."[20]

On the Yakama Reservation in Washington State, as a result of the government policy to give individual ownership of land ("allotments") to Indians, so many non-Indians rented that land for their own use that by 1902 it became necessary to establish public schools to serve non-Indian children. Since these schools enrolled Indian children as well, this process achieved an integration that did not occur within the federally operated Indian schools. The government agent on the reservation observed that "Indian children progress much faster when thus thrown in contact with white children than they do when they are all kept together with whites excluded."[21]

Nationwide, however, the results of integration policies were limited, since the federal government in the United States, like that in Canada, has no authority over local school systems. By 1908, as racism nationwide reached something of a climax, there were only four school districts in the United States willing to accept the Indian children who lived nearby,[22] while in Canada in 1911 it was observed that "a very marked prejudice exists . . . generally among the whites against association with Indian children," and Indian pupils in several public schools were told to stop attending.[23] Among countless incidents of this sort, "in 1929, three Indian children were refused admittance to West Saanich [British Columbia] school even though the municipal authorities were prepared to allow them to enter because some white parents protested their presence."[24] As late as the mid-1930s, there were public school districts in the United States refusing to admit Indian pupils.[25]

Even when Indian pupils were accommodated in local public schools, the results were often unsatisfactory. Federal oversight of how local schools treated Indian pupils was very limited, and Indian parents had the impression that the government simply wanted to wash its hands of all responsibility, leaving their children at the mercy of white prejudices and low expectations. When the Bureau of Indian Affairs decided to close the Rainy Mountain school in Oklahoma, serving Kiowa pupils, local whites wrote to their congressmen in Washington to protest that the Kiowas were not ready to enter the public schools. "The Indian standard of living is centuries behind that of the ordinary American. . . . The Indian child is a menace to all of his associates until he has been taught the laws of hygiene and clean living," which should occur in a boarding school like Rainy Mountain. The superintendent of the local public schools added that "Indian children responded 'very reluctantly' to public school methods of instruction; his school was not equipped to provide the special environment that Indians needed. . . . 'We submit that the Indian is greatly handicapped by the futile attempt to civilize him by trying to get him to learn what he cannot understand'." Some of his teachers would refuse to accept classes that included Indian children, who "were almost always dirty and bred disease." Assigning the Kiowa pupils after the closing of Rainy Mountain "would be a menace to the safety and progress of his schools."[26]

The common reluctance of local school districts to accept Indian pupils undoubtedly reflected the attitude of white parents to the presence of children characterized, as in Canada, by " their dirty habits, their undisciplined behaviour, and their speaking another language," but there was also a financial reason. Public schools in most states were then, as now but to an even greater degree, funded by local property taxes, and Indian land was not taxable; thus Indian parents were not contributing to the cost of the local public schools. It was through individual arrangements between the Federal Department of the Interior and local school boards that payments were made by the government in lieu of taxation. Through such arrangements, and despite many difficulties, there was a steady increase in the number and proportion of Indian pupils attending local public schools; by 1928, they outnumbered those attending schools operated by the federal government.[27]

In 1928, the United States Senate began hearings on Indian affairs; considerable frustration was expressed with the evident failure of the government's schools to prepare Indian youth to adapt to the demands of contemporary American society. "If you cannot instill into them [the Indians] the idea that it is necessary for them to go out and hold jobs and take their

Table 14.1 Distribution of Indian pupils

	BIA day schools	BIA boarding schools	Mission and private schools	Local public schools
1890	3,967	12,410	N/A	N/A
1900	5,120	19,810	1,275	246
1911	6,121	19,912	2,739	10,265
1920	5,765	21,659	3,518	30,858
1930	3,983	28,333	3,558	34,775

Source: Adapted from Reyhner and Eder (2004), 151.

place in the world," a senator from North Dakota opined, "then it seems to me the spending of money on them is more or less of a loss."[28] Integration into local public schools received an impetus, at least at the policy level, from the influential "Meriam Report" released the same year, which emphasized that "Indian children brought up in public schools with white children have the advantage of early contacts with whites while still retaining their connection with their own Indian family and home. This would seem to be a good thing for both sides."[29]

Given the long-standing principle that education was a state responsibility (virtually every state constitution so asserts, whereas the United States Constitution does not mention education at all), such arrangements were not only a bureaucratic headache but also legally anomalous. Increasingly, therefore, federal Indian Bureau officials preferred to deal with state education officials who, by the early decades of the twentieth century, were playing an increasingly active role in general. Finally, in 1934, Congress passed the Johnson-O'Malley Act, which authorized the Secretary of the Interior to contract with state and territorial governments to provide for educational and other services for Indians.

During the 1930s, there was a major effort by the American federal government to reach the large number of Indian children not attending school at all by enrolling them in existing public schools or by creating new government day schools on reservations. After a lull as a result of the distraction of the Second World War, the effort continued. On the Navajo Reservation, which had an especially low proportion of school attendance, by 1960–1961 there were 13,000 pupils in on-reservation boarding schools and border town programs, 6,000 in off-reservation boarding schools, 7,500 in reservation public schools, and another 3,500 in trailer, mission, and day schools, six times the number of students enrolled in 1939."[30]

Between 1930 and 1970, the proportion of Indian children attending local public schools in the United States—with the costs of this schooling subsidized by the federal government—increased from 53 to 65 percent, with the intention that the proportion would continue to increase as integration took hold and the isolation of reservation life was broken down. Starting in the 1950s the "Impact Aid" program, designed initially to assist public schools in areas impacted by military families living on non-taxable government property, was extended to schools serving Indian families in similar circumstances. By 1970, 129,000 Indian pupils were attending local public schools at partial federal expense, while only 51,000 attended schools operated by the federal government.[31] The process has continued: by 2007, 88–89 percent of Indian pupils in the United States were attending local public schools, 6–7 percent were attending Bureau of Indian Education schools, and the balance in private and religious schools.[32]

The same strategy of placing Indian pupils in local schools was officially adopted in Canada after the Second World War, based on a growing belief in integration but also on the conclusion that it would be cheaper to pay for the enrolment of Indian pupils in provincial public schools wherever proximity to Indian communities allowed. A legislative study in 1946 "proposed that wherever possible young Indians be schooled together with non-Indian children."[33]

> By 1951, the federal government had replaced the missionaries' authority with a perceived unlimited power to demand integrated education. In the 1951 revisions, parliament unilaterally terminated the chief's and band council's authority to frame rules and regulations for education, leaving the minister of Indian Affairs with the exclusive authority. The act, however, continued the religious affiliation of Indian schools and attendance and truancy provisions. In addition, the minister of Indian Affairs was authorized to enter into agreements with provincial and territorial governments for Indian education. Under these agreements, the federal government paid local school boards for Indian tuition, but the agreements did not confer rights of supervision over the curriculum, administration of teaching personnel, or methods or materials of instruction or management.[34]

The intention was that Indians be integrated into the national mainstream, and that their children be "encouraged to attend provincial schools or a private school run by one of the religious denominations that had previously operated federal residential and day schools. This had the financial advantage for the government of making it unnecessary to build its own secondary schools on the reservations, and for local public schools, this new arrangement "quickly became a 'cash cow',"[35] but Indian pupils were left at the mercy of educational administrators and teachers who usually had little experience with or interest in their needs. By 1961, 128 school contracts were in effect, and 15 years later there were 550. Although, in 1947, there were only 137 Indian children in public school classrooms, by 1961 there were 10,822, or 25 percent of school-aged Indians, and 40 percent were in local public schools by 1963.[36]

In Ontario, by 1968, about half of the Indian children were in schools operated by local boards rather than by the federal or mission organizations.[37] Two years earlier, a major study entitled *A Survey of the Contemporary Indians of Canada*, characterizing its recommendations as "essentially one special part of the government's war on poverty," recommended that Indians be encouraged to leave their reserves in order to take advantage of employment opportunities in the Canadian economy, and that "a large and increasing part of an expanded Indian Affairs Branch budget should be used to support Indians who wish to leave their reserves."[38]

There was a similar policy development in New Zealand in 1955.[39] In effect, in all three countries, native peoples were given the same status as that of immigrant minority groups.[40] This was the strategy recommended by Richard Henry Pratt in his autobiography, warning that

> If we had adopted the segregating Indian system for each language group of immigrants and held them in racial communities on reservations remote from the environment of our American life, it would have just as effectually prevented their Americanization. We have unlimited proof that Americanization is easily accomplished for hundreds of thousands of diverse-language immigrants yearly, and also ample evidence that it can just as readily be accomplished for our few Indians. . . . The great powers of schools, especially when located among the Indians and administratively utilized to that end, have easily become potential racial and tribal promoters of cohesion.[41]

"Cohesion" in this case denoted the separate group solidarity that Pratt deplored as leading inevitably to poverty and backwardness. The analogy with immigrants was by no means welcomed by all Native leaders in the three countries. Many insisted that, unlike immigrants, they had not voluntarily accepted a cultural and linguistic as well as geographical displacement, and that they had every right to remain separate and distinct.

The integration efforts did in general provide access for Indian children to better-resourced schools; in Canada, "as late as 1947 . . . the federal government was spending $45 a year per aboriginal pupil in a federal day school compared with about $200 that the British Columbia government allocated per pupil in a public school."[42] But attending local public schools did not necessarily lead to a better education. Catholic authorities asserted frequently that the education experience of Indian pupils in specialized Indian schools—many of which, of course, were Catholic—was better fitted to their needs than that available in local public schools, which could be indifferent or hostile to Indians and not focused on how best to help them make a transition to Canadian society. A Catholic spokesman warned, in 1958, that "instead of favouring the pupils['] acculturation towards our Canadian society, attendance at the non-Indian school will, on the contrary, add to his sense of separateness." There was considerable evidence that this was the case, at least in the short term. Catholic leaders claimed that "at recent meetings held [by the church] in the West a number of families had expressed a strong objection to sending their children to non-Indian schools" because their "children did not feel at ease among non-Indians." As a sign of this alienation, Indian pupils dropped out of school at a high rate, disproving the claim of federal officials that where integrated education had "taken hold, there [was] plenty of evidence to show that it [had] given impetus to education among the Indians and has helped to instill respect for the benefits of education among Indian children." As a result, "[a]boriginal political leaders . . . opposed integrated education because it was in many minds 'ill-equipped if not totally unprepared to cope with the special learning problems of native children'."[43]

This change of strategy also created the unintended consequence of an increased vulnerability to the ineptitude or ill will of local officials. As would happen later with the funding under the 1965 Elementary and Secondary Education Act, intended to benefit pupils from low-income families, the Johnson-O'Malley funds were often diverted by local school districts into their general revenues. In addition, the efforts that were under way at the federal level in the 1930s to give a larger role to Indian cultures and even languages in the instructional program were often not supported by local school authorities. "Without the protective federal involvement to maintain their unique status as sovereign domestic nations . . . American Indians were relegated to the same status as other American ethnic groups"[44] in a period when there was a strong emphasis on the assimilation of immigrant pupils to majority norms.

Just as the strategy of residential schools did not live up to its promise, so the emphasis on integration into local public schools proved to have significant shortcomings. Philleo Nash, an anthropologist and former U.S. Commissioner of Indian Affairs, reflecting in 1970 on the Rough Rock model of community-controlled schooling, told an interviewer that "the reason that Rough Rock was so long in coming, in my opinion, was obeisance to the public schools. It was thought that because Indian children were American citizens, they ought to be educated like other American children in a public school. . . . In the 1950s this policy was aggressively pursued in spite of the deterioration of the public schools." Unfortunately, he said, "Of all the ills afflicting the education of Indian children, few are being substantially corrected within the existing public schools." As a result, at the BIA, "[W]e began to take a close look at what was being done in some of the districts and concluded that we had better concentrate on improving the quality of education in our own federally operated schools."[45]

The failure of integration of Indian children into local school systems in the United States was asserted powerfully in 1969 by a Special Subcommittee on Indian Education of Congress, the so-called "Kennedy Report," which concluded that the "dominant policy of the Federal Government towards the American Indian had been one of coercive assimilation," and that this policy "has had disastrous effects on the education of Indian children. . . . Schools attended by Indian children have become a kind of battleground where the Indian child attempts to protect his integrity and identity as an individual by defeating the purposes of the school"; these schools have failed to "understand or adapt to, and in fact often denigrate, cultural differences"; the schools have blamed "their own failures on the Indian student," which reinforces his "defensiveness"; the schools have failed "to recognize the importance and vitality of the Indian community"; and the community and child have retaliated "by treating the school as an alien institution."[46]

The committee called for less coercive approaches to meeting the goal of assimilation, but it did not call that goal into question. Others, among the Indian leadership, were doing so, insisting that Indians were not simply another ethnic minority group but were sovereign nations under treaties made by the United States government during the period of westward expansion. Thus, in the words of a white supporter of Indian self-sufficiency, "American Indians only stand to lose by integration into the larger society."[47] In effect, counters a recent book that is highly critical of many aspects of current policy toward American Indians, "with little debate outside the parochial circles of Indian affairs, a generation of policymaking has jettisoned the long-standing American ideal of racial unity as a positive good and replaced it with a doctrine that, seen from a more critical angle, seems disturbingly like an idealized form of segregation, a fact apparently invisible in an era that has made a secular religion of passionate ethnicity."[48]

Economic realities have dictated that many Indian families now live in urban areas where they are in a small minority and, even if they seek out other Indians in churches and community organizations, those they associate with commonly have different tribal traditions. A study of Indian schoolchildren in Chicago in 1970 found that "[k]nowledge of their tribal language and culture was slight. . . . When asked whether they would like to speak their tribal language, three fourths expressed interest. On the other hand, most have no actual plans to do so."[49]

The same study, however, found that Indian youth in cities were more alienated from the majority culture than were those who are more isolated geographically.[50] The former group, in effect, may be alienated from *both* cultures. A study in 1969, in Minneapolis, found a disturbing pattern of adult Indian militants "bent upon persuading the young that education is not 'the Indian way' . . . viable alternative approaches to Indian education are not proposed by these militants, perhaps because they are not capable of doing so. The community of Indians in Minneapolis, then, is further divided on the issue of the meaning and importance of formal education to the American Indian."[51]

CHAPTER 15

Have We Learned Anything?

One thing should be clear from all this sad history: there is no satisfactory solution to the complicated problem of educating children considered by the dominant members of the society so *different* as to make them incapable of benefitting fully from the sort of education provided to children of the majority. It is not a question of resources only, or of technique, or of the structure of schooling, but more fundamentally of the whole enterprise of "minority education." Inevitably, such education, even with the best of intentions, is a preparation to occupy (and to internalize) a separate and inferior position. As a result, public schools, which Horace Mann and his allies saw as "the great equalizers of the conditions of men," have been reproducers and confirmers of inequality for Indian pupils for many decades. Some schools have subtracted rather than added value, and have sent Indian youth out into the world *less* competent and less capable of learning life's lessons than they would have been without such schooling.

This is not to call for a "one-size-fits-all" education. Some pedagogical strategies are especially effective with pupils from one sort of background, with one set of childhood experiences, or with a particular set of interests and abilities. There is growing evidence that a flourishing diversity of approaches, determined at the school level in response to immediate challenges, while informed by the shared experience of networks of schools that are committed to particular methods of instruction and school organization, is what is needed to confront the problems of educating poor children well.[1]

Some advocates for the education of Indians in the United States and in Canada insist that the answer is to provide "Indian education," schools controlled by tribal authorities and placing a strong emphasis on a distinctive Indian understanding of the goals of education. From this perspective, the problem with the earlier separate schooling was not that it was separate but that it was under the control of non-Indians.

In effect, this position is consonant with the call, over recent decades, for Afro-centric schooling and for black community control of schools in black residential areas.[2] As with Afro-centric schools, the outcomes of Indian-controlled schools with respect to the competencies required for successful participation in North American societies have been decidedly mixed. The American Indian Public Charter School in Oakland, California, for example, attempted to place a strong emphasis on tribal culture and arts, but with disastrous academic results that were only reversed when the school abandoned its cultural emphasis and focused strongly on academic effort.

AIPCS was founded in 1996 to "integrate [Indian] culture in all subjects. Students will be involved in various ethnic-related projects from planting crops and learning traditional cooking to Native American storytelling and researching their individual tribes. Other activities students will participate in include pottery, making musical instruments, basket-weaving, and cultural art." Educationally, it was a disaster, "a caricature of almost everything that can go wrong with a parent-driven, multicultural school. . . . Student achievement was pitiful," and enrolment had dwindled down to 27. Then a new principal was appointed, a Lumbee Indian from North Carolina who grew up poor but became a successful businessman. Ben Chavis "eliminated every multicultural offering, requiring instead that students have a minimum of three hours of English language arts and math each morning that followed state-adopted textbooks, step-for-step." Just as important, he created a strong sense of community and commitment to the students, almost all of them poor and many from disrupted homes. Measured achievement shot up, and AIPCS "is currently the highest performing middle school in the Oakland area," with its students scoring far above the statewide goals on the California Academic Performance Index. Every tenth grader passed the California high school exit exam on the first try, though half of those in Alameda county failed to do so. There are now about 700 students in middle and high schools operated by AIPCS.[3]

There are many other examples of both public and private schools serving at-risk students that have abandoned the racial essentialism that calls for distinctive educational approaches based on the assumption that Indian (or black or Latino) pupils are somehow fundamentally different from other youth and have instead insisted on high expectations, while providing the consistent support and constant encouragement that are necessary for at-risk youth to meet those expectations. What these schools have in common is that they are free from the constraints of bureaucracy with its pressure to implement a one-size-fits-all model of instruction, and that they refuse to hide behind—or let their students hide behind—excuses for why they cannot be expected to achieve. In other respects, in instructional methods and the structuring of school life, they differ greatly.

Education policy-makers should abandon, once and for all, the harmful illusion that the diversity to which schooling should respond is a diversity defined by *race*. Attempts to define the appropriate education for *all* Indians have been profoundly misguided. This has been true even when those attempts have been motivated by the most benevolent and sympathetic intentions. They rest, finally, on a form of racial essentialism, the assumption that the differences "go all the way down" and that it is possible to generalize about members of those groups on the basis of what is, finally, an ascribed identity.

There was, after all, no common "Indian" identity three or four generations ago, except as a way for white Americans and Canadians to lump together peoples whose languages, belief-systems, traditions, and ways of life have been, for many centuries, enormously dissimilar. The emergence of an "Indian" identity has been in reaction to white aggressions and—as we have seen—was greatly fostered by the residential schools, so much criticized today, that brought together Indians from different peoples and ways of life and imposed on them a common language, English or French. While there are many organizations, today, that include "American Indian" in their names, it is fair to say that this is essentially an invented identity, like "Latino" for individuals deriving from 20 and more different national traditions, or "Asian" for individuals who do not even share a common language, much less culture and history.

To say that an identity has been invented does not, of course, mean that it is insignificant or inauthentic, but that its significance and authenticity are derived from those who embrace it. Contemporary "Indian" identity is not the sum total of Cherokee and Hopi and Cree and Sioux and 200 other traditions and cultures, or their lowest common denominator, but something new, drawing upon elements of those traditions for symbolic purposes, to be sure, but doing so primarily as a way of asserting a common project *over against* the white majority. It is an invention—no disparagement is meant by this word—of activists for what they perceive as common Indian interests, which means essentially benefits to be demanded as a matter of right from the government.

As an instrument of political mobilization and leverage, it could not be expected that this recently minted Indian identity would penetrate deeply among two million Americans and Canadians who are Indian by descent. For those who live on reserves or reservations, the tribal identity is surely predominant; for those—more all the time—who live in cities, even that may grow faint. In the National Assessment of Education Progress in 2007, pupils in the United States who were identified by their schools as Indian were less likely to report that they were Indian than were pupils of other groups to agree with the schools about their own racial/ethnic identity. More than one in four of the fourth graders and nearly one in five of the eighth graders identified as Indian by their schools did not volunteer that identity, indicating that Indian identity may be rather weakly held, at least for those not living on reservations. Of those who did identify as Indian, less than half could give the name of their tribes.[4]

One of the results of the dispersal of Indian families into urban areas across North American has been the attempt to substitute a generic "Indian" culture for the different—and often very different—tribal cultures. This was evident in Bielenberg's study of an urban charter school that served pupils from more than 30 different tribal groups:

> For the director, parents, and teachers involved with this school this means inserting American Indian literature, cultural studies, and history into the curriculum. While the content is different from what is taught in most public schools, there is little evidence that other aspects of the structure of schooling has [sic] changed to better meet the needs of the children. Culturally appropriate curriculum has been defined as a curriculum that "uses materials that link traditional or cultural knowledge originating in Native home life and community to the curriculum of the school". . . . But what happens when your students come from a variety of tribal backgrounds and range from traditional to highly assimilated? This is certainly a major issue in urban settings such as the one observed in this study, and it is likely to be an issue even in some of the fairly isolated Pueblos of the Southwest. There is no idealized, homogenous group of Indian children, especially in urban areas. The charter school at which Bernita teaches has chosen to deal with this problem by incorporating a sort of Pan-Indian curriculum that can be applied to anyone who attends the charter school. Rather than originating in the home, the concepts for the curriculum are strongly driven by the understanding of Indian culture of the director and teachers of the charter school.[5]

Continuing to emphasize generic "Indian" separateness detached from specific tribal identities and cultures benefits the virtuosi of identity, those who make it their business to be accepted as ethnic leaders or spokesmen. We can see a parallel among immigrant groups in the United States: a new type of leadership emerged in the 1920s, less concerned with maintaining traditions and more with mobilizing members to exert political pressure "to maximize material and social gains in the larger society."[6] Such ethnic leaders may seek to maintain the distinct ethnic community that is the basis of their status, and characteristics (especially language) that keep it separate, even if that cuts their followers off from successful participation in the host society. Those working in the ethnic media, or in cultural and mutual-support organizations, or in ethnic political pressure groups, have a direct stake in the continuing existence of a distinct minority community. Becoming expert in "the manipulation of the symbolic, the instrumental, and the affective," they may themselves achieve a high level of participation in the host society while depending on the continued existence of a group of followers who are precisely not integrated.[7] Ironically, they tend themselves to be thoroughly bicultural, while sometimes resisting measures that would enable members of the groups for whom they speak to achieve the same competence. Teachers in programs designed for minority children, social workers and community organizers, ethnic elected and appointed officials, professors and researchers specializing in minority cultures and languages, and leaders in advocacy groups may seek (as they might put it) to "develop community awareness and separate identity through various forms of consciousness raising," though themselves are entirely capable of functioning in the host society.

The situation is much more serious when it comes to those who claim to speak for Indians in the United States and Canada, because the demand for special treatment is often made not only on the basis of a deprived condition but also on what is represented to be a racially based and significantly distinct mode of functioning that only the racial virtuoso understands and can prescribe for. This has the effect of reviving the assumptions about fundamental racial differences that have been so profoundly harmful to the education of Indian youth. Caution is essential in forming generalizations about the ways in which Indian pupils in general (a category which is meaningless) learn, or the pedagogies and forms of school organization that are best suited to their needs. It is time to listen to the warnings uttered by Miller on the basis of a detailed study of residential schools for Indians in Canada.

> First, the root of the problem with residential schools was not religious instruction, inadequate teaching, insufficient vocational training, or any other specific feature of the schools' operation. The essence of the problem was the assumption of Euro-Canadians—churches, governments, people—that they, because of their racial superiority to Aboriginal people, *knew better* than the Native communities and their leaders what was in the best interest of those dependent groups. Is that attitude dead? Or has it been transmuted into something apparently different though fundamentally the same? The second cautionary note concerns recent events that show that the we-know-best-what's-good-for-you attitude is still alive and kicking.[8]

Surely the time has come to recognize that individual Indians and Indian families will make different choices about how they confront the twenty-first century. The United States and Canada should implement public policies that as far as possible are neutrally supportive of any choices that are not harmful to children. It is possible to predict to some extent what these choices are likely to be.

For many families of Indian ancestry, especially those living in cities or in off-reservation rural areas, that identity is likely to become more and more residual, as Richard Alba, Mary Waters, and others have shown in their studies of ethnicity in America. Tribal languages will be lost, apart perhaps from a few phases of greeting, and cultural elements will become residual. The educational policy priority for the children of these families should be effective instruction and support, leading to successful participation in the wider society and economy and avoiding marginalization, not "Indian education."

For others, probably a smaller number, it seems likely that tribal identity will continue to be salient or in fact be reclaimed, either as a central life-project leading to some degree of separation from the mainstream of American and Canadian society, or as an important supplement to participation in that society. Education policy *should respect this choice*, and make it possible for those families to choose publicly funded schools that have a distinct tribal character and—if this is what parents want—promote competence in an Indian language. So long as such schools are accountable for ensuring that their pupils acquire the knowledge and skills essential to effective adulthood in the wider society, a pluralistic nation should support the choice of parents to provide for their children an education based upon a distinctive worldview.

This suggestion is consistent with the findings of Batchelder's survey of Navajo adults about whether and to what extent Navajo language and culture should be a component of the instruction provided in schools. She found a wide range of opinions, with some wishing them excluded completely, others insisting that the maintenance of language and culture should be a central mission of the schools, and every variation in between, leading to her conclusion that "if the Navajo Nation is to continue to rely on schools to help preserve its linguistic and cultural heritage, then more than one model of how to make this partnership successful needs to be acknowledged."[9] If this is true for those living on the largest reservation, it is presumably even more so for the hundreds of thousands of Indians who have chosen off-reservation life.

The *Universal Declaration of Human Rights* (1948) asserts that "[p]arents have a prior right to choose the kind of education that shall be given to their children," a principle that had already been affirmed by the United States Supreme Court in *Pierce v. Society of Sisters*, 268 U.S. 510 (1925). It is time that this principle be applied to the education of those Indian children whose parents wish an education informed by ancestral perspectives, as indeed to all families whose religious convictions call for a distinctive education, subject always to protection of the child's right to an effective preparation for adult responsibilities.

Charter schools, the independent public schools authorized in most states and in Alberta, are one vehicle for providing an education that responds directly to the educational concerns of parents, including in some cases a concern for help in passing on a distinctive language and culture to their children. Culture, rightly understood, is almost invariably rooted in religious perspectives that should normally be made explicit—without seeking to proselytize—as part of education. Unfortunately, the legal conditions under which most charter schools operate in the United States push them toward the sort of superficial engagement with culture—whether Indian or mainstream—described in the case of the urban charter school studied by Bielenberg.

As we have seen repeatedly in the course of this narrative, it has often been schools sponsored by religious organizations that have provided an alternative to the homogenizing effects of government sponsored schools, an alternative respectful of native language and culture. Because these faith-based schools have been dependent on voluntary participation and sometimes on financial support from the Indian peoples they have served, the forms in which they have incorporated local language and culture have usually been based on what was demanded by families, not on the prescriptions of anthropologists and curriculum theorists.

This leads to the final suggestion, that a long-overdue correction of America's exclusion of faith-based schools from public funding, either as charter schools or through a wider availability of educational vouchers, would make it possible to provide schooling to Indian youth in a rich variety of modes responsive to the great diversity among Indian families, culturally, linguistically, and in what they want for their children.

Notes

Introduction

1. Statistics from nas_http://nces.ed.gov/nationsreportcard/nies/nies_2009/sum_02.asp.

Chapter 1

1. http://www.census.gov/prod/cen2010/briefs/c2010br-02.pdf.
2. Bordewich (1997), 55.
3. DeJong (1993), 195.
4. www12.statcan.gc.ca/english/census06/data/topics/RetrieveProductTable.cfm?ALEVEL=3&APATH=3&CATNO=97-555-XCB2006057&DETA, accessed February 17, 2009.
5. Friesen and Friesen (2005), 15–16.
6. Milloy (1999), 305.
7. Friesen and Friesen (2005), 21.
8. Stancavage and others (2006), 9.
9. National Center for Education Statistics (2008b), 14, (2005), 38–41.
10. Fuchs and Havighurst (1983), 158.
11. National Center for Education Statistics (2005), 50–63, 66; (2008a), 8–10.
12. Battiste (1995), xii.
13. Mackay and Myles (1995), 158.
14. Cummins (1997), 418.
15. National Center for Education Statistics (2008b), 8.

Chapter 2

1. King (1981), 111.
2. See, for example, Cantor (1963); Cohn (1970); Desmond and Moore (2009); Dyer (1980); Frederickson (1987); Jordan (1969); Newby (1965); and Ruchames (1970).
3. Vanderwerth (1971).
4. Jordan (1969), 239.
5. In Miller (1996), 40.

6. Jefferson (1984), 266; Jordan (1969), 477–78.
7. Morant (1958), 38.
8. Desmond and Moore (2009), 154.
9. Gossett (1965), 237.
10. Lomawaima and McCarty (2006), 45.
11. Parsons (1973), 357.
12. In Reyhner and Eder (2004), 45.
13. Tocqueville (2000), 312–13.
14. In Handlin (1959), 33.
15. Gossett (1965), 243–44.
16. Barman, Hébert, and McCaskill (1986b), 4, 8.
17. Handlin (1959), 35.
18. Bordewich (1997), 54.
19. In Miller (1996), 187.
20. Gossett (1965), 240, 242.
21. Desmond and Moore (2009), 93, 161, 375, 289.
22. Lyons (1975) 57, 87, 89, 93, 110.
23. Jordan (1969), 478.
24. In Grant (2008), 300.

Chapter 3

1. Jaenen (1986), 46.
2. In Miller (1996), 39, 47.
3. In Szasz (2007), 53–54.
4. Salisbury (1974), 29; Pratt (2004), 272.
5. In Jaenen (1986), 47.
6. Ibid., 46–59.
7. Handlin (1959), 27.
8. Szasz (2007), 259.
9. Naeher (1989), 346.
10. Van Lonkhuyzen (1990), 396.
11. Salisbury (1974), 31.
12. In Naeher (1989), 361.
13. Szasz (2007), 126.
14. In Salisbury (1974), 47.
15. Monaghan (1990), 508.
16. Simmons (1979), 214.
17. Monaghan (1990), 496.
18. Ibid., 499.
19. Bushnell (1953), 208, 218.
20. Van Lonkhuyzen (1990), 406.
21. Tanis (1970), 316–17.
22. Van Lonkhuyzen (1990), 409–10.

23. Naeher (1989), 355–56.
24. Szasz (2007), 127.
25. Thomas (1975), 8.
26. Szasz (2007), 58, 104, 54.
27. Ibid., 67, 259.
28. Ibid., 185, 191.
29. Ibid., 185.
30. Lindquist (1944), 113.
31. Szasz (2007), 218–30.
32. In Bordewich (1997), 280.
33. In Miller (1996), 51.
34. See Hamilton (1975), 36–45.
35. Wilson (1986), 66.

Chapter 4

1. In McLoughlin (1993), 376–77.
2. Reyhner (1992), 42.
3. Miller (1996), 97–99.
4. In Prucha (2000), 91.
5. Ibid., 103–4.
6. In Adams (1995), 15.
7. Milloy (1999), 11–12.
8. Flanagan (2000), 120–21.
9. In Parsons (1973), 344.
10. In Milloy (1999), 11, 14.
11. In Prucha (1970), 214.
12. Trafzer, Keller, and Sisquoc (2006), 8.
13. In Prucha (1970), 37.
14. Ibid., 39.
15. Reyhner and Eder (2004), 41.
16. Adams (1995), 6.
17. In McLoughlin (1986), 33.
18. Engs (1999), 125.
19. In DeJong (1993), 38–39.
20. Ibid., 41.
21. Trafzer, Keller, and Sisquoc (2006), 10.
22. McLoughlin (1986), 207.
23. In Prucha (1970), 225.
24. Ibid., 224.
25. In Prucha (2000), 57.
26. Ibid., 72–73.
27. In McLoughlin (1986), 449.
28. Miller (1996), 77.

29. Wilson (1986), 71–72.
30. In Milloy (1999), 17–18.
31. Flanagan (2000), 45.
32. Reyhner and Eder (2004), 36.
33. Henderson (1995), 248–50.
34. Milloy (1999), 6.
35. Wilson (1986), 75.
36. Blair and Fredeen (1995), 35.
37. Flanagan (2000), 72–73.

Chapter 5

1. McLoughlin (1993), 87–88.
2. McLoughlin (1986), 16–17.
3. Mihesuah (1998), 10, 7.
4. McLoughlin (1986), 337–38.
5. Ibid., 31.
6. Ibid., 328, 67, 169, 173.
7. Ibid., 355.
8. Szasz (2006), 193.
9. Mihesuah (1998), 16.
10. McLoughlin (1986), 335.
11. Ibid., 314.
12. Bordewich (1997), 41.
13. In DeJong (1993), 95.
14. Szasz (2006), 192.
15. Mihesuah (1998), 18–19, 46.
16. Ibid., 46, 21.
17. Ibid., 46.
18. Ibid., 22, 5.
19. Ibid., 22.
20. Ibid., 27.
21. In ibid., 81, 80.
22. Ibid., 82–83.
23. In McLoughlin (1993), 93.
24. Ibid., 95.
25. Mihesuah (1998), 105–6.
26. Ibid., 107–9.
27. In Dyer (1980), 71.
28. McLoughlin (1993), 95.
29. Ibid., 125.
30. DeJong (1993), 92.
31. Sizer (1964), 34.
32. Szasz (2006), 193–95.

33. Mihesuah (1998), 48, 110.
34. Leupp (1910), 332, 335.
35. Leupp (1914), 47–48.
36. In DeJong (1993), 101.
37. Szasz (2006).
38. McLoughlin (1993), 376.
39. DeJong (1993), 87.
40. Fuchs and Havighurst (1983), 130.

Chapter 6

1. Ellis (2006), 77.
2. In Prucha (1976), 281.
3. Daily (2004), 17.
4. Rayman (1981), 396.
5. DeJong (1993), 59.
6. McLoughlin (1986), 76.
7. Rayman (1981), 398–400.
8. McLoughlin (1986), 73; see Schutt (1998).
9. Prucha (1970), 219.
10. In Prucha (2000), 33.
11. In Mitchell and Skelton (1966), 41.
12. Reyhner and Eder (2004), 43.
13. Prucha (1970), 220.
14. In Reyhner and Eder (2004), 44.
15. Lomawaima (1994), 2.
16. In Prucha (1970), 221.
17. Ibid., 233n.
18. Wilson (1986), 67–69.
19. Milloy (1999), 14, 17.
20. Friesen and Friesen (2005), 75.
21. Lipka and McCarty (1994), 273.
22. McLoughlin (1986), 248.
23. Ibid., 433–37.
24. Ibid., 249.
25. Brown (1996), 170.
26. Prucha (1970), 222.
27. McLoughlin (1986), 423, 440.
28. Parsons (1973), 339–40, 356–57.
29. In DeJong (1993), 65.
30. Rayman (1981), 398–400.
31. In DeJong (1993), 42.
32. In Prucha (1970), 246.
33. In Reyhner and Eder (2004), 50.

34. Ibid., 53.
35. McLoughlin (1986), 365–65.
36. McLoughlin (1993), 91.
37. In Prucha (2000), 63.
38. Prucha (1976), 32.
39. Hoxie (2001a), 3.
40. In McLoughlin (1993), 249.
41. Garland (1970), 51, 110.
42. In Prucha (2000), 105.
43. Ellis (1996), 30–31.
44. Ibid., 35.
45. In ibid., 6.
46. In Prucha (2000), 111.
47. In McCarty (2002), 23.
48. Ellis (1996), 36.
49. In Prucha (2000), 132.
50. Adams (1995), 8.
51. In Prucha (2000), 123.
52. In ibid., 124.
53. DeJong (1993), 35.
54. Reyhner and Eder (2004), 68.
55. In Prucha (2000), 156.
56. In Mitchell and Skelton (1966), 42–43.
57. DeJong (1993), 272.
58. Coleman (1987), 475.
59. Prucha (1976), 290–91.
60. In Prucha (2000), 163.
61. In Miller (1996), 103.
62. Ashworth (1979), 16.
63. Milloy (1999), 53–55.
64. Ibid., 56.
65. Coates (1986), 133–36, 141, 145.

Chapter 7

1. Hoxie (2001a), 43, 148.
2. Mitchell and Skelton (1966), 42.
3. Reyhner and Eder (2004), 73.
4. Mitchell and Skelton (1966), 43–44.
5. Adams (1995), 321.
6. Pratt (2004), 273.
7. DeJong (1993), 74.
8. In ibid., 73.
9. Ibid., 76–77; Reyhner and Eder (2004), 86.

10. See Bendroth (1999).
11. Prucha (1976), 307.
12. In Adams (1995), 27.
13. In Prucha (1976), 313.
14. Mitchell and Skelton (1966), 51.
15. DeJong (1993), 79.
16. In Mitchell and Skelton (1966), 44.
17. In ibid., 47.
18. In ibid., 45.
19. Green (1980), 373; DeJong (1993), 75.
20. DeJong (1993), 81.
21. In ibid., 81.
22. Rathbun (2006), 156–57.
23. Leupp (1910), 297.
24. In DeJong (1993), 85.
25. Reyhner and Eder (2004), 89.
26. In DeJong (1993), 154.
27. Holst (1944), 103.
28. Lindquist (1944), 135.
29. Daily (2004), 66, 69.
30. Miller (1996), 123.
31. Barman (1995), 71.
32. Milloy (1999), 307, 220, 234.
33. Battiste (1995).
34. McCarty (2002), 92.
35. In Goodluck, Lockard, and Yazzie (2000), 13.
36. Milloy (1999), 235.
37. Green (1980), 374.
38. Daily (2004), 106, 25.
39. Ashworth (1979), 34.
40. In Hoxie (2001b), 95–96.
41. Samuel A. Eliot in Lindquist (1944), 116.
42. Leupp (1910), 30–31.

Chapter 8

1. Wesley (1957), 126.
2. Goffman (1961).
3. Szasz (2006), 188.
4. Barman (1995), 57.
5. In Cummins (1997), 417.
6. Milloy (1999), xiv, xvii.
7. Barman (1995), 73.
8. Cummins (1997), 418.

9. Adams (1995).
10. DeJong (1993), ix.
11. See Glenn (1988).
12. Lomawaima and McCarty (2006), 47.
13. Trafzer, Keller, and Sisquoc (2006), 1.
14. Gresko (1986), 88–89.
15. Mihesuah (1998), 111.
16. Lomawaima (1994), 71.
17. Reyhner and Eder (2004), 200.
18. Gresko (1979), 102.
19. Szasz (2006), 197.
20. Miller (1996), 430.
21. Milloy (1999), 24.
22. Owen (1992), 41.
23. Lindquist (1944), 119.
24. Lomawaima (1994), 33.
25. Ashworth (1979), 37–38.
26. In Wilson (1986), 72.
27. Adams (1995), 29–30.
28. Milloy (1999), 13, 17.
29. In Ellis (1996), 13.
30. In Milloy (1999), 25, 27.
31. Ellis (1996), xii.
32. Ashworth (1979), 4–5.
33. Ibid., 11–14, 16.
34. In Barman (1995), 59.
35. Reyhner and Eder (2004), 71.
36. Ashworth (1979), 17.
37. John Collier, Jr., in Fuchs and Havighurst (1983), 203.
38. Trafzer, Keller, and Sisquoc (2006), 12.
39. Adams (1995), 142, 118–19.
40. Miller (1996), 203.
41. Titley (1993), 372.
42. McLoughlin (1993), 319.
43. Adams (1995), 45.
44. Engs (1999), 118–23.
45. Washington (1965), 77.
46. Spack (2002), 59.
47. Engs (1999), 128.
48. Adams (1995), 327.
49. Reyhner and Eder (2004), 134.
50. Pratt (2004), 213.
51. Ibid., 5.
52. Adams (1995), 51.

53. Bordewich (1997), 282.
54. Adams (1995), 53.
55. Pratt (2004), 259, 265.
56. Utley (2004), xxi.
57. Lomawaima (1994), 18.
58. Reyhner and Eder (2004), 138–39.
59. Pratt (2004), 311.
60. Leupp (1910), 122–23.
61. Adams (2004), xiii.
62. Reyhner and Eder (2004), 73.
63. In DeJong (1993), 109.
64. Milloy (1999), 16.
65. In Wilson (1986), 76.
66. Miller (1996), 83.
67. Titley (1993), 372–74.
68. Milloy (1999), 7.
69. In Titley (1993), 379.
70. In Gresko (1979), 95.
71. Miller (1996), 171.
72. Lomawaima (1994), 150.
73. Miller (1996), 203.
74. Adams (2006), 49.
75. See Jenkins (2007).
76. Adams (1995), 255, 266.
77. Ellis (2006), 66–68.
78. Miller (1996), 341.
79. Adams (1995), 59, 63.

Chapter 9

1. In Fuchs and Havighurst (1983), 223.
2. In Miller (1996), 126.
3. Milloy (1999), 66.
4. Ibid., xiv, 103.
5. Ibid., 162.
6. In Barman (1995), 65.
7. Ibid., 68.
8. Lindquist (1944), 120.
9. In Barman (1995), 69.
10. Milloy (1999), 162–63.
11. Ibid., 131–33.
12. In ibid., 51, 77.
13. In Hoxie (2001a), 195–96.
14. Titley (1986), 136–37.

15. In Milloy (1999), 67.
16. Allen (1970), 102.
17. In Spack (2002), 101.
18. McKay and McKay (1987), 67.
19. Ellis (1996), 96–97.
20. Reyhner and Eder (2004), 233–34.
21. James (1988), 614.
22. In Jaenen (1986), 58.
23. Trafzer, Keller, and Sisquoc (2006), 16, 28.
24. Lomawaima (1994), 34.
25. In Adams (1995), 260.
26. In Milloy (1999), 157.
27. In Jaenen (1986), 50.
28. In McLoughlin (1986), 352.
29. Milloy (1999), 158.
30. In ibid., 159.
31. In Adams (1995), 285, 277, 291.
32. In Adams (2004), xv.
33. In Prucha (2000), 199.
34. Coates (1986), 136.
35. Leupp (1910), 119.
36. Adams (1995), 300.
37. Wilson (1986), 83.
38. In Miller (1996), 379.
39. In Reyhner and Eder (2004), 194.
40. Barman (1986), 126.
41. Reyhner and Eder (2004), 201–2.
42. Adams (1995), 300–1.
43. Szasz (1999), 76.
44. Lindquist (1944), 145.
45. Spack (2002), 90.
46. Adams (2006), 45.
47. In Reyhner and Eder (2004), 91.
48. Kluckhohn and Leighton (1962), 141.
49. Wilson (1986), 64.
50. Gresko (1986), 102.
51. Trafzer, Keller, and Sisquoc (2006), 3.
52. Peshkin (1997), 104–5.
53. Ibid., 113.
54. Ibid., 114.
55. Titley (1992), 67.
56. Barman, Hébert, and McCaskill (1986b), 12.
57. In Ellis (2006), 90.
58. Ellis (1996), 180.

59. Hoxie (2001b), 171.
60. Fuchs and Havighurst (1983), 242.
61. Spack (2002), 173.
62. Pratt (2004), 303.
63. Fuchs and Havighurst (1983), 13.
64. In Szasz (1999), 109.
65. Riney (2006), 136.
66. Dixon and Trafzer (2006), 234.
67. Milloy (1999), 190, 214.
68. Fuchs and Havighurst (1983), 81.

Chapter 10

1. Lomawaima (1994), 86.
2. In DeJong (1993), 135.
3. In Lomawaima and McCarty (2002), 286–87.
4. In Prucha (2000), 221.
5. In Szasz (1999), 23.
6. In DeJong (1993), 141.
7. In Lomawaima (1994), 31.
8. In Kelly (1983), 228.
9. In Daily (2004), 48.
10. Ibid., 44.
11. In Kelly (1983), 272.
12. Hoxie (2001a), 99.
13. Daily (2004), 47, 49.
14. In Fuchs and Havighurst (1983), 13.
15. Szasz (1999), 107.
16. In McCarty (2002), 55–56.
17. Daily (2004), 151.
18. In McCarty (2002), 61.
19. In Milloy (1999), 6.
20. Adams (1995), 17.
21. Henderson (1995), 254.
22. Flanagan (2000), 166.
23. Adams (1995), 297.
24. Flanagan (2000), 170.
25. Seymour (1944), 59–60.
26. See account in Daily (2004), 80–100.
27. Daily (2004), 83, 85.
28. Seymour (1944), 64.
29. Duchs and Havighurst (1983), 35.
30. Persson (1986), 160.
31. Miller (1996), 391.

32. Bashford and Heinzerling (1987), 128.
33. In Ashworth (1979), 43.
34. Battiste (1995), x.
35. Barman, Hébert, and McCaskill (1987), 7.
36. Reyhner and Eder (2004), 321.
37. Flanagan (2000), 5.
38. Ibid., 97, 101, 103.
39. Ibid., 173–75.
40. Ibid., 177.
41. Friesen and Friesen (2005), 25.
42. In Dyer (1980), 81.
43. Daily (2004), 33, 39.
44. In Fuchs and Havighurst (1983), 321.
45. Lindquist (1944), 15.
46. Flanagan (2000), 99, 195–96.
47. In Lomawaima and McCarty (2002), 298.
48. Szasz (1999), 113.
49. Prucha (2000), 254.
50. In ibid., 255.
51. DeJong (1993), 211.
52. National Center for Education Statistics (2005), 82.
53. In Prucha (2000), 255.
54. Battiste (1986), 36.
55. Persson (1986), 165.
56. Barman, Hébert, and McCaskill (1986), 15.
57. Miller (1996), 402.
58. Cardinal, quoted by Barman, Hébert, and McCaskill (1986), 15.
59. Barman, Hébert, and McCaskill (1986), 15.
60. In Ashworth (1979), 43.
61. In ibid., 43.
62. In Barman, Hébert, and McCaskill (1987), 2.
63. Birch (1989), 175.
64. Longboat (1987), 25.
65. In Longboat (1987), 29.
66. Hampton (1995), 37.
67. Prucha (2000), 316.

Chapter 11

1. Fishman (2001b), 5.
2. Crystal (2000), 121.
3. Blair and Fredeen (1995), 31.
4. Bunge (1992), 377.

5. Crawford (1995), 19, 18.
6. McCarty (2002), 179–80; McCarty (2003), 148.
7. McAlpine and Herodier (1994), 129.
8. National Center for Education Statistics (2005), 78.
9. Stancavage and others (2006), 17.
10. Spack (2002), 4.
11. Miller (1996), 68.
12. McLaughlin (1989), 282–84.
13. Lindquist (1944), 118.
14. Murdoch (1985), 520.
15. Jaenen (1986), 54.
16. Murdoch (1985), 518–19.
17. Spolsky and Holm (1971), 64.
18. Barrington (1991), 310.
19. Battiste (1986), 75.
20. Wilson (1986), 71.
21. Spack (2002), 7, 18, 50, 80.
22. Reyhner and Eder (2004), 78–79, 58.
23. McLoughlin (1993), 317.
24. Spolsky (2004), 203.
25. Persson (1986), 159.
26. Van Lonkhuyzen (1990), 424.
27. In Wilson (1986), 82; in this spirit, the Wycliffe Bible Translators (www.wycliffe.org) work around the world producing scripture portions in hundreds of indigenous languages.
28. Miller (1996), 84–85.
29. McLoughlin (1993), 236.
30. In Prucha (2000), 106.
31. In Reyhner and Eder (2004), 74.
32. Prucha (1976), 284.
33. Spack (2002), 19, 28–29.
34. Prucha (1976), 25.
35. McLoughlin (1993), 87–89.
36. Reyhner and Eder (2004), 76.
37. Quoted by Leibowitz (1971), 3.
38. Reyhner and Eder (2004), 76.
39. In Prucha (1976), 285–86.
40. In Prucha (2000), 173.
41. In Reyhner and Eder (2004), 77.
42. In Spack (2002), 33–34.
43. Ibid., 35.
44. Prucha (1976), 287–88.
45. Milloy (1999), 38.
46. Ibid., 183, 185.

47. Gresko (1986), 97.
48. Miller (1996), 199.
49. Szasz (1999), 12.
50. Persson (1986), 155, 158.
51. Gresko (1986), 93–94.
52. McAlpine, Brophy, and Crago (1996), 395.
53. Ellis (1996), 133.
54. Ibid., 151.
55. Hoxie (2001a), 163.
56. Szasz (1999), 71, 73.
57. Reyhner and Eder (2004), 97; Ellis (1996), 150.
58. Adams (1995), 313–14; Gossett (1965), 155.
59. Reyhner and Eder (2004), 100.
60. Dewey (1966), 232, 342.
61. In McCarty (2002), 75.
62. Ellis (1996), 147.
63. Lomawaima and McCarty (2006), 71.
64. In Reyhner and Eder (2004), 7.
65. Szasz (1999), 32.
66. Holst (1944), 104.
67. Szasz (1999), 78, 80.
68. Reyhner and Eder (2004), 207.
69. In DeJong (1993), 135.
70. Leupp (1910), 126.
71. James (1988), 602.
72. Collier (1983), xvi.
73. Reyhner and Eder (2004), 214.
74. Szasz (1999), 101.
75. Collier (1983), xii–xiii.
76. See Kelly (1983), 32–101, 103.
77. Garland (1970), 57.
78. Ibid., 81, 412–13.
79. Bordewich (1997), 71–72.
80. Kelly (1983), 98.
81. Daily (2004), 5.
82. Lindquist (1944), 16.
83. In ibid., 142.
84. Szasz (1999), 44–45.
85. Reyhner and Eder (2004), 228–29.
86. James (1988), 602, 605.
87. In Kelly (1983), 133.
88. Reyhner and Eder (2004), 128; Daily (2004), 11, 60.
89. Lindquist (1944), 79–80.
90. Daily (2004), 77–78.

91. In Battiste (1987), 122.
92. 921 F.2d 1055.

Chapter 12

1. Spolsky and Holm (1971), 63.
2. Reyhner and Eder (2004), 224.
3. Boyce (1974), 97.
4. Holst (1944), 108.
5. McCarty (2002), 60.
6. Reyhner and Eder (2004), 225.
7. Lee and McLaughlin (2001), 25.
8. James (1988), 613.
9. Bauer (1971), 30.
10. Bauer (1970), 224.
11. Fuchs and Havighurst (1983), 266–67.
12. McCarty (2002), 67.
13. Collier (1988), 257.
14. Ibid., 258.
15. In Erickson and Schwartz (1969), 1.3.
16. Fuchs and Havighurst (1983), 42, writing in the early 1970s, report the same phenomenon of other Indian schools being the major source of employment in their areas, and one may infer from their account a similar "mission creep."
17. Reyhner and Eder (2004), 263.
18. McCarty (2002), 83, 131, 89.
19. Ibid., 88.
20. Ibid., 83.
21. Ibid., 52.
22. Spolsky (1982), 147.
23. See Glenn with de Jong (1996).
24. Erickson and Schwartz (no date), 1.
25. McCarty (2002), 115.
26. In ibid., 102.
27. Ibid., 108.
28. Erickson and Schwartz (1969), 3.54–55.
29. McCarty (2002), 84, 106–7.
30. Erickson (1970a), 78; Erickson and Schwartz (1970), 31; Reyhner and Eder (2004), 266.
31. Schwartz (1969), 5.19n.
32. In Reyhner and Eder (2004), 264.
33. Erickson (1970a), 80.
34. Ibid., 79.
35. Ibid., 82–83.
36. Erickson (1970b), 111; Erickson and Schwartz (1969), 3.10.

37. Erickson (1970a), 90.
38. McCarty (2002), 110.
39. Wax (1970), 71.
40. Muskrat (1970), 72–75.
41. Emerson (1970), 96.
42. Erickson (1970a), 82–84.
43. Erickson (1970b), 113.
44. Collier (1988), 263.
45. Reyhner and Eder (2004), 269.
46. McCarty (2002), 140.
47. Ibid., 134–35.
48. Ibid., 136.
49. McCarty, Wallace, Lynch, and Benally (1991), 46.
50. McCarty (2002), 132n, 198.
51. Collier (1988), 263, 266.
52. McCarty (2002), 172.
53. http://www.roughrock.bia.edu.
54. Erickson and Schwartz (1969), 2.29.
55. Holm and Holm (1990), 172.
56. Ibid., 177.
57. Erickson and Schwartz (1969), 3.37; 5.18; 5.21; 7.23; 7.37.
58. Ibid., 6.19; Reyhner and Eder (2004), 271–73.
59. Reyhner and Eder (2004), 274.
60. In Goodluck, Lockard, and Yazzie (2000), 9.
61. Ashworth (1979), 40.
62. Barman, Hébert, and McCaskill (1987b), 12.
63. Crystal (2000), 16–18.
64. McAlpine and Herodier (1994), 130.
65. Blair and Fredeen (1995), 43.
66. McAlpine and Herodier (1994), 131.
67. Blair and Fredeen (1995), 36.
68. Crystal (2000), 115, 126.
69. Blair and Fredeen (1995), 38.
70. Persson (1986), 166.
71. Diamond (1987), 90.
72. Barman, Hébert, and McCaskill (1986b), 16.
73. Persson (1986), 150.
74. McKay and McKay (1987), 66.
75. Reyhner and Eder (2004), 37.
76. McAlpine and Herodier (1994), 130.
77. Ibid., 132.
78. McAlpine, Brophy, and Crago (1996), 393.
79. Ibid., 399, 409.
80. Ibid., 407–8.
81. Reyhner and Eder (2004), 37.

82. See Ermine (1995).
83. Barman, Hébert, and McCaskill (1987b), 4.
84. Hampton (1995), 19.
85. McCaskill (1987), 164, 176.
86. Ibid., 165.

Chapter 13

1. Lee and McLaughlin (2001), 33–35.
2. Spolsky and Holm (1971), 60–61.
3. Crawford (1995), 21.
4. In Batchelder (2000), 1.
5. Fillerup (2000), 23.
6. McCarty (2002), 15.
7. Lee and McLaughlin (2001), 31.
8. McCarty (2002), 181; emphasis in original.
9. Ibid., 183.
10. Lee and McLaughlin (2001), 25–26.
11. Fishman (2002), xii–xiii.
12. Henze and Davis (1999), 3–4.
13. Spolsky (1982), 148.
14. Lee and McLaughlin (2001), 36.
15. McAlpine and Herodier (1994), 138.
16. Spolsky (1982), 147.
17. Lee and McLaughlin (2001), 33, 63.
18. Szasz (1999), 177–78.
19. Lee and McLaughlin (2001), 37.
20. Fillerup (2000), 33.
21. Blair and Fredeen (1995), 39, 43.
22. Fuchs and Havighurst (1983), 207, 288.
23. Reyhner and Eder (2004), 329.
24. Fishman (1989), 399–400.
25. Reyhner and Eder (2004), 221.
26. Kramer (1991), 298–99.
27. Leap (1991), 21–24, 28.
28. Martinez (2000), 211, 217.
29. Spolsky (1982), 142–43.
30. Martinez (2000), 214.
31. Spolsky (1982), 149.
32. In Lomawaima (1994), 36.
33. Martinez (2000), 215–16, 218.
34. Robinson (1985), 524–27.
35. Tennant (1971), 35–36.
36. McCarty (2002), 117.
37. Predaris (1984), 27.

38. Pitman (1995), 2.
39. Ohannessian (1971), 69.
40. In Reyhner and Eder (2004), 219.
41. Spolsky (1978), 278.
42. Ibid., 279.
43. Spolsky (2004), 205–6.
44. National Center for Education Statistics (2008b), 12, 22, 18
45. Crystal (2000), 81.
46. Ibid., 29.
47. Leavitt (1995), 128.
48. In Crawford (1992), 155.
49. Freeman, Stairs, Corbière, and Lazore (1995), 53.
50. In Crawford (1992), 379.
51. In ibid., 380.
52. Crystal (2000), 119, 122.
53. Fishman (1985), 340.
54. Crystal (2000), 124.
55. Kramer (1991), 302.
56. Fuchs and Havighurst (1983), 306.

Chapter 14

1. Gutmann (1987).
2. In DeJong (1993), 110–12.
3. In Adams (1995), 18.
4. Ibid., 319.
5. Prucha (1970), 13.
6. Szasz (2007), 262–63,142.
7. Hoxie (2001a), 208.
8. Hendrick (1976), 165.
9. Fuchs and Havighurst (1983), 98–101.
10. Barman (1995), 59–61.
11. Barman (1986), 114, 119, 126.
12. Barman (1995), 62.
13. In DeJong (1993), 177.
14. Hendrick (1976) 175–76.
15. Hoxie (2001a), 66.
16. Spack (2002), 94.
17. Szasz (1999), 89.
18. Ellis (1996), 25.
19. DeJong (1993), 104, 177.
20. Leupp (1914), 81.
21. Szasz (1999), 11.
22. Hoxie (2001a), 190.

23. Barman (1986), 113.
24. Ashworth (1979), 41.
25. Szasz (1999), 102.
26. Ellis (1996), 187–88.
27. Szasz (1999), 89–90.
28. In Szasz (1999), 35.
29. In DeJong (1993), 156.
30. McCarty (2002), 64.
31. Szasz (1999), 89.
32. National Center for Education Statistics (2008b), 22.
33. Barman, Hébert, and McCaskill (1986b), 13.
34. Henderson (1995), 253.
35. Barman (1995), 72; Henderson (1995), 253.
36. Milloy (1999), 201.
37. Stamp (1982), 235.
38. In Flanagan (2000), 178.
39. Barrington (1991), 317.
40. Kramer (1991), 293.
41. Pratt (2004), 270–71.
42. Barman (1995), 69.
43. Milloy (1999), 222–24, 235.
44. Kramer (1991), 293.
45. In Allen (1970), 100–103.
46. In Szasz (1999), 150–51.
47. Kramer (1991), 302.
48. Bordewich (1997), 328.
49. Fuchs and Havighurst (1983), 112–13.
50. Ibid., 131.
51. In ibid., 284.

Chapter 15

1. Whitman (2008).
2. See Glenn (1995).
3. Whitman (2008), 68–89.
4. National Center for Education Statistics (2008b), 29.
5. Bielenberg (2000), 144.
6. Barton (1978), 170.
7. Kastoryano (1992), 174.
8. Miller (1996), 436.
9. Batchelder (2000), 7; unfortunately, she does not provide the proportion of respondents who took each position.

References

Adams, David Wallace, *Education for Extinction: American Indians and the Boarding School Experience, 1875–1928*, University Press of Kansas, 1995.
———, "Foreword," in Pratt, 2004.
———, "Beyond Bleakness: The Brighter Side of Indian Boarding Schools, 1870–1940," in Trafzer, Keller, and Sisquoc, 2006.
Allen, Ray A., "Whither Indian Education? A Conversation with Philleo Nash," *The School Review*, vol. 79, no. 1 (November, 1970), 99–108.
Angel, Frank, "Social Class or Culture?" in B. Spolsky, editor, *A Fundamental Issue in the Education of Culturally Different Students. The Language Education of Minority Children*, Rowley: Newbury House Publishers, 1972.
Archibald, Jo-Ann, "Locally Developed Native Studies Curriculum: An Historical and Philosophical Rationale," in Battiste and Barman, 1995.
Ashworth, Mary, *The Forces Which Shaped Them: A History of the Education of Minority Group Children in British Columbia*, Vancouver: New Star Books, 1979.
Axelrod, Paul, *The Promise of Schooling: Education in Canada, 1800–1914*, University of Toronto Press, 1997.
Barman, Jean, "Separate and Unequal: Indian and White Girls at All Hallows School, 1884–1920," in Barman, Hébert, and McCaskill, 1986.
———, "Schooled for Inequality: The Education of British Columbia Aboriginal Children," in *Children, Teachers and Schools in the History of British Columbia*, edited by Jean Barman, Neil Sutherland, and J. Donald Wilson, Calgary: Detselig, 1995.
Barman, Jean, and Neil Sutherland, "Royal Commission Retrospective," in Barman, Sutherland, and Wilson, 1995.
Barman, Jean, Y. Hébert, and D. McCaskill, editors, *Indian Education in Canada: Volume 1: The Legacy*. Vancouver: University of British Columbia Press, 1986a.
———, "The Legacy of the Past: An Overview," (1986b) in Barman, Hébert, and McCaskill, 1986a.
———, editors, *Indian Education in Canada: Volume 2: The Challenge*, Vancouver: University of British Columbia Press, 1987a.
———, "The Challenge of Indian Education: An Overview," (1987b) in Barman, Hébert, and McCaskill, 1987a.

Barman, Jean, Neil Sutherland, and J. Donald Wilson, editors, *Children, Teachers and Schools in the History of British Columbia*, Calgary: Detselig Enterprises, 1995.

Barrington, John M., "The New Zealand Experience: Maoris," in *Minority Status and Schooling*, edited by Margaret A. Gibson and John U. Ogbu, New York: Garland, 1991.

Barton, Josef J., "Eastern and Southern Europeans," in *Ethnic Leadership in America*, edited by John Higham, Baltimore: Johns Hopkins University Press, 1978.

Bashford, Lucy, and Hans Heinzerling, "Blue Quills Native Education Centre: A Case Study," in Barman, Hébert, and McCaskill, 1987a.

Batchelder, Ann, "Teaching Diné Language and Culture in Navajo Schools," in Reyner, Martin, Lockard, and Gilbert, 2000.

Battiste, Marie, "Micmac Literacy and Cognitive Assimilation," in Barman, Hébert, and McCaskill, 1986a.

———, "Mi'kmaq Linguistic Integrity: A Case Study of Mi'kmawey School," in Barman, Hébert, and McCaskill, 1987a.

———, "Introduction," in Battiste and Barman, 1995.

Battiste, Marie, and Jean Barman, editors, *First Nations Education in Canada: The Circle Unfolds*, Vancouver: University of British Columbia, 1995.

Bauer, Evelyn, "Bilingual Education in BIA Schools," *TESOL Quarterly*, vol. 4, no. 3 (September, 1970), 223–229.

———, "A History of Bilingual Education in BIA Schools," in *Bilingual Education for American Indians*, Washington: Bureau of Indian Affairs, 1971.

Begay, Sally, Galena Sells Dick, Dan W. Estell, Juanita Estell, Teresa L. McCarty, and Afton Sells, "Change from the Inside Out: A Story of Transformation in a Navajo Community School," *Bilingual Research Journal* 19 (1), 1995.

Bendroth, Margaret, "Rum, Romanism, and Evangelism: Protestants and Catholics in Late-Nineteenth-Century Boston," *Church History*, vol. 68, no. 3 (September, 1999), 627–647.

Bielenberg, Brian, "Charter Schools for American Indians," in Reyner, Martin, Lockard, and Gilbert, 2000.

Blair, Heather, and Shirley Fredeen, "Do Not Go Gentle into That Good Night. Rage, Rage, against the Dying of the Light," *Anthropology & Education Quarterly*, vol. 26, no. 1 (March), 1995, 27–49.

Bordewich, Fergus M., *Killing the White Man's Indian: Reinventing Native Americans at the End of the Twentieth Century*, New York: Anchor Books, 1997.

Boyce, George A., *When Navajos Had Too Many Sheep: The 1940s*, San Francisco: Indian Historian Press, 1974.

Brown, Richard D., *The Strength of a People: The Idea of an Informed Citizenry in America, 1650–1870*, Chapel Hill: University of North Carolina Press, 1996.

Bunge, Robert, "Language: The Psyche of a People," in Crawford, 1992.

Bushnell, David, "The Treatment of the Indians in Plymouth Colony," *The New England Quarterly*, Vol. 26, No. 2. (June, 1953), pp. 193–218.

Cantor, Milton, "The Image of the Negro in Colonial Literature," *The New England Quarterly*, Vol. 36, No. 4. (Dec., 1963), pp. 452–477.

Coates, Ken, "A Very Imperfect Means of Education: Indian Day Schools in the Yukon Territory, 1890–1955," in Barman, Hébert, and McCaskill, 1986.

Cohn, Jay, "The Negro Character in Northern Magazine Fiction of the 1860's," *The New England Quarterly*, Vol. 43, No. 4. (Dec., 1970), pp. 572–592.

Coleman, Michael C., "The Responses of American Indian Children to Presbyterian Schooling in the Nineteenth Century: An Analysis through Missionary Sources," *History of Education Quarterly*, Vol. 27, No. 4. (Winter, 1987), pp. 473–497.

Collier, John, Jr., "Foreword: An Introduction to John Collier," in Kelly, 1983.

———, "Survival at Rough Rock: A Historical Overview of Rough Rock Demonstration School," *Anthropology & Education Quarterly*, vol. 19, no. 3 (September, 1988), 253–269.

Coombs, L. Madison, "A Summary of Pertinent Research in Bilingual Education," in *Bilingual Education for American Indians*, Washington, DC: Bureau of Indian Affairs, 1971.

Crawford, James, editor, *Language Loyalties*, Chicago: University of Chicago Press, 1992.

———, "Endangered Native American Languages: What Is To Be Done, and Why?" *Bilingual Research Journal*, 19 (1), 1995.

Crystal, David, *Language Death*, Cambridge University Press, 2000.

Cummins, Jim, "Minority Status and Schooling in Canada,"*Anthropology & Education Quarterly*, Vol. 28, No. 3, (September, 1997), pp. 411–430.

Daily, David W., *Battle for the BIA: G. E. E. Lindquist and the Missionary Crusade against John Collier*, Tucson: University of Arizona Press, 2004.

DeJong, David H., *Promises of the Past: A History of Indian Education*, Golden, CO: North American Press, 1993.

Desmond, Adrian, and James Moore, *Darwin's Sacred Cause*, Boston: Houghton Mifflin Harcourt, 2009.

Dewey, John, *Democracy and Education* (1916), New York: The Free Press, 1966.

Diamond, Billy, "The Cree Experience," in Barman, Hébert, and McCaskill, 1987a.

Dixon, Patricia, and Clifford E. Trafzer, "The Place of American Indian Boarding Schools in Contemporary Society," in Trafzer, Keller, and Sisquoc, 2006.

Doolittle, J. R., "A Report on Boarding Schools for Indians in Oregon (1867)," in *Education in the United States: A Documentary History*, pages p. 1734–1735, edited by Sol Cohen, New York: Random House, 1974.

Dyer, Thomas G., *Theodore Roosevelt and the Idea of Race*, Baton Rouge: Louisiana State University Press, 1980.

Ellis, Clyde, *To Change Them Forever: Indian Education at the Rainy Mountain Boarding School, 1893–1920*, Norman: University of Oklahoma Press, 1996.

———, "'We Had a Lot of Fun, but of Course that Wasn't the School Part': Life at the Rainy Mountain Boarding School, 1893–1920," in Trafzer, Keller, and Sisquoc, 2006.

Emerson, Gloria J., "The Laughing Boy Syndrome," *The School Review*, vol. 79, no. 1 (November), 1970, 94–98.

Engs, Robert Francis, *Educating the Disfranchised and Disinherited: Samuel Chapman Armstrong and Hampton Institute, 1839–1893*, Knoxville: University of Tennessee Press, 1999.

Erickson, Donald A., "Custer *Did* Die for Our Sins!" *The School Review*, vol. 79, no. 1 (November, 1970a), 76–93.

———, "Failure in Navajo Schooling," *Parents Magazine* (September 1970b), 66–68, 109–113.

———, and Henrietta Schwartz, *Community School at Rough Rock: An Evaluation for the Office of Economic Opportunity*, April 1969.

———, "What Rough Rock Demonstrates," *Integrated Education*, March–April 1970, 21–34.

———, "Rough Rock Study: Summary of Methods, Findings, and Conclusions," typescript, no date, provided by D. Erickson, February 2009.

Ermine, Willie, "Aboriginal Epistemology," in Battiste and Barman, 1995.

Fillerup, Michael, "Racing Against Time: A Report on the Leupp Navajo Immersion Project," in Reyner, Martin, Lockard, and Gilbert, 2000.

Fishman, Joshua A., "The Ethnic Revival in the United States: Implications for the Mexican-American Community," in *Mexican-Americans in Comparative Perspective*, edited by Walker Connor, Washington: The Urban Institute, 1985.

———, *Language and Ethnicity in Minority Sociolinguistic Perspective*, Clevedon (United Kingdom): Multilingual Matters, 1989.

———, editor, *Can Threatened Languages Be Saved?* Clevedon, UK: Multilingual Matters, 2001.

———, "Why is it so Hard to Save a Threatened Language?" in Fishman, 2001.

———, "Foreword," in *A Place to be Navajo: Rough Rock and the Struggle for Self-Determination in Indigenous Schooling*, Mahwah (NJ): Lawrence Erlbaum Associates, 2002.

Flanagan, Tom, *First Nations? Second Thoughts*, Montreal: McGill-Queen's University Press, 2000.

Frederickson, George M., *The Black Image in the White Mind: The Debate on Afro-American Character and Destiny, 1817–1914*, Wesleyan University Press, 1987.

Freeman, Kate, Arlene Stairs, Evelyn Corbière, and Dorothy Lazore, "Ojibway, Mohawk, and Inuktitut Alive and Well? Issues of Identity, Ownership, and Change," *Bilingual Research Journal*, 19 (1), 1995.

Friesen, John W., and Virginia Lyons Friesen, *First Nations in the Twenty-First Century*, Calgary: Detselig, 2005.

Fuchs, Estelle, and Robert J. Havighurst, *To Live On This Earth: American Indian Education*, Albuquerque: University of New Mexico Press, 1983.

Garland, Hamlin, *The Captain of the Gray-Horse Troop*, New York: Harper & Brothers, 1902; republished Upper Saddle River, NJ: Gregg Press, 1970.

Glenn, Charles L., *The Myth of the Common School*, Amherst: University of Massachusetts Press, 1988.

———, "Minority Schools on Purpose," in *Changing Populations, Changing Schools: 94th Yearbook of the National Society for the Study of Education*, Part II, edited by Erwin Flaxman and A. Harry Passow, Chicago: National Society for the Study of Education, 1995.

Glenn, Charles L., with Ester de Jong , *Educating Immigrant Children: Schools and Language Minorities in 12 Nations*, New York: Garland Publishing, 1996.

Goffman, Erving, *Asylums, Essays on the Social Situation of Mental Patients and Other Inmates*, Garden City (NY): Doubleday Anchor, 1961.

Goodluck, Mary Ann, Louise Lockard, and Darlene Yazzie, "Language Revitalization in Navajo/English Dual Language Classrooms," in Reyner, Martin, Lockard, and Gilbert, 2000.

Gossett, Thomas F., *Race: The History of an Idea in America*, New York: Schocken Books, 1965.

Grant, Colin, *Negro with a Hat: The Rise and Fall of Marcus Garvey*, Oxford University Press, 2008.

Green, Michael, "What Happened to the Indians in the War Between the Catholics and the Protestants?" *Reviews in American History*, vol. 8, no. 3 (September), 1980, 372–376.

Gresko, Jacqueline, "White 'Rites' and Indian 'Rites': Indian Education and Native Responses in the West," in *Shaping the Schools of the Canadian West*, edited by David C. Jones, Nancy M. Sheehan, and Robert M. Stamp, Calgary: Detselig, 1979.

———, "Creating Little Dominions within the Dominion: Early Catholic Indian Schools in Saskatchewan and British Columbia," in *Indian Education in Canada: Volume I: The Legacy*, edited by Barman, Hébert, and McCaskill, Vancouver: University of British Columbia Press, 1986.

Gunther, Erna, "Cultural Backgrounds," in Lindquist, 1944.

Gutmann, Amy, *Democratic Education*, Princeton University Press, 1987.

Haig-Brown, Celia, "Taking Control: Contradiction and First Nations Adult Education," in Battiste and Barman, 1995.

Hamilton, Milton W., *Sir William Johnson and the Indians of New York*, Albany: New York State American Revolution Bicentennial Commission, 1975.

Hampton, Eber, "Towards a Redefinition of Indian Education," in Battiste and Barman, 1995.

Handlin, Oscar, *Race and Nationality in American Life*, Garden City (NY): Doubleday Anchor, 1959.

Henderson, James [sákéj] Youngblood, "Treaties and Indian Education," in Battiste and Barman, 1995.

Hendrick, Irving G., "Federal Policy Affecting the Education of Indians in California, 1849–1934," *History of Education Quarterly*, Vol. 16, No. 2. (Summer, 1976), pp. 163–185.

Henze, Rosemary, and Kathryn A. Davis, "Authenticity and Identity: Lessons from Indigenous Language Education," *Anthropology of Education Quarterly*, Vol. 30, No. 1 (March, 1999), 3–21.

Henze, Rosemary, and Lauren Vanett, "To Walk in Two Worlds: Or More? Challenging a Common Metaphor of Native Education," *Anthropology & Education Quarterly*, Vol. 24, No. 2. (June, 1993), pp. 116–134.

Holm, Agnes, and Wayne Holm, "Rock Point, a Navajo Way to Go to School: A Valediction," *Annals of the American Academy of Political and Social Science*, 508 (March 1990), 170–184.

———, "Navajo Language Education: Retrospect and Prospects," *Bilingual Research Journal*, Vol. 19, No. 1 (1995).

Holst, John H., "Educational Developments and Trends," in Lindquist, 1944.

Hoxie, Frederick E., *A Final Promise: The Campaign to Assimilate the Indians, 1880–1920*, Lincoln: University of Nebraska Press, 2001a.

———, editor, *Talking Back to Civilization: Indian Voices from the Progressive Era*, Boston: Bedford/St. Martin's, 2001b.

Jaenen, Cornelius J., "Education for Francization: The Case of New France in the Seventeenth Century," in Barman, Hébert, and McCaskill, 1986a.

James, Thomas, "Rhetoric and Resistance: Social Science and Community Schools for Navajos in the 1930s," *History of Education Quarterly*, Vol. 28, No. 4. (Winter, 1988), pp. 599–626.

Jefferson, Thomas, *Writings*, New York: The Library of America, 1984.

Jenkins, Sally, *The Real All Americans: The Team That Changed a Game, a People, a Nation*, New York: Doubleday, 2007.

Jordan, Winthrop D., *White over Black: American Attitudes Toward the Negro 1550–1812*, New York: Penguin Books, 1969.

Kach, Nick, and Kas Mazurek, editors, *Exploring Our Educational Past: Schooling in the North-West Territories and Alberta*, Calgary: Detselig Enterprises, 1992.

Kastoryano, Riva, "Relations interethniques et formes d'intégration," in *Face au racisme, 2: Analyses, hypothèses, perspectives*, edited by Pierre-André Taguieff, Paris: Éditions La Découverte, 1992.

Kelly, Lawrence C., *The Assault on Assimilation: John Collier and the Origins of Indian Policy Reform*, Albuquerque: University of New Mexico Press, 1983.

King, James C., *The Biology of Race*, Revised Edition, Berkeley: University of California Press, 1981.

King, Richard, "Role Shock in Local Control of Indian Education," in Barman, Hébert, and McCaskill, 1987a.

Kluckhohn, Clyde, and Dorothea Leighton, *The Navaho*, Garden City (NY): Doubleday Anchor, 1962.

Kramer, Betty Jo, "Education and American Indians: The Experience of the Ute Indian Tribe," in *Minority Status and Schooling*, edited by Margaret A. Gibson and John U. Ogbu, New York: Garland, 1991.

Leap, William L., "Pathways and Barriers to Indian Language Literacy-Building on the Northern Ute Reservation," *Anthropology & Education Quarterly*, Vol. 22, No. 1. (March, 1991), pp. 21–41.

Leavitt, Robert, "Language and Cultural Context in Native Education," in Battiste and Barman, 1995.

Lee, Tiffany S., and Daniel McLaughlin, "Reversing Navajo Language Shift, Revisited," in Fishman, 2001.

Leibowitz, Arnold H., "A History of Language Instruction in American Indian Schools: The Imposition of English by Government Policy," in *Bilingual

Education for American Indians, Washington: Bureau of Indian Affairs, 1971.

Leupp, Francis E., *The Indian and His Problem*, New York: Charles Scribner's Sons, 1910.

———, *In Red Man's Land: A Study of the American Indian*, New York: Fleming H. Revell Company, 1914.

Lindquist, G. E. E., *The Indian in American Life*, New York: Friendship Press, 1944.

Lipka, Jerry, and Teresa L. McCarty, "Changing the Culture of Schooling: Navajo and Yup'ik Cases," *Anthropology & Education Quarterly*, Vol. 25, No. 3, Alternative Visions of Schooling: Success Stories in Minority Settings (September, 1994), pp. 266–284.

Lomawaima, K. Tsianina, *They Called It Prairie Light: The Story of Chilocco Indian School*, Lincoln: University of Nebraska Press, 1994.

Lomawaima, K. Tsianina, and Teresa L. McCarty, "When Tribal Sovereignty Challenges Democracy: American Indian Education and the Democratic Ideal," *American Educational Research Journal*, vol. 39, no. 2 (Summer, 2002), 279–305.

———, *"To Remain an Indian": Lessons in Democracy from a Century of Native American Education*, New York: Teachers College Press, 2006.

Longboat, Dianne, "First Nations Control of Education: The Path to Our Survival as Nations," in Barman, Hébert, and McCaskill, 1987a.

Lyons, Charles H., *To Wash an Aethiop White: British Ideas About Black Educability, 1530–1960*, New York: Teachers College Press, 1975.

Mackay, Ron and Lawrence Myles, "A Major Challenge for the Education System: Aboriginal Retention and Dropout," in Battiste and Barman, 1995.

Martinez, Rebecca Blum, "Languages and Tribal Sovereignty: Whose Language Is It Anyway?" *Theory into Practice*, vol. 39. no. 4 (Autumn, 2000), 211–219.

May, Stephen, and Sheila Aikman, "Indigenous Education: addressing current issues and developments," *Comparative Education*, vol. 39, no. 2 (2003), 139–145.

McAlpine, Lynn, Alice Eriks-Brophy, and Martha Crago, "Teaching Beliefs in Mohawk Classrooms: Issues of Language and Culture," *Anthropology & Education Quarterly*, vol. 27, no. 3 (September, 1996), 390–413.

McAlpine, Lynn, and Daisy Herodier, "Schooling as a Vehicle for Aboriginal Language Maintenance: Implementing Cree as the Language of Instruction in Northern Quebec," *Canadian Journal of Education*, vol. 19, no. 2 (Spring, 1994), 128–141.

McCarty, Teresa L., *A Place to be Navajo: Rough Rock and the Struggle for Self-Determination in Indigenous Schooling*, Mahwah (NJ): Lawrence Erlbaum Associates, 2002.

———, "Revitalizing Indigenous Languages in Homogenising Times," *Comparative Education*, vol. 30, no. 2 (May, 2003), 147–163.

———, Regina Hadley Lynch; Stephen Wallace; and AnCita Benally "Classroom Inquiry and Navajo Learning Styles: A Call for Reassessment," *Anthropology & Education Quarterly*, vol. 22, no. 1. (March, 1991), pp. 42–59.

McCaskill, Don, "Revitalization of Indian Culture: Indian Cultural Survival Schools," in Barman, Hébert, and McCaskill, 1987a.

McKay, Alvin, and Bert McKay, "Education as a Total Way of Life: The Nisga'a Experience," in Barman, Hébert, and McCaskill, 1987a.

McLaughlin, Daniel, "The Sociolinguistics of Navajo Literacy," *Anthropology and Education Quarterly*, vol. 20, no. 4 (December, 1989), 275–290.

McLoughlin, William G., *Cherokee Renascence in the New Republic*, Princeton University Press, 1986.

———, *After the Trail of Tears: The Cherokees' Struggle for Sovereignty, 1839–1880*, Chapel Hill: University of North Carolina Press, 1993.

Mihesuah, Devon A., *Cultivating the Rosebuds: The Education of Women at the Cherokee Female Seminary, 1851–1909*, Urbana: University of Illinois Press, 1998.

Miller, J. R., *Shingwauk's Vision: A History of Native Residential Schools*, Toronto: University of Toronto Press, 1996.

Milloy, John S., *"A National Crime": The Canadian Government and the Residential School System, 1879 to 1986*, Winnipeg: University of Manitoba Press, 1999.

Mitchell, Frederic, and James W. Skelton, "The Church-State Conflict in Early Indian Education," *History of Education Quarterly*, vol. 6, no. 1 (Spring, 1966), 41–51.

Monaghan, E. Jennifer, "'She Loved to Read in Good Books': Literacy and the Indians of Martha's Vineyard, 1643–1725," *History of Education Quarterly*, vol. 30, no. 4, Special Issue on the History of Literacy (Winter, 1990), pp. 492–521.

Morant, G. M., *The Significance of Racial Differences*, Paris: UNESCO, 1958.

Murdoch, John, "Canadian Hunter-Gatherer Adaptive Strategies and Indigenous Language Development," *International Journal of American Linguistics*, vol. 51, no. 4 (October, 1985), 518–521.

Muskrat, Joseph, "The Need for Cultural Empathy," *The School Review*, vol. 79, no. 1 (November, 1970), 72–75.

Naeher, Robert James, "Dialogue in the Wilderness: John Eliot and the Indian Exploration of Puritanism as a Source of Meaning, Comfort, and Ethnic Survival," *The New England Quarterly*, vol. 62, no. 3 (September, 1989), 346–368.

National Center for Education Statistics, Institute of Education Sciences, *Status and Trends in the Education of American Indians and Alaska Natives*, Washington, DC: U.S. Department of Education, 2005.

———, *National Indian Education Study 2007: Part I, Performance of American Indian and Alaska Native Students at Grades 4 and 8 on NAEP 2007 Reading and Mathematics Assessments*, Washington, DC: U.S. Department of Education, 2008a.

———, *National Indian Education Study 2007: Part II, The Educational Experiences of American Indian and Alaska Native Students in Grades 4 and 8, Statistical Analysis Report*, Washington, DC: U.S. Department of Education, 2008b.

Newby, I. A., *Jim Crow's Defense: Anti-Negro Thought in America, 1900–1930*, Baton Rouge: Louisiana State University Press, 1965.

Ohannessian, Sirarpi, "Planning Conference for a Bilingual Kindergarten Program for Navajo Children," in *Bilingual Education for American Indians*, Washington, DC: Bureau of Indian Affairs, 1971.

Osborne, A. Barry, "Insiders and Outsiders: Cultural Membership and the Micropolitics of Education among the Zuni," *Anthropology & Education Quarterly*, vol. 20, no. 3. (September, 1989), pp. 196–215.

Owen, Michael, "Brokers of Cultural Change: British Wesleyan Missionaries in Rupert's Land, 1840–1854," in *Exploring Our Educational Past: Schooling in the North-West Territories and Alberta*, edited by Nick Kach and Kas Mazurek, Calgary: Detselig, 1992.

Parsons, Lynn Hudson, "'A Perpetual Harrow upon My Feelings': John Quincy Adams and the American Indian," *The New England Quarterly*, vol. 46, no. 3. (September, 1973), pp. 339–379.

Persson, Diane, "The Changing Experience of Indian Residential Schooling: Blue Quills, 1931–1930," in Barman, Hébert, and McCaskill, 1986a.

Peshkin, Alan, *Places of Memory: Whiteman's Schools and Native American Communities*, Mahwah, NJ: Lawrence Erlbaum, 1997.

Pitman, A. Lynette, "The Debacle of Native American Education," typescript (paper for seminar with the author), 1995.

Pratt, Richard Henry, *Battlefield and Classroom Four Decades with the American Indian, 1867–1904*, edited by Robert M. Utley, Norman: University of Oklahoma Press, 2004.

Predaris, Theodora G., "American Indian/Alaskan Native Program Study," in *Educating the Minority Language Student: Classroom and Administrative Issues*, Rosslyn, VA: National Clearinghouse for Bilingual Education, 1984.

Prucha, Francis Paul, *American Indian Policy in the Formative Years: The Indian Trade and Intercourse Acts, 1790–1834*, Lincoln: University of Nebraska Press, 1970.

———, *American Indian Policy in Crisis: Christian Reformers and the Indian, 1865–1900*, Norman: University of Oklahoma Press, 1976.

———, editor, *Documents of United States Indian Policy*, Lincoln: University of Nebraska Press, 2000.

Rathbun, Tanya L., "The Catholic Experience at St. Boniface Indian School," in Trafzer, Keller, and Sisquoc, 2006.

Rayman, Ronald, "Joseph Lancaster's Monitorial System of Instruction and American Indian Education, 1815–1838," *History of Education Quarterly*, vol. 21, no. 4 (Winter, 1981), 395–409.

Regnier, Robert, "The Sacred Circle: An Aboriginal Approach to Healing Education at an Urban High School," in Battiste and Barman, 1995.

Reyhner, Jon, "Policies toward American Indian Languages: A Historical Sketch," in Crawford, 1992.

Reyhner, Jon, and Jeanne Eder, *American Indian Education: A History*, Norman: University of Oklahoma Press, 2004.

Reyhner, Jon, Joseph Martin, Louise Lockard, and W. Sakiestewa Gilbert, editors, *Learn in Beauty: Indigenous Education for a New Century*, Flagstaff: Northern Arizona University, 2000.

Riner, Reed D., "American Indian Education: A Rite That Fails." *Anthropology & Education Quarterly*, vol. 10, no. 4. (Winter, 1979), pp. 236–253.

Riney, Scott, "Loosening the Bonds: The Rapid City Indian School in the 1920s," in Trafzer, Keller, and Sisquoc, 2006.

Robinson, Patricia, "Language Retention among Canadian Indians: A Simultaneous Equations Model with Dichotomous Endogenous Variables," *American Sociological Review*, vol. 50 (August, 1985), 515–529.

Ruchames, Louis, *Racial Thought in America: I. From the Puritans to Abraham Lincoln*, New York: Grosset and Dunlap, 1970.

Salisbury, Neal, "Red Puritans: The 'Praying Indians' of Massachusetts Bay and John Eliot," *The William and Mary Quarterly*. 3rd Series, vol. 31, no. 1 (January 1974), 27–54.

Schutt, Amy C., "'What Will Become of Our Young People?' Goals for Indian Children in Moravian Missions," *History of Education Quarterly*, vol. 38, no. 3. (Autumn, 1998), pp. 268–286.

Schwartz, Henrietta, "Teaching and Learning in General," in Erickson and Schwartz, 1969.

Seymour, Flora Warren, "Indian-White Relations," in Lindquist, 1944.

Simmons, William S., "Conversion from Indian to Puritan," *The New England Quarterly*, vol. 52, no. 2. (June, 1979), pp. 197–218.

Sizer, Theodore, editor, *The Age of the Academies*, New York: Teachers College, 1964.

Spack, Ruth, *America's Second Tongue: American Indian Education and the Ownership of English, 1860–1900*, Lincoln: University of Nebraska Press, 2002.

Spolsky, Bernard, "Bilingual Education in the United States," in *International Dimensions of Bilingual Education*, edited by James E. Alatis, Washington: Georgetown University, 1978.

———, "Sociolinguistics of Literacy, Bilingual Education, and Tesol," TESOL Quarterly, vol. 16, no. 2 (June, 1982), 141–151.

———, *Language Policy*, Cambridge University Press, 2004.

Spolsky, Bernard, and Wayne Holm, "Literacy in the Vernacular: The Case of Navajo," in *Bilingual Education for American Indians*, Washington: Bureau of Indian Affairs, 1971.

Stamp, Robert M., *The Schools of Ontario, 1876–1976*, Toronto: University of Toronto Press, 1982.

Stancavage, Frances B., and others, *National Indian Education Study, Part II: The Educational Experiences of Fourth- and Eighth-Grade American Indian and Alaska Native Students, Statistical Analysis Report* (NCES 2007: 454), Washington, DC: U.S Department of Education, National Center for Education Statistics, Institute of Education Sciences, 2006.

Stanley, Timothy J., "White Supremacy and the Rhetoric of Educational Indoctrination: a Canadian Case Study," in Barman, Sutherland, and Wilson, 1995.

Sterling, Shirley, "Quaslametko and Yerko: Two Grandmother Models for Contemporary Native Education Pedagogy," in Battiste and Barman, 1995.

Szasz, Margaret Connell, *Education and the American Indian: The Road to Self-Determination, 1928–1998*, University of New Mexico Press, 1999.

———, "Through a Wide Angle Lens: Acquiring and Maintaining Power, Position, and Knowledge through Boarding Schools," in Trafzer, Keller, and Sisquoc, 2006.

———, *Indian Education in the American Colonies, 1607–1783*, Lincoln: University of Nebraska Press, 2007.

Tanis, Norman Earl, "Education in John Eliot's Indian Utopias, 1646–1675," *History of Education Quarterly*, vol. 10, no. 3. (Autumn, 1970), pp. 308–323.

Tefft, Stanton K., "Anomy, Values and Culture Change Among Teen-Age Indians: An Exploratory Study," *Sociology of Education*, vol. 40, no. 2. (Spring, 1967), pp. 145–157.

Tennant, Edward A., "The Bilingual Education Act and the American Indian," in *Bilingual Education for American Indians*, Washington, DC: Bureau of Indian Affairs, 1971.

Thomas, G. E., "Puritans, Indians, and the Concept of Race," *The New England Quarterly*, vol. 48, no. 1. (March, 1975), pp. 3–27.

Tippeconnic, John W., III, "Tribal Control of American Indian Education: Observations since the 1960s with Implications for the Future," in *Next Steps: Research and Practice to Advance Indian Education*, edited by Karen Gayton Swisher and John W. Tippeconnic, ERIC Clearinghouse RS 021 798, 1999.

Titley, E. Brian, "Indian Industrial Schools in Western Canada," in *Schools in the West: Essays in Canadian Educational History*, edited by Nancy M. Sheehan, J. Donald Wilson, and David C. Jones, Calgary: Detselig, 1986.

———, "Red Deer Indian Industrial School: A Case Study in the History of Indian Education," in *Exploring Our Educational Past: Schooling in the North-West Territories and Alberta*, edited by Nick Kach and Kas Mazurek, Calgary: Detselig, 1992.

———, "Industrial Education for Manitoba Natives: The Case of Rupert's Land Indian School," in *Issues in the History of Education in Manitoba*, edited by Rosa del C. Bruno-Jofré, Lewiston: Edwin Mellen Press, 1993.

Tocqueville, Alexis de, *Democracy in America*, translated by Harvey V. Mansfield and Delba Winthrop, Chicago: University of Chicago Press, 2000.

Trafzer, Clifford E., Jean A. Keller, and Lorene Sisquoc, "Introduction: Origin and Development of the American Indian Boarding School System," in *Boarding School Blues: Revising American Indian Educational Experiences*, Lincoln: University of Nebraska Press, 2006.

Utley, Robert M., "Introduction," in Pratt, 2004.

Vanderwerth, W. C., editor, *Indian Oratory*, New York: Ballantine Books, 1971.

Van Lonkhuyzen, Harold W. "A Reappraisal of the Praying Indians: Acculturation, Conversion, and Identity at Natick, Massachusetts, 1646–1730," *The New England Quarterly*, vol. 63, no. 3. (September, 1990), pp. 396–428.

Washington, Booker T., *Up From Slavery*, New York: Dell, 1965.

Wax, Murray L., "Gophers or Gadflies: Indian School Boards," *The School Review*, vol. 79, no. 1 (November, 1970), 62–71.

Wesley, Edgar B., "Forty Acres and a Mule and a Speller," *History of Education Journal*, Vol. 8, No. 4. (Summer, 1957), pp. 113–127.
Whitman, David, *Sweating the Small Stuff: Inner-City Schools and the New Paternalism*, Washington, DC: Thomas B. Fordham Institute, 2008.
Wilson, J. Donald, "'No Blanket to be Worn in School': The Education of Indians in Nineteenth-Century Ontario," in Barman, Hébert, and McCaskill, 1986a.
Wilson, Peggy, "Trauma of Sioux Indian High School Students," *Anthropology & Education Quarterly*, vol. 22, no. 4. (December, 1991), pp. 367–383.

Index

Index of Indian Peoples

Algonquian, 20, 25, 128
Apache, 62, 82, 120
Arapahoe, 62
Athapaskan, 128

Cherokee, 5–6, 13–14, 21–2, 31–2, 35, 39–46, 52–3, 55–6, 58, 62–3, 84–6, 99, 115, 129–31, 172
Cheyenne, 62, 133, 172
Chickasaw, 39, 45, 143
Choctaw, 33–4, 39, 41, 45, 57, 63, 129, 143
Comanche, 60–2, 82, 97
Cree, 99, 115, 127, 130, 134–5, 147, 160–2, 167, 172, 175, 195
Creek, 21, 39, 45
Crow, 172

Dakota/Lakota, 129, 132–3, 172
Delaware, 31

Hopi, 99, 102, 148, 169–70, 195
Huron, 19–20

Inuit, 8, 66, 127, 162–3
Inuktikut, 127
Iroquois, 26–7

Kiowa, 60–2, 82, 92, 97, 106, 185

Lumbee, 181

Maori (of New Zealand), 128–9
Micmac, 19, 129, 167

Mohawk, 23, 27, 90, 129, 135, 162–3, 176
Montagnais, 99

Navajo, 5–6, 12, 61, 74, 78, 81, 97, 103–4, 107, 111–22, 127–9, 136–7, 142, 145–60, 165–8, 172–3
Nisga'a, 97, 162

Ojibwa, 29, 35, 54, 127–8
Osage, 57

Paiute, 139, 183
Papago, 148
Passamaquoddy, 172
Pottawatamie, 45
Pueblo, 8, 104–6, 111, 140–1, 144, 148, 167, 170–2

Sechelt, 81
Seminole, 35, 39
Seneca, 51, 53, 75
Shawnee, 103
Shuswap, 78
Sioux, 2, 61–2, 81, 96, 129, 131, 133, 135, 141, 148

Tewa, 139

Ute, 170, 172, 177

Wampanoag, 22

Yakama, 184
Yuk, 172

Zuñi, 172

Index of Denominations

Anglican, 16, 27, 35, 37, 54, 65, 73, 89–90, 94–5, 101–2, 127, 129–30, 134, 182

Baptist, 41, 45, 58, 69, 73

Catholic, 19, 25, 27, 49, 51, 54, 58, 63, 65, 68–71, 73–4, 82, 92, 94, 99, 116–7, 128–9, 134–5, 188–9
Christian Reformed, 144
Congregationalist, 41, 52, 58, 63, 68–9, 85

Episcopalian, 63, 68–9, 133
evangelical, 25, 56, 155

Lutheran, 71

Methodist, 35, 41, 45, 54, 58–9, 63, 69, 81, 94, 106, 128, 134
Moravian (United Brethren), 41, 53, 57

Native American Church, 145, 168, 174

Orthodox, 55

Presbyterian, 41, 45, 52, 57, 63–4, 68–9, 73–4, 94, 99, 129

Quaker (Society of Friends), 55, 60–1, 63, 68–9, 151

traditional Indian religions, 20, 45, 73, 104, 144–5, 164, 171, 175

United Church of Canada, 6, 73, 94

General Index

achievement, academic, 3, 6–8, 105, 122, 158, 163, 194
Adams, President John Quincy, 13, 31, 42, 56
Agassiz, Louis, 16
aggression
 by Indians, 70, 117
 by whites, 31–5, 46, 55, 103, 184–5, 195
Alabama, 33, 56
Alaska, 54–5, 83–4, 114
Alberta, 6, 79, 114, 124, 134, 162, 199
Alford, Thomas Wildcat, 103
allotment of land. *See* individual land ownership
American Board of Commissioners for Foreign Missions, 39, 41, 52, 57, 129
American Indian Federation, 98
American Indian Public Charter School, 194
Armstrong, Samuel Chapman, 85–6

Ashagashe, 35
assimilation of Indians into white society and culture, 29, 45, 50, 56, 74, 77, 87, 102, 104, 111, 113, 121, 123, 128, 130, 134, 141, 182, 189–90
Atkins, John D. C., 132–3

Bagot Commission, 81
Beatty, Willard, 139
Blue Quills Indian School, 116–17, 134–5, 162
Blumenbach's racial categories, 11
Board of Indian Commissioners, 61
Brainerd Mission, 39, 52
British Columbia, 6, 65, 75, 77–8, 80–2, 95, 97, 102, 108, 162, 181–4, 188
British government in Canada, 15, 27, 30–2, 35
Bureau of Catholic Indian Missions (BCIM), 70–1

Index • 235

Calhoun, John C., 13, 33, 53
California, 126, 141, 181–4, 194
Canadian Royal Commission on Aboriginal Peoples, 117–18
Carlisle Indian School, 2, 25, 50, 64, 78, 84, 86–8, 90–1, 96, 98, 100, 106–7, 110, 120, 133, 179–80
Catholic schooling, opposition to, 67–70
Chavis, Ben, 194
Chicago, 190
Child, Lydia Maria, *Appeal for the Indians*, 131
Chilocco Indian School, 81, 91, 171
Chrétien, Jean, 124
"Civilization Fund," 33, 41, 56
Civil War, 45–6, 59
Clay, Henry, 14
Collier, John, 73, 97, 103, 115–16, 139–45, 148, 158, 169
Columbian Exposition, 107, 136
'common school' as a focus of policy, 2, 57, 68, 180–2
Connecticut, 25
Cooper, James Fenimore, 16
corrupting influence
  of Indian families, 36–7, 88–9, 101, 109
  of white civilization, 15, 34–5, 83, 128
culture
  of Indian peoples, 20–3, 44, 47, 49–50, 55, 73–4, 79, 81, 86, 91, 97–8, 101, 103, 104–7, 110–12, 118, 121, 124–91, 194–6, 198–9
  of the white majority, 40, 43, 45, 47, 64, 98, 101, 103, 121, 131, 134, 136, 142, 157, 163, 168, 177, 191

Dakota, North and South, 5, 67, 85, 91, 96, 102, 145, 184
Dartmouth, Indians attending, 26, 31
Darwin, Charles, 17
Declaration of the First Nations, 124
Deloria, Vine, 156
Dewey, John, 137

Director of Indian Education, 103, 136
disappearance of Indians
  belief in, 13–15, 30, 32, 35, 53, 59, 136, 184
  contrary to the evidence, 5, 15
  distribution of land. *See* individual land ownership
Dodge, Chee, 97
Dodge, Mabel, 111
Dorchester, Daniel, 69
Dugua, Pierre, 19

Eastman, Charles, 2, 135
Eliot, John, 13, 21–4
Emerson, Gloria, 155–6
Erickson, Donald, 152–6
"Evangelical United Front," 56
Evans, James, 128

Far North of Canada, 54, 66, 101, 114, 162–3
Fishman, Joshua, 125, 169
"Five Civilized Nations," 37, 39–47, 62, 114
Florida, 25, 85
Folger, Peter, 22
Frelinghuysen, Theodore, 56
"Friends of the Indian," 61, 64, 69, 114, 155

gambling casinos, 119–20, 177–8
Garland, Hamlin, 60, 141–2
George, Chief Dan, 75
Georgia, 13, 31–2, 41, 52, 56
General Federation of Women's Clubs, 140
Grant, President Ulysses S., 60

Hall, G. Stanley, 136–7
Hampton, Eber, 103
Hampton Institute, 2, 32, 62, 85–6, 89, 97, 103
Hare, Bishop William, 133
Harvard, Indians attending, 22
Haskell Institute, 84, 91

Head Start Programs, 165, 168
Holm, Wayne, 166
Holmes, Oliver Wendell, 14
Hudson's Bay Company, 54, 81, 114
Hurston, Zora Neale, 17
Huxley, Aldous, 111

identity
  generic Indian, 50, 80, 113, 123, 135, 145, 178, 195–8
  tribal, 5, 23–4, 73, 80, 91, 101, 160, 163, 166, 181, 198
immigrants, 2, 29, 49, 68, 134, 141, 160, 169, 175–6, 178–9, 188–9, 196
Indian Affairs
  Annual Report on (Canada), 90
  Bureau of (US),49, 72, 77–8, 89, 107, 116, 120, 122, 185
  colonial officials for, 22
  Commissioner of (US), 29, 30–1, 34, 46, 58–63, 67–71, 75, 79, 83–4, 88, 97, 100–3, 109, 132, 138–43, 169, 182, 184, 189
  Committee on (US), 31, 86, 112, 185
  Department of (Canada), 31, 74, 94, 106, 114, 119, 123–4, 134, 188
  Minister of (Canada), 124, 187
  Office of (US),14, 53, 70–1, 183
Indian Control of Indian Education, 117, 123, 168
"Indian New Deal," 73, 102, 140–3
Indian population
  in Canada, 6
  in the United States, 5–6, 63, 67
Indian Rights Association, 71
Indian Rights Movement, 80
individual land ownership, 36, 46, 62, 113, 115, 141–2, 150, 184
industrial education. *See* manual labor schools
Ireland, John, 49

Jackson, President Andrew, 35, 52
James Bay and Northern Quebec Agreement, 162
Jamestown, 20
Jefferson, President Thomas, 12, 17, 32, 51–2

Kansas, 84
"Kennedy Report," 121–2, 190
Kentucky, 14, 33, 41, 56
King Philip's War, 23–4
Knox, Henry, 32

Lac La Ronge Indian Band, 161
Lacombe, Father, 96
Lake Mohonk Conference of the Friends of the Indian, 61, 64, 69–70, 111
language, Indian
  loss of, 7, 45, 52, 57, 84, 97, 104, 125–7, 130–4, 136–7, 149, 157, 160–1, 165–78, 190, 198
  maintenance of, 7, 43–4, 50, 64, 68, 73–4, 125, 127–30, 133–5, 147–62, 165, 167–75, 189, 198–9
laws, Canada
  Act to Encourage the Gradual Civilization of the Indian Tribes (1857), 36
  British North America Act (1867), 36
  Civilization and Enfranchisement Act (1858), 36
  Indian Act (1876), 36
  Indian Advancement Act (1884), 36
laws, United States
  Curtis Act (1898), 46, 114
  General Allotment Act of 1887 (Dawes Act), 113, 141
  Indian Appropriation Act (1896), 46
  Indian Education Act of 1972, 172
  Indian Self-Determination and Education Assistance Act of 1975, 124
  Johnson-O'Malley Act (1934), 186, 189
  Native American Language Act of 1992, 176
  Tribally Controlled Community College Assistance Act (1978), 124

Tribally Controlled Schools Act (1988), 124
Wheeler-Howard Act (1934), 115
Le Jeune, Paul, 12
League of Indians of Western Canada, 106
Leupp, Francis, 46, 75, 88, 136, 139, 184
Los Angeles, 2
Ludlow, Helen, 32

Macdonald, Prime Minister Sir John A., 64, 113
Manitoba, 94, 118, 128
Mann, Horace, 3, 13, 42, 193
manual labor schools, 52, 54, 56, 62, 69, 80–1, 84, 87–90, 94, 97, 101, 132
Manuel, George, 81
Martha's Vineyard, 22–4
Massachusetts, 13, 20–6, 42, 57
Mather, Cotton, 130
Mayhew, Thomas, 22–4
Medill, William, 59
Meriam Report, 72, 109–11, 139, 186
Minneapolis, 191
missionaries, 13, 20, 23, 25, 27, 33–4, 39, 42–3, 45, 49–59, 64–5, 68, 73–5, 82, 99, 111–12, 114, 127–31, 133–4, 145, 183, 187
Mississippi, 129
Missouri, 57
mixed-blood Indians
  among Cherokees, 39–45, 58, 85
  Métis, in Canada, 6, 29, 67
monitorial method of instruction, 57
Monroe, President James, 52
Montezuma, Carlos, 120
Morgan, Jacob, 97–8
Morgan, Thomas Jefferson, 69, 137, 182
Morton, Samuel, 16
Murray, Sir George, 30

Nash, Philleo, 189
Natick, 21, 23–4
National Assessment of Educational Progress, 6, 8, 47, 127, 174, 195

National Congress of American Indians, 113
National Indian Brotherhood, 117, 123, 168
National League for the Protection of American Institutions, 69
National Study of American Indian Education, 8, 47, 120, 149, 169, 178
Navajo Mental Health Project, 151
New Age spirituality, 144, 164
New France, 12, 19–20, 26, 98–9, 128
New Mexico, 6, 47, 111, 140–1, 170
New York, 25, 27
North Carolina, 25, 32, 39, 181
Northwest Ordinance, 31

Ohio, 31, 33–4
Oklahoma, 6, 30, 33, 39, 46–7, 52, 60, 62, 80–1, 87, 97, 106, 131
Ontario, 6, 8, 27, 35, 54, 89–90, 101, 130, 164, 188

parents
  grandparents, 127, 149, 166
  Indian, 1–2, 9, 12, 36, 41, 52, 61, 70, 72, 79, 81–3, 89–91, 93, 95–101, 103, 107, 117, 123, 125, 133–5, 138, 140, 147–51, 154, 156–9, 161–2, 164, 166, 169–70, 172, 185, 194, 196, 198–9
  non-Indian, 95, 106, 117, 123, 179, 181–4
Parker, Arthur C., 75
Parkman, Francis, 14
Peace Commission and Peace Policy, 59, 62, 130
Pennsylvania, 2, 25, 55, 180
Peshkin, Alan, 8, 104–5
Pierce v. Society of Sisters, 199
Plymouth, 22–3
Porter, P. B., 55–6
poverty, of Indians, 7–8, 118–19
Pratt, Richard Henry, 50, 68, 83–88, 91, 100, 107, 114, 120, 133, 137, 179–80, 188

Progressive Education, 57
public schools, 2–3, 46, 50, 69–70, 73, 88, 95, 106, 110, 114, 116–17, 122, 124, 140–1, 162, 171, 174, 179–91, 193

Qu'Appelle school and Pow Wow, 79, 135
Quebec, 8, 126, 162

race, belief in significance of, 3, 9, 11–17, 30, 35, 40, 85–7, 111, 136–7, 194–7
Reel, Estelle, 96, 137
religious activities, government funding of, 34, 53–9, 62–5, 67, 69–71, 73–4, 93–4, 199
reservations, 7, 15, 30, 36, 51, 58, 60–2, 68, 73–4, 82, 86–7, 90–1, 96–120, 132–3, 136–41, 144–5, 147–52, 158, 161, 165–70, 180, 184, 186–8, 195
residential schools, 6, 26, 35, 44, 50, 64–5, 67, 73, 79–108, 120, 122, 134–5, 182, 189, 195, 197
Reuben Quick Bear v. Leupp, 72
Riel, Louis, 29
Rock Point, 78, 81, 127, 137, 145, 158–60, 165–6
Roessel, Robert, 150–3
Roosevelt, President Franklin, 115, 143
Roosevelt, President Theodore, 41, 45, 75, 119
Rough Rock, 74, 78, 81, 116, 118, 121, 142, 149–60, 166, 173, 189
Rupert's Land, 80–1, 90
Ryan, W. Carson, 140
Ryerson, Egerton, 3, 54, 89–90

Saskatchewan, 6, 96, 161, 164
separate schooling of Indian children and youth, 2–3, 77–92, 179, 193
Sequoyah (George Gist or Guess), 130
slavery among Cherokees, 40, 45, 58
Society of American Indians, 75, 80

Spencer, Herbert, 17
Spolsky, Bernard, 129, 151, 167, 172–3
Standing Bear, Luther, 96
Stockbridge, Massachusetts, 25
Strachan, John, 35, 54, 129
Superintendent of Indian Education, 42, 69, 88

Taos artistic colony, 111
teachers
  Indian, 3, 21, 23, 26, 42, 45, 74, 87, 99, 103, 118, 124, 129, 132, 139, 149, 151, 153–4, 157, 159, 163, 165, 168–9, 171, 173–4, 178, 181, 183
  New Englanders, 39, 43
Tennessee, 33, 39, 52, 55
Tocqueville, Alexis de, 14
Toronto, 73
treaties with Indians, 1, 13, 29–35, 37, 39, 42–3, 51, 55, 61–3, 65, 71, 114, 117, 123, 173, 181, 190
Treaty of Fort Laramie (1868), 61
Treaty of Hopewell (1785), 32
Trudeau administration "White Paper," 117, 123

Universal Declaration of Human Rights (1948), 198–9

Virginia, 25

War on Poverty, 116
Washington, Booker T., 85
Washington, President George, 12, 14, 32, 51
Wheelock, Eleazar, 26
William and Mary, Indians attending, 25
Winnipeg, 81
Worcester, Samuel Austin, 52

Yukon, 65–6, 101

Zelman v. Simmons-Harris, 72

GPSR Compliance

The European Union's (EU) General Product Safety Regulation (GPSR) is a set of rules that requires consumer products to be safe and our obligations to ensure this.

If you have any concerns about our products, you can contact us on

ProductSafety@springernature.com

In case Publisher is established outside the EU, the EU authorized representative is:

Springer Nature Customer Service Center GmbH
Europaplatz 3
69115 Heidelberg, Germany

www.ingramcontent.com/pod-product-compliance
Lightning Source LLC
LaVergne TN
LVHW051913060526
838200LV00004B/125